THE FRIEDMAN ARCHIVES

Best of the Blog 2

The most popular postings, lessons, and observations taken from the Friedman Archives Blog from 2014 - 2017. www.FriedmanArchives.com/blog

by Gary L. Friedman

Version 1.0

ISBN 978-1-387-36834-1

Published By

The Friedman Archives Press

TABLE OF CONTENTS

SECTION 0	INTRODUCTION	5
SECTION 1	TRAVEL STORIES	7
1.1	A Month in Oceania	7
1.2	5 Lessons from the UK	23
SECTION 2	LIGHTING INSIGHTS	47
2.1	Classical Environmental Portraits	47
2.2	A Gift for my Wife	51
2.3	Product Lighting	54
2.4	How I Lit This Child Prodigy	56
2.5	Better Pictures Using your Smartphone	63
2.6	How to Shoot a Bharatanatyam Arangetram	68
2.7	Newborn Photography Secrets	78
2.8	5 Types of Outdoor Portrait Lighting	90
2.9	A Tale of Two Portraits	97
SECTION 3	PHOTOGRAPHIC MISCELLANY	103
3.1	I found a Use for 14-bit RAW	103
3.2	How High-Megapixels Can Lead to Sharper Pictures	112
3.3	Baseball with RBS (Really Bad Shadows)	124
3.4	Air Show in RBL (Really Bad Light)	129
3.5	Shooting Star Trails	145
3.6	The Published Photographer's Perpetual Nightmare	152
3.7	Mythbusting!	159
3.8	Fun with Green Screens	168
3.9	Shooting Your First Wedding	174
3.10	Full-Frame vs. Small Sensor (don't laugh...)	182
3.11	A real-world example of Induced Moiré	196
3.12	Turn your iPad into a High-Resolution Film Scanner	201

3.13	MY PERSONAL WORKFLOW	210
3.14	ETTR REVISITED	217

SECTION 4   **NOTHING TO DO WITH PHOTOGRAPHY** **223**

4.1	POSSIBLE SOLUTIONS TO THE HOT SHOE DESIGN PROBLEM	223
4.2	4 KICKSTARTER IDEAS	229
4.3	WHY AMERICANS BEHAVE THE WAY THEY DO	237
4.4	I KNOW WHAT I DID LAST SUMMER	239

SECTION 0 INTRODUCTION

I've now been writing a photography blog for 10 years, which upon reflection is kind of jarring. (Where did the time go?) Unlike most blogs, I try to ensure there's always a teachable moment. And because I don't like being bombarded by content either, I usually post every six weeks or so (partly because these take so much time to assemble!), and make sure that I actually have something useful to say before I do.

Four years ago, I published the "Best of the Blog" (now retroactively labeled "Volume 1") which was quite popular. It's not hard to understand why – how many times have you rummaged through a person's years-long blog posts just to find the good stuff? Probably not many. And so the sheer convenience of packaging material and making it approachable and easy to read on a Kindle made it worth the modest price. In this edition I'm also including some of my favorite contributions to Cameracraft from the past 5 years, making this a great collection of content you just can't find anywhere for free.

I use the blog as a personal indulgence – I can show off, I can gripe, I can propose new ideas (some of which have nothing to do with photography), and I can publicly demonstrate that I'm not being paid by Sony. The platform also allows me to state an honest opinion without being subject to too many trolls. (That alone is worth the price of admission. ☺)

The other, secondary goal of the blog is to discuss issues about photography that have little to do with gear (one of the reasons I like being associate editor for Cameracraft magazine as well). So the blog tries a little bit to balance that out a little too.

Okay, enough of this. I hope you enjoy this collection of insights, wisdom, and of course images!

-Gary

SECTION 1   TRAVEL STORIES

1.1   A MONTH IN OCEANIA

First published November, 2015 in Cameracraft Magazine

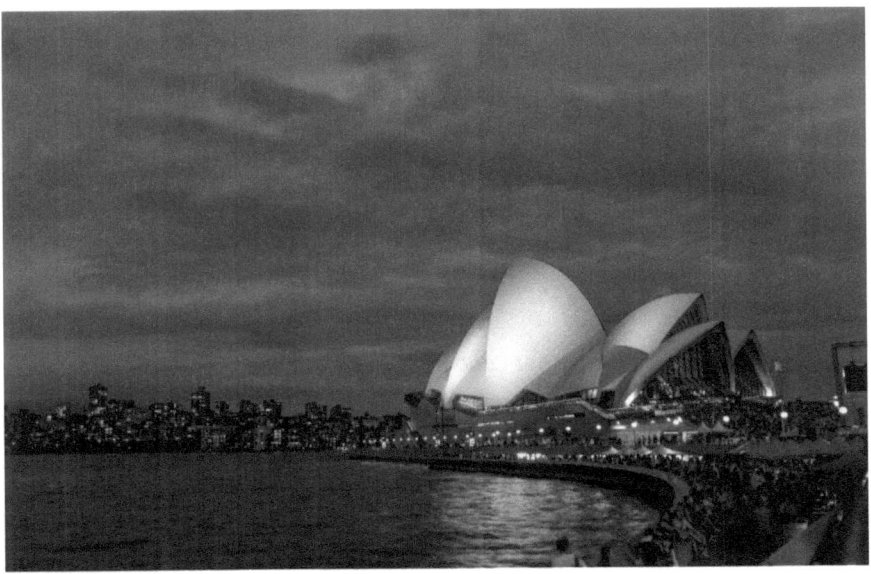

It started out as a mere business trip. Just do a couple of seminars in Australia then fly home. Maybe 1.5 weeks, tops.

"But you can't fly all the way to Australia and not take time to tour!". Fair enough. Now it's a 3-week trip.

"But I hear New Zealand is absolutely beautiful! We can't go all the way there and not see New Zealand as well!" So now it's a 4-week trip and a 3rd seminar was added on the North island.

Of course you know what happened next. Those countries are huge, and with 3 anchor weekends and time needed to travel from one event to the next, the trip

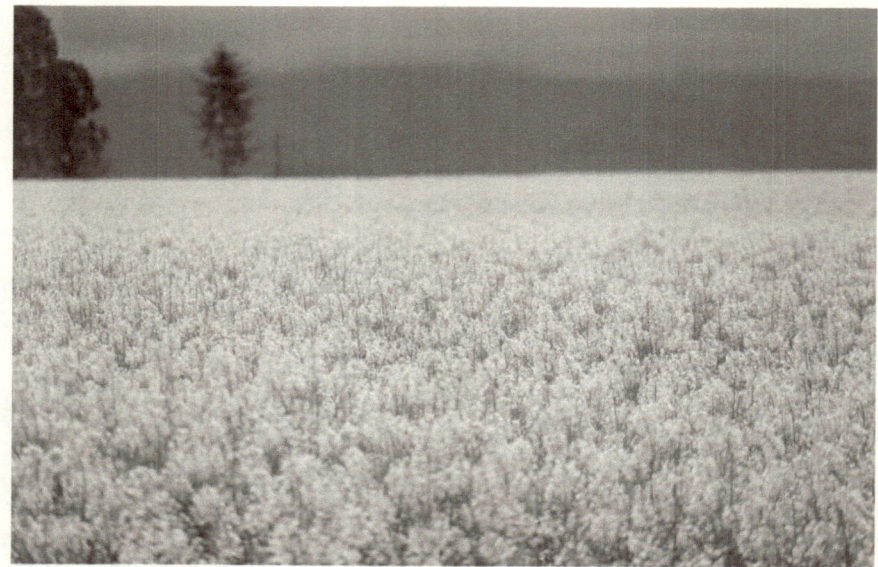

Rape plants, from which we get Canola oil, in New Zealand.

became filled with too much to see, too much distance between places, a ton of driving, and not enough time to make the visit meaningful.

This is my world. I've always grown up believing that when you visit a place, you should spend some quality time there and not concentrate on doing touristy things. You should research places, famous photos, etc. and make a plan on how you plan to do better. Not this time. We only had a rough itinerary – all we had were airline tickets and hotels for the anchor weekends, and everything else was up in the air. We'll have to decide on what to do each day and each night we find a hotel when we're tired.

This trip will either be wonderful or be a disaster.

My Equipment

I was expecting a ton of landscape opportunities, and so I packed accordingly. In my bag I brought a Sony A7r II (with A7 as a backup), the Zeiss 16-35 f/4, and the hugely underrated 24-240 superzoom from Sony. This lens is awesome for travel, especially if you have no idea what you're going to see next. To cover its mild deficiencies at the long end, whenever I'd shoot highly detailed subjects at long distances (like Koalas and Wallabies) I'd switch to the 70-200 f/4 lens from Sony. Add to that a Samyang 14mm fisheye lens (which never got used), a Nissin Di700a wireless flash and radio trigger, tripod, laptop and backup drives and you end up with a camera bag weighing 20 pounds! (I also had my trusty RX-100 IV. I never go anywhere without that.)

One of the eternal challenges of being a travel stock photographer is the need to get something different from what everyone else has. And so while we did visit some popular tourist places (Sydney Opera House, the Great Barrier Reef, the Great Ocean Road), we also tried to spend most of our time in the out-of-the-way places that most travelers would never find. What follows are some of the highlights of the trip.

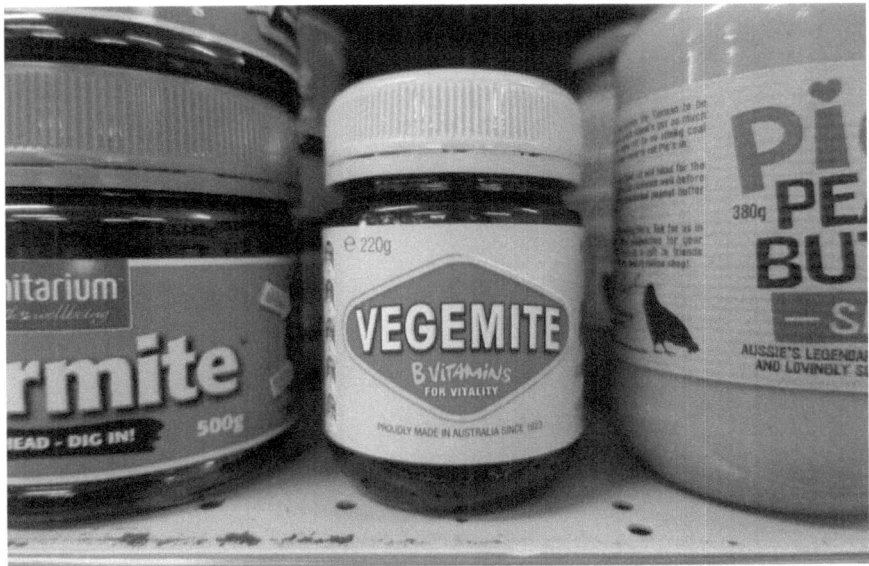

An establishing shot. Nothing says "Australia" like Vegemite.

New Zealand

Beautiful country. Good light and low haze. Sheep everywhere. 7 days driving both islands and 2 days seminaring (that's a word!). The only reason people don't flock there for the beauty and quality of life is because their immigration department is very stringent on who they let in. Didn't see a single Kiwi bird. We made careful notes of where we want to explore further when we return in a few years – this time we'll spend several weeks there instead of several days.

In Australia we hugged the East coast, between Sydney and Cairns (the most popular jump-off point for the great barrier reef.) We also flew to Adelaide and drove the Great Ocean Road to Melbourne. That drive alone was worth the price of admission.

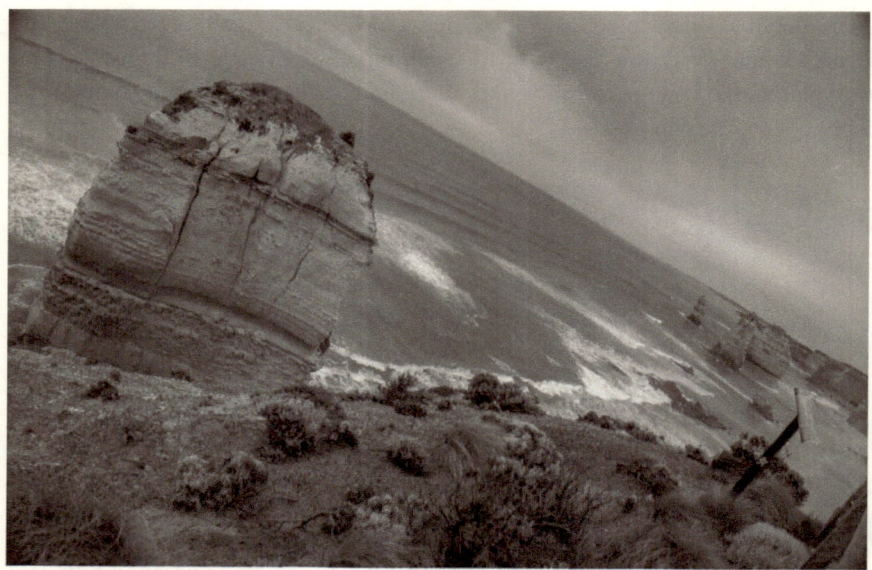

The "12 Apostles" natural rock formations along Australia's southern coast. To try to get a different image I shot at an angle to add some energy to the composition.

So what did I look for?

It's difficult to articulate what images I seek when I travel. Establishing shots are a given – these convey where you are in one picture, and are heavily licensable, especially when you shoot at 42 megapixels as there's not as much out there at such high resolutions. Landscapes can be profitable too but it can be hard to establish a sense of place – a beautiful coastline could be anywhere. Am I getting a unique shot that (probably) nobody else has taken?

I also find environmental portraits – images that show the person in the environment in which they thrive -- can be a good seller as well as long as you get model releases. This usually involves talking with people and getting permission to shoot first, but the shots are unique and they do tell a story and are popular on travel brochures.

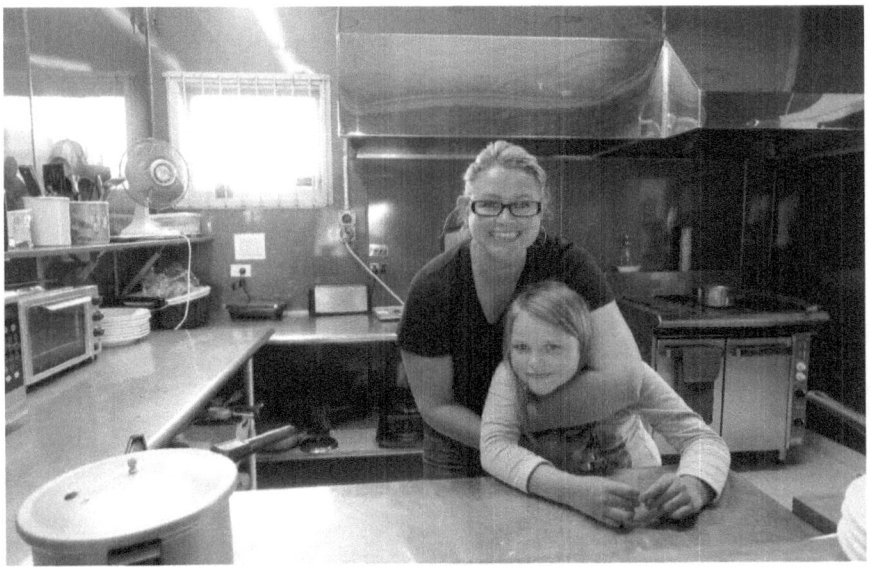

Environmental Portrait – A restaurant owner and her daughter. Taken in "Ned's Place, a licensed Café – Bistro in New Zealand.

Biggest Disappointment

Expectations determine happiness. And all of my life I heard the Great Barrier Reef was immense and beautiful and amazing. The reef itself had wonderful biodiversity but from a photographic point of view it was disappointing. Poor light and poor visibility. Had I been serious I would have rented an underwater housing with a huge flash. Clearly I wasn't serious. Tried to process a RAW file to show what it should have looked like but was reminded yet again that nothing can truly fix bad light.

History You Never Hear At Home

While planning my shot of the Sydney Opera House, I learned of the theater's history, how it was a financial boondoggle from the beginning, how the architect had no idea how to build it nor how the performance space would be transformed to accommodate both opera and ballet (each has different requirements), how the architect was eventually fired and the project was finished using a government architect. Iconic as it may be, it has never paid for itself and in fact has been a large financial drain on the government. Two days after the stock shot at the top of this article was taken, the terrorist attacks happened in Paris and the colors on the roof mirrored that of the French flag. (Lebanon, who suffered a similar terrorist attack at about the same time, complained about being ignored.)

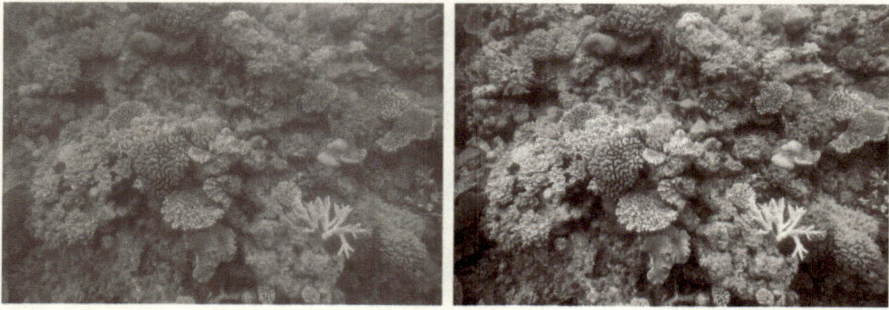

The Great Barrier Reef was quite a disappointment. After we returned home, we heard news reports that it was officially "dying".

I also heard from an Aussie that the whole reason the British infested the continent was that after the American colonies had revolted, they needed someplace new to send their prisoners. If this is true, I now feel guilty.

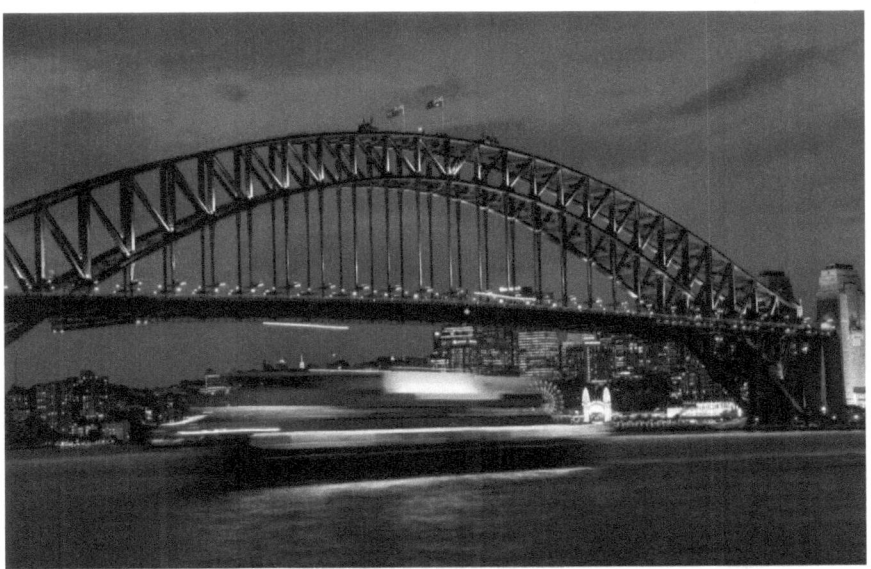

The Sydney Harbor Bridge. I put a blurred ship in the foreground just to make this image stand out.

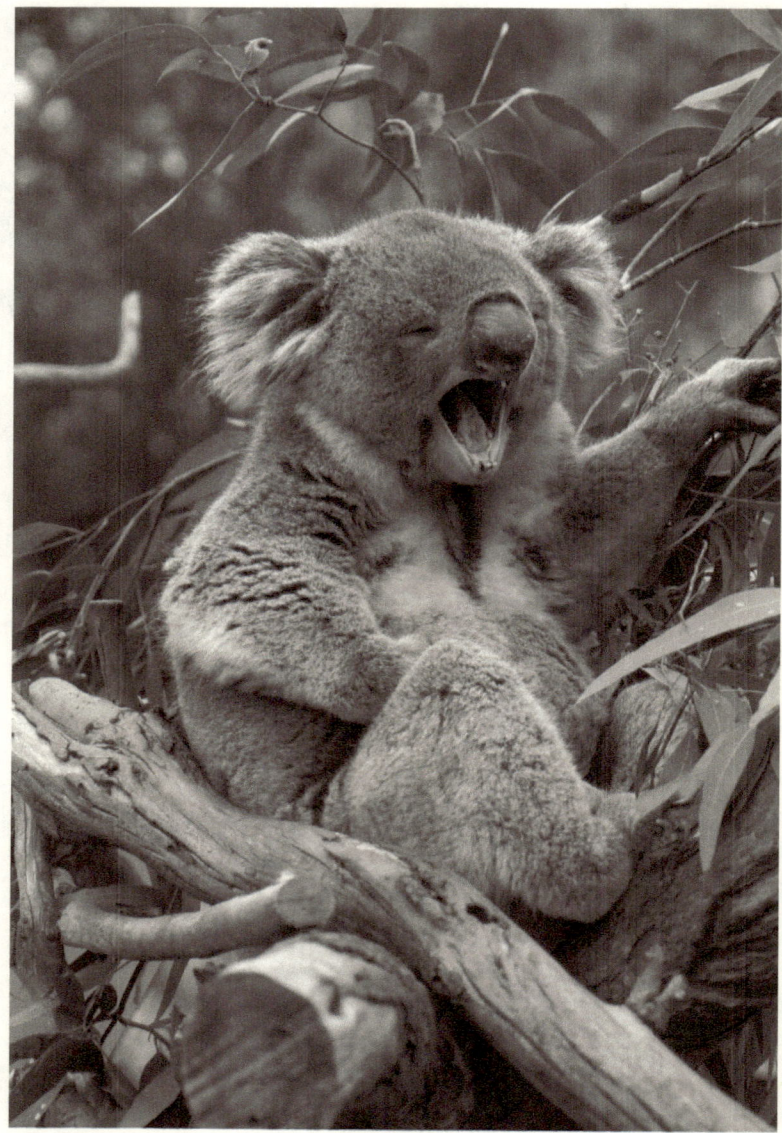

Super-zooms fall short when shooting fine-detailed subjects from a distance. For such occasions I brought the white Sony 70-200 f/4 lens which is quite sharp and captures every hair.

Stressed Out Koalas

Recent scientific research suggested that when tourists hold Koalas it kind of stresses them out, and based on this discovery tourists were no longer allowed to pay to do this. Except in the state of Queensland, where the tourism industry would have suffered. It is said that the Koalas there are being raised specially for this purpose (implying they won't suffer the same kind of stress) but that's difficult to believe.

Identifying Your Winners in 5 Seconds

Every day was full and there was barely enough time to sleep. But I had to post occasional shots on Facebook because my ego (well, my friends too) demands it.

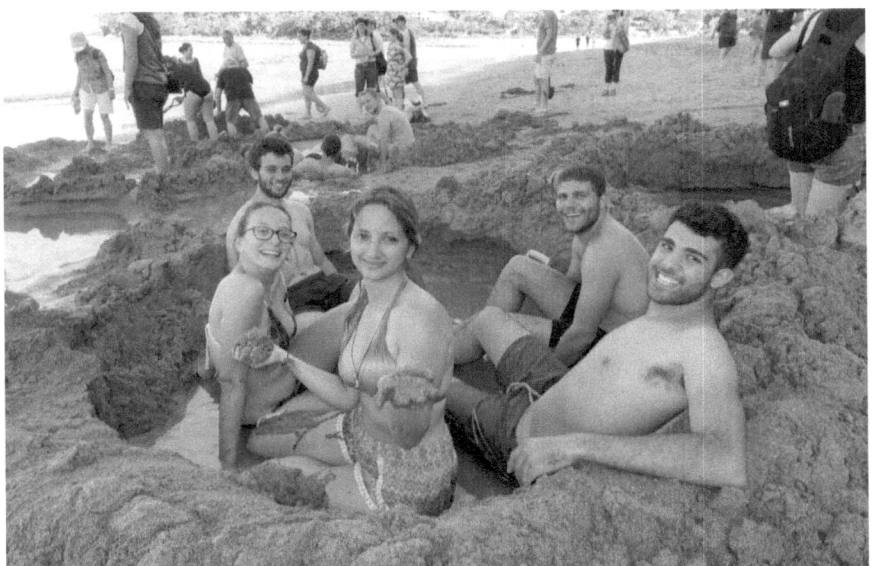

The ocean water is freezing... however a part of Hot Water Beach sits atop a geothermal vent. Bring a shovel and dig in the right place and hot water fills the hole. Instant spa! RX-100 with fill flash set to -1.

So rather than do Lightroom editing every night for hours to find my best images, I did what we used to do in the days of slides: View everything in thumbnail size, take off my glasses, and the images with the strongest composition and best light would be instantly recognizable. I'd then take these best images and post them to facebook, straight from the camera. See how many hours of life energy I just saved?

Elusive Penguins

After the 3rd seminar in Melbourne, we had just one day leftover. My wife and I decided to head over to Philip Island specifically to see the blue "little penguins" (that's actually the technical name!) in a wildlife sanctuary.   At sunset they all come out of the ocean and head over to their boroughs after mating season. After paying all sorts of money to participate, and even paying extra to get a front-row seat for the "Penguin Parade" across the beach, we were told at the last minute that photos were not allowed. "The flash bothers the animals" was the official reason. "So why not just ban flash photography?" "Because the [certain stereotyped Asian ethnicity deleted] will just ignore the rules and shoot anyway. It's easier to

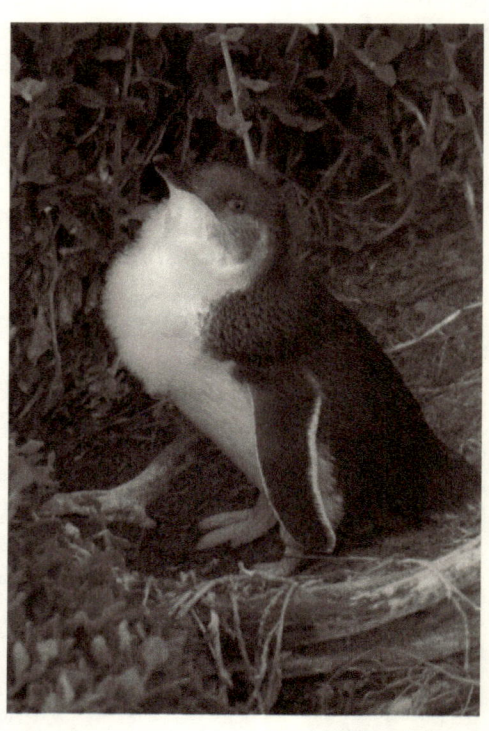

Too noisy to license; but not so much that it can't print in a magazine.

just ban photography altogether." Oh, so many holes in that logic! It's times like these it pays to just let go of the outcome (and the associated anger and cost) and just enjoy the moment. I snuck in a couple of shots but the light was so low that they're not really licensable.

Now What?

This plagues me after every trip. When I get home, I'll feverishly go through my selection / editing / tweaking workflow, step back and look at what I ended up with... and be totally and completely dissatisfied with it. "Not enough anchor images!" "Not enough 'Wow!' shots." "I should have come back at a different time of day." "If only I had pulled off the road and took that picture at sunset as I had contemplated!" You know... thoughts like that which waste the gift of consciousness. Then I'll walk away from it for about 3 weeks and look at the work again with a fresh set of eyes. "Not as bad as I thought." "Actually, there are some good ones in there." I've been going through this cycle since my early 20's. You'd figure I'd learn by now. But clearly it means I still care about my work. (At least that's what I tell myself.)

More Shots From the Trip

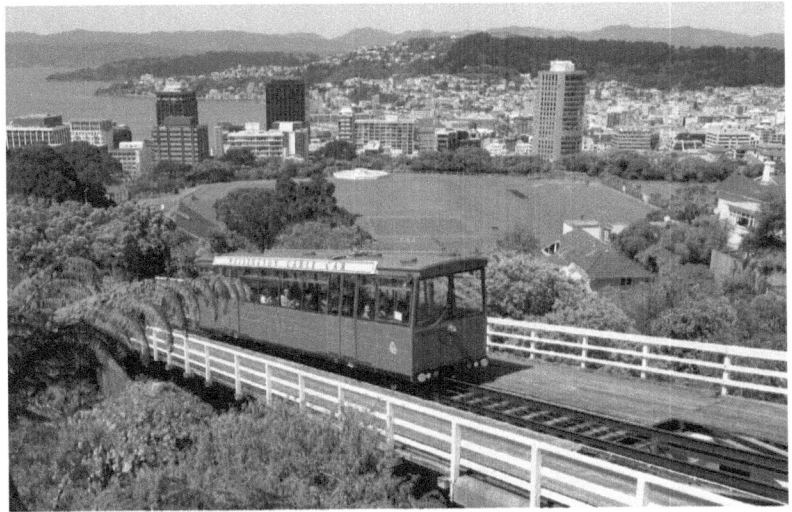

A stock shot in Wellington. Everyone who's ever visited has this exact same shot. Other than sheer megapixels mine's not any better. Sometimes you have to just cover your bases.

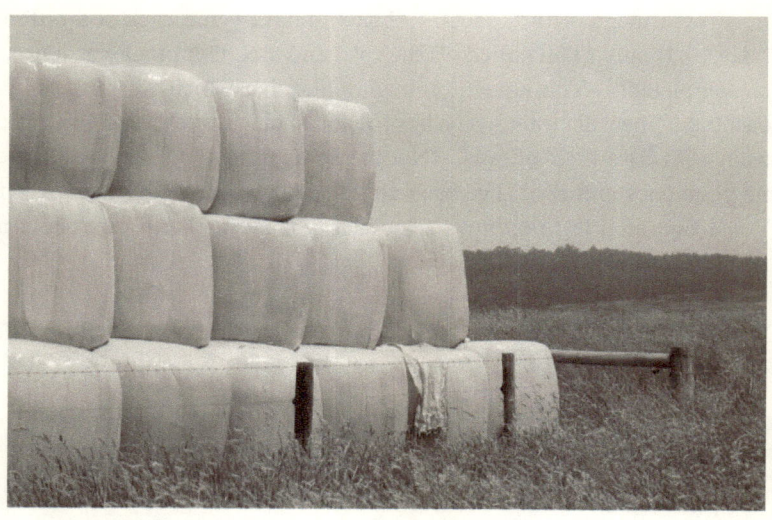

I've always wondered where mint-flavored marshmallows were grown...

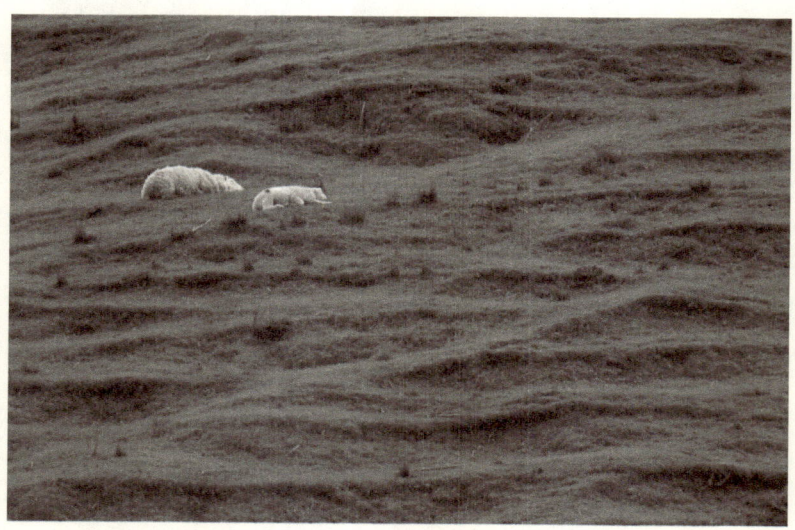

New Zealand is beautiful and covered in green. Sheep are as plentiful as mass shootings in the U.S.

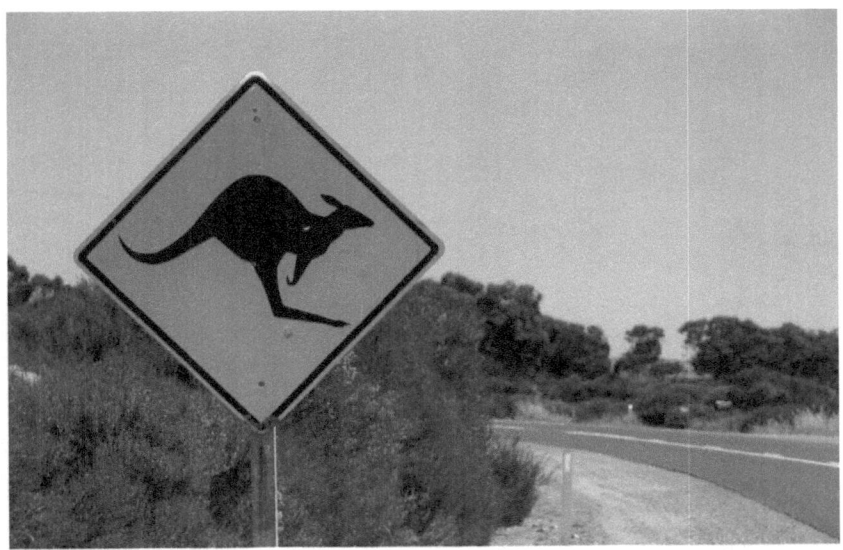

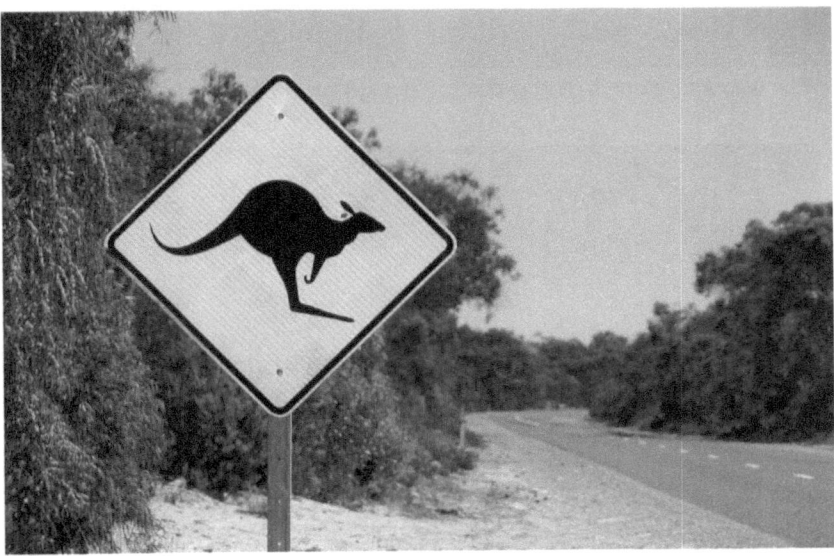

Trick of Trade - signage usually contains highly directional reflective coating. If your subject doesn't "pop" then even using a small flash can illuminate it quite strongly. Now I can license this.

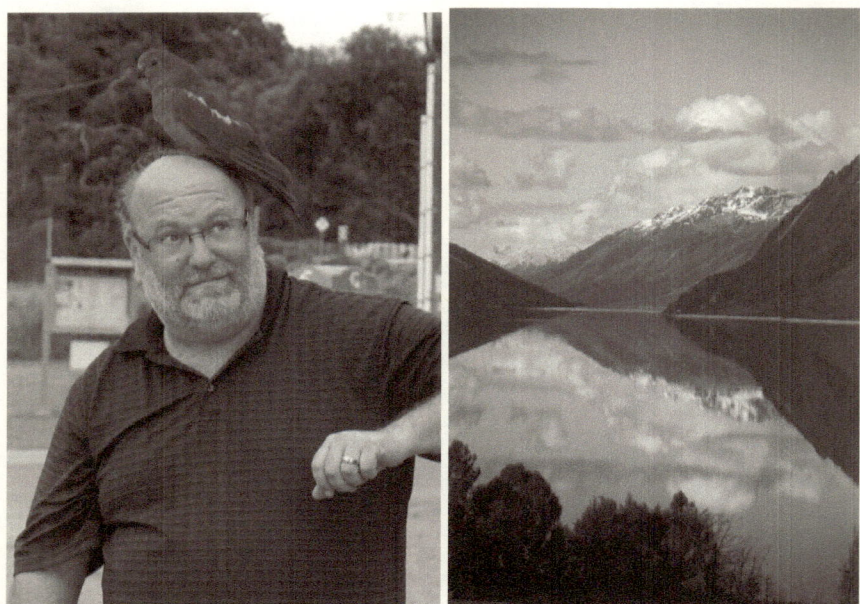

Left: A wild King Parrot. Not in a zoo. :-) Right: More natural beauty.

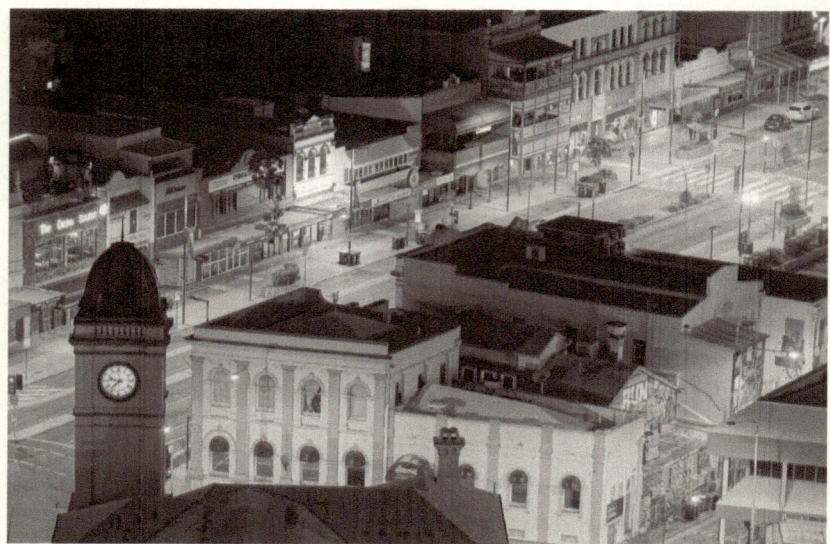

The City of Townsville. (Cue Power Puff Girls music...)

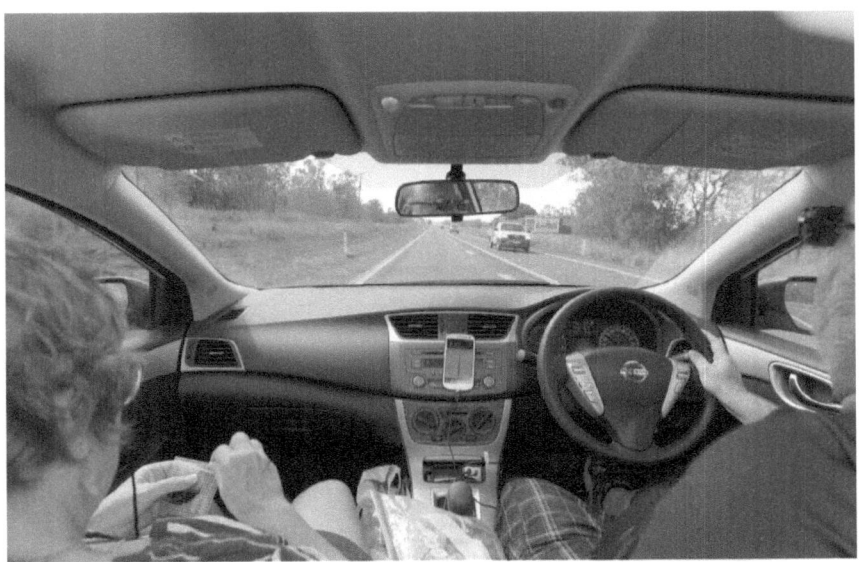

This was originally taken as a challenge for the grandkids: "Find two unusual things about this picture" To take this shot, I set exposure compensation = -1 (otherwise the camera would average the windshield and the dashboard and blow out the windshield). I also used wireless flash to lighten the interior, pointing to the ceiling from the back seat, with Flash Exposure Compensation set to -1 because it's normally too strong for my tastes. Camera mounted on a tripod sitting on the back seat and fell over every time I made a mild turn. Oh, the lengths I go to to take even the most boring shot!

Other tidbits: Keep your old mobile phones after you upgrade - they're still plenty useful as standalone GPS units using Nokia HERE maps. That's my old Galaxy S3 guiding us to the next roundabout mounted on the dashboard using a bit of velcro..

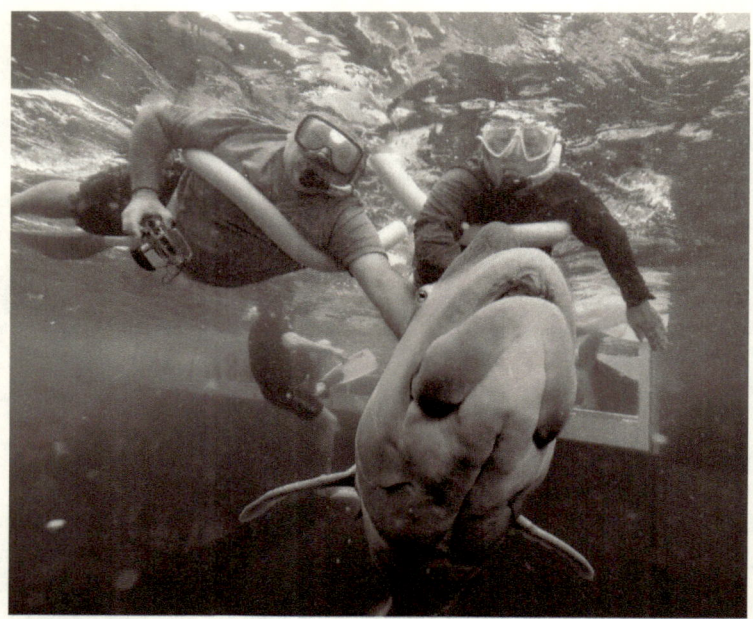

Snorkeling on the Great Barrier Reef and petting a Maori Wrasse.

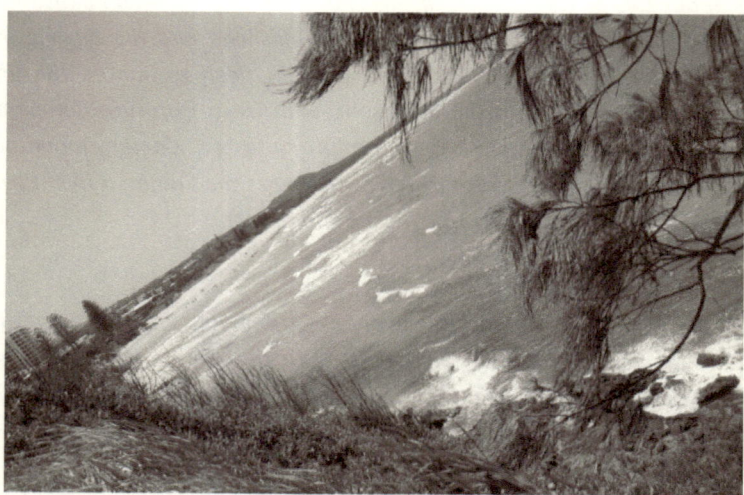

The beaches in Brisbane are amazing. But the water got muddy once you went North.

First published July 2017

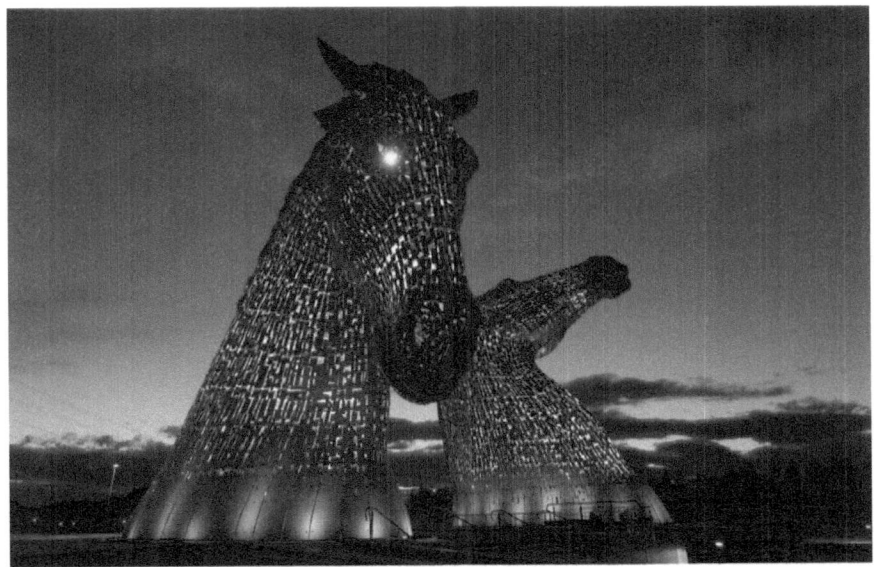

We just returned from a month of travel, first giving 2 seminars in the UK (England and Scotland), and then vacationing in Southern Ireland (EU, not UK). The light was poor to average; it rained a lot, and I did the best I could with the six total minutes of good light I had. :-)

Lots of pictures to share and lessons regarding those pictures. I'll be as brief as I can.

1. Overcoming Lightroom's Small Slider Range

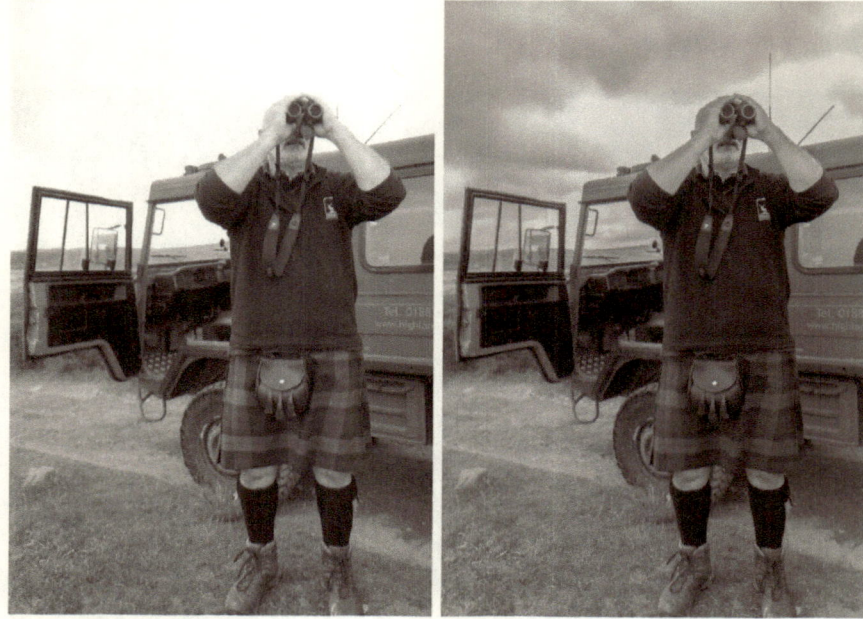

Do Jewish Scotsmen get a Kilty conscience?

An overcast sky can provide nice soft light for portraiture (as long as the sky isn't in the shot), but pretty awful conditions for landscapes. Here shooting RAW is essential for its expanded dynamic range compared to jpg. BUT, programs like Lightroom may not allow you to slide the controls enough to do all the correcting you need.

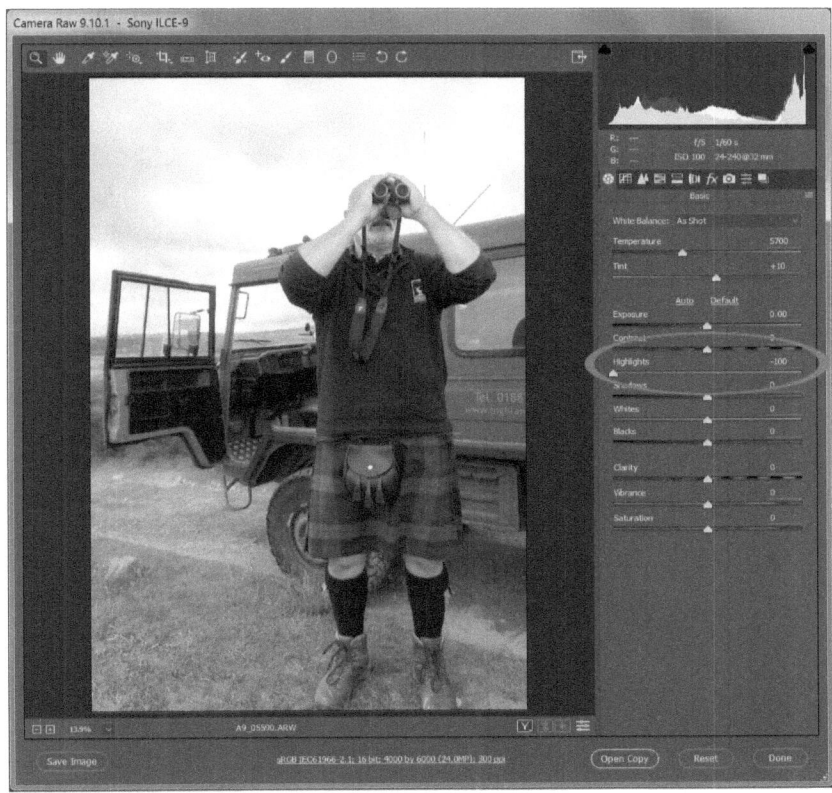

The "Highlights" slider in both Lightroom and Adobe Camera Raw (part of Photoshop) can be used to recover some of the nearly-blown-out highlights in the sky. But as you can see, it doesn't slide to the left far enough.

Fortunately, Photoshop has a feature that lets you apply the same controls multiple times until you get what you need. Just go to FILTER -> CAMERA RAW FILTER... and voila! The same set of import controls pop up again, allowing you (in this case) to slide the "highlights" slider to the left for even more correction. I had to reduce the highlights 3 times in order to get the sky dark enough in the Scotsman looking through Binoculars shot (see right example, two images earlier).

This technique was also used in the image below, photographing an amazingly huge public artwork sculpture called "The Kelpies" in Scotland:

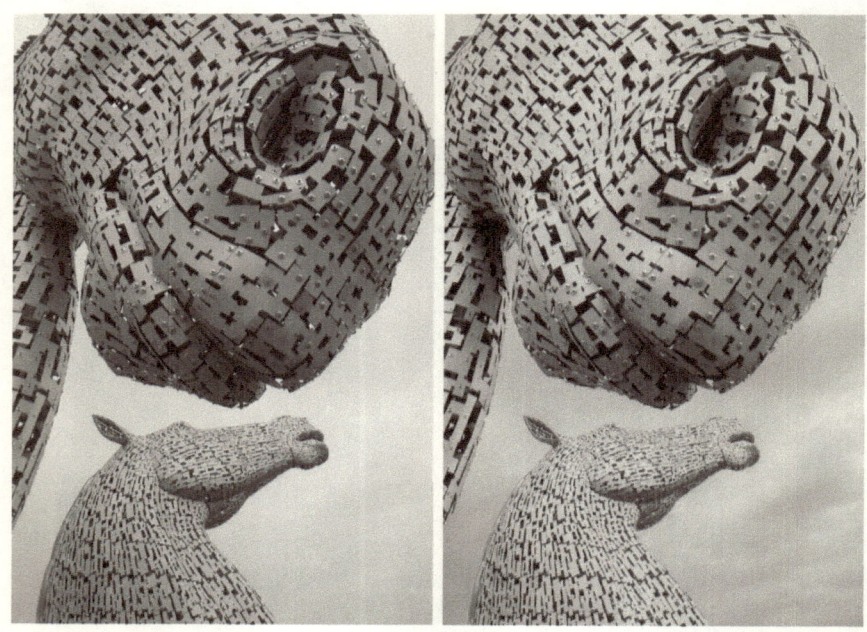

I really hate overcast skies, for it can sometimes lead to blah (and therefore unlicensable) images.   Shooting RAW can often allow you to recover the highlights that get blown out in the .jpg.

2. B&W Can Often Save RBL

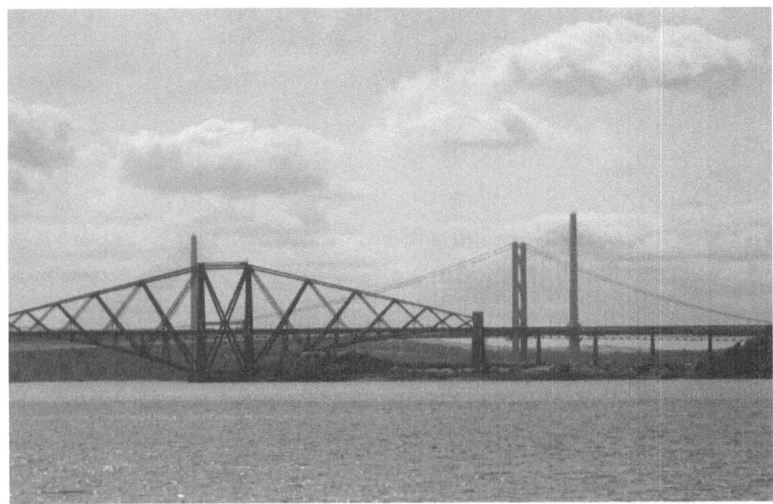

The Forth bridge (on the left) might be an engineering marvel for its day - the longest cantilever bridge span in the world – a title it held for 27 years. But it's hard to be impressed with bad light.

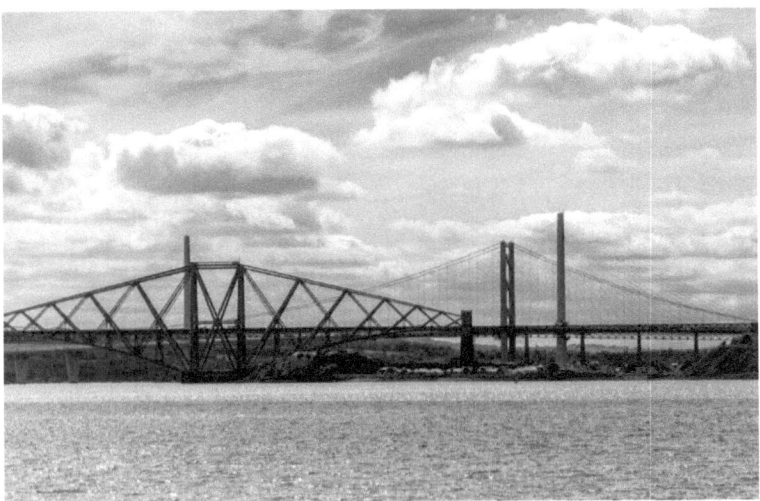

That's a bit better.

RBL stands for Really Bad Light. (The bane of all photographers.) Another trick I have up my sleeve for dealing with it is to convert the image to high-contrast black-and-white, using Photoshop's IMAGE --> ADJUSTMENTS --> B&W Control. Unlike simply desaturating the colors, the B&W control allows you to specify a shade of grey for each color that you have. Do you want the blue sky to come out dramatically dark? Slide the blue control to the left. Light vegetation? Slide the green control to the right. Then use the curves tool to place your whites and blacks (for maximum "punch") and you've gone from hopelessly boring to "Wow! That's a great picture! What kind of camera do you have?".

3. Lush Landscapes Require Underexposure

This one's not intuitive. Most shots you take in the forest, of mountainscapes, and of vegetation in general will come out overexposed, no matter what brand of camera you shoot with. Why? Because your camera's built-in exposure meter is assuming that your subject is reflecting back 18% of the light that hits it. (Your average subject has 18% reflectivity. It thinks you're shooting something average. And by definition, most of the time, you are.)

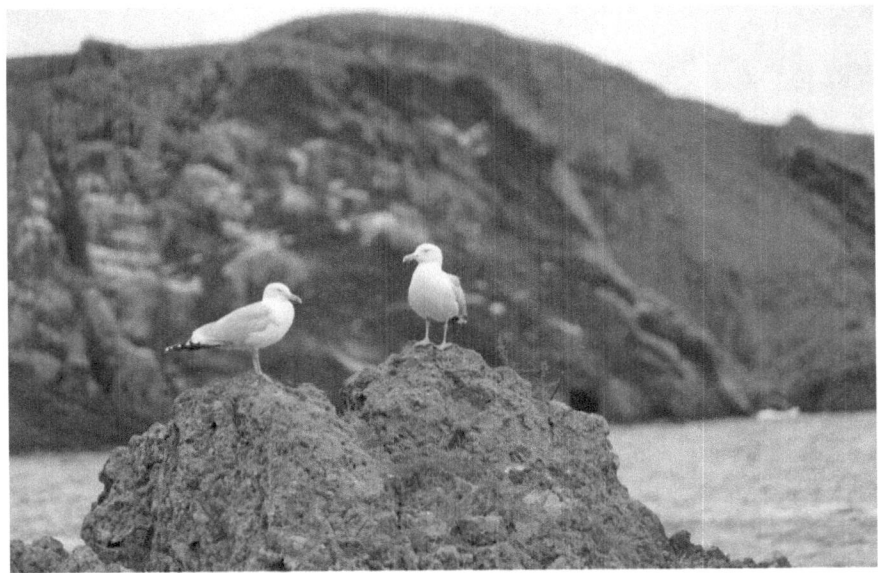

The dark rocks and moss reflect back MUCH less than 18% of the light that hits it. Your camera's meter says, "I need to let in more light in order for the average brightness to look like an average scene!" And so it looks washed out.

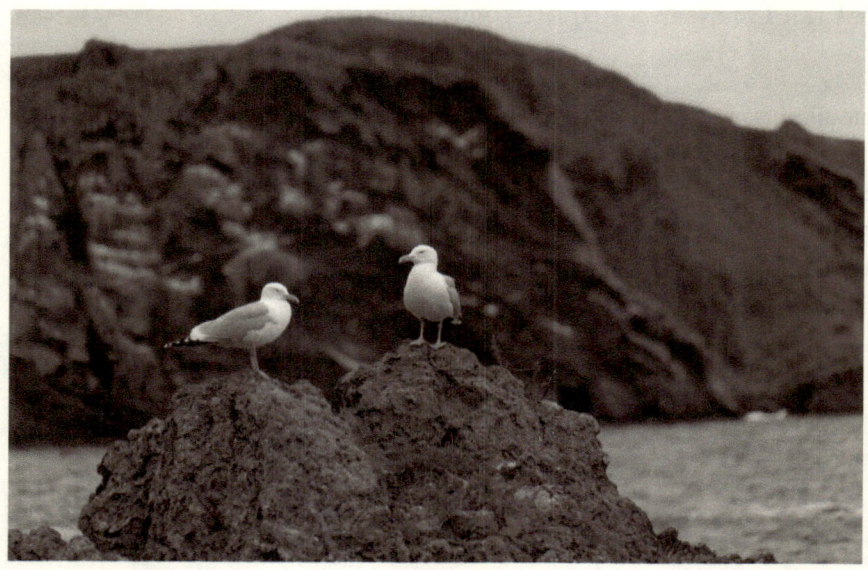

Setting your Exposure Compensation to -1 will usually make it look the same way it looked to your eye.

Anyway, forests, mountains, and landscapes in general (discounting the sky) tend to reflect back much less, and so your camera says "OMG! I have to let in more light to make this look average!" and so it does. This is why I set my exposure compensation to -1 when I'm out in the field like this – it corrects for it in the camera. Many of you might look at the 2nd image and say "That's a little dark for my taste"; however it was an overcast and dark day and these pictures accurately depict how it looked to my eye.

4. Forcing the Blue Hour using White Balance

I'm a big fan of twilight shots take at "the blue hour", like the example below:

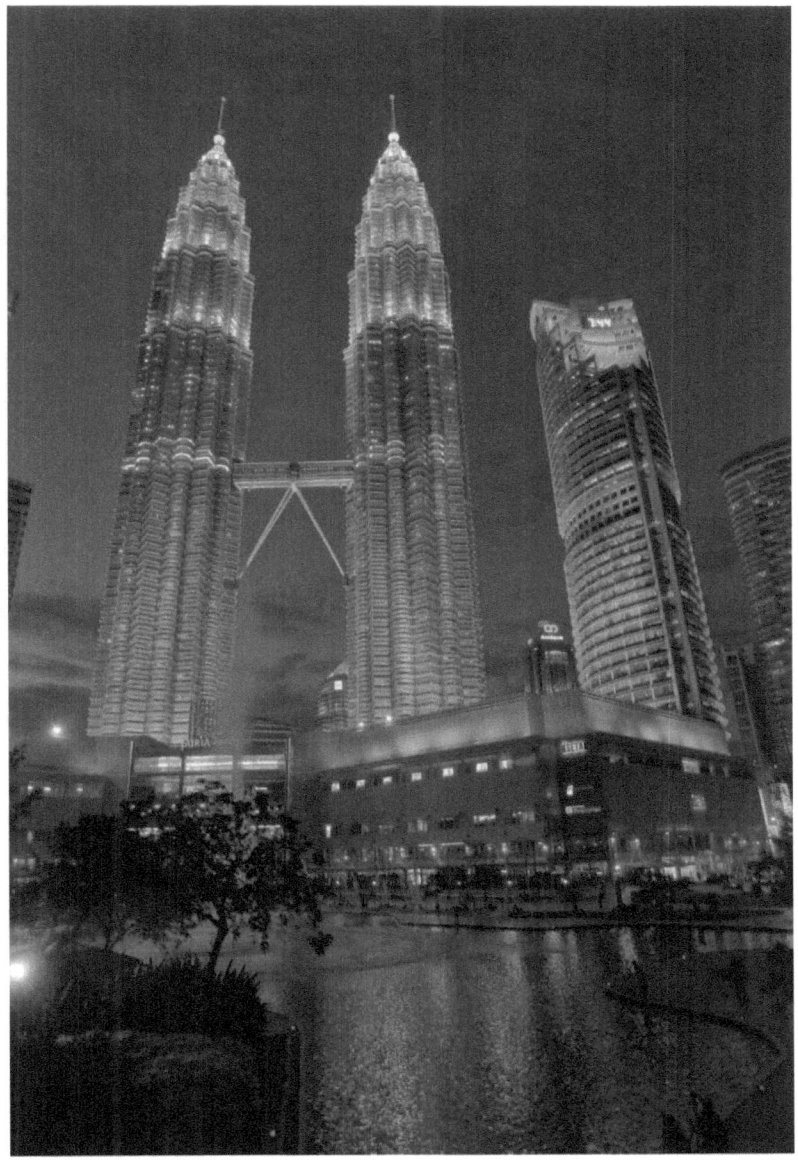

The Petronas Towers in Kuala Lumpur. Wait for the sky to darken and the subject to lighten, and when the two are close, that's the best time to shoot.

This is the kind of shot I had envisioned when we returned to the Kelpies to shoot the sculptures at night. But sometimes the sky doesn't turn blue after sunset, instead turning a yuckky grey-blue to which nobody will say "Wow!":

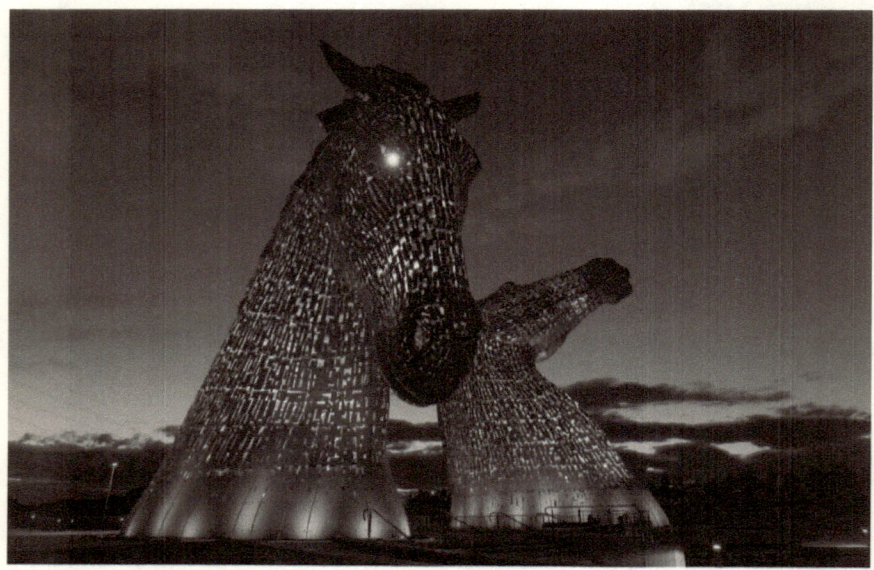

It's OK; but not what I had pre-visualized. So I decided to try changing the camera's White Balance to "Tungsten", which applies an overall bluish tint to the entire image. It worked!

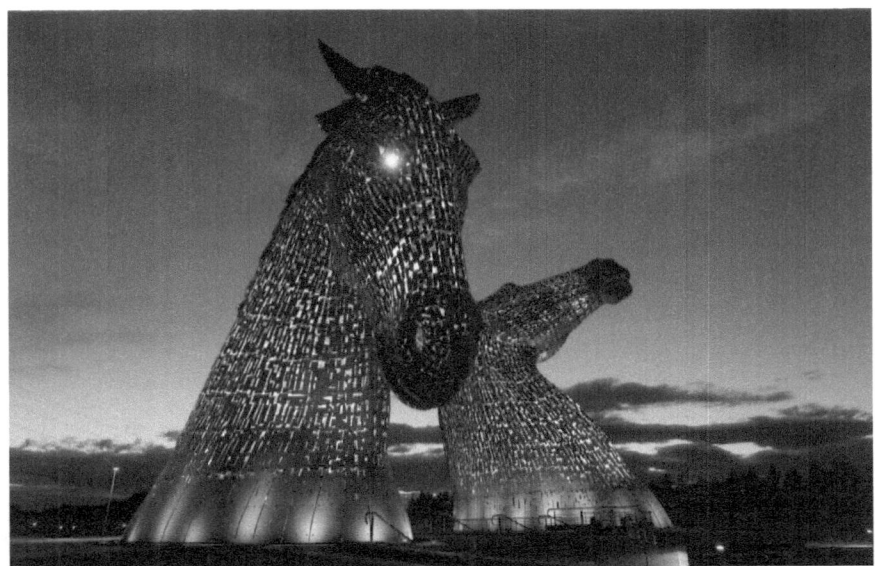

Normally this is a dangerous technique, since it also casts a blue cast over your subject as well. But the illumination at this particular moment was an incandescent yellow, which I knew would cancel the blue cast, making the subject appear white. There were about a dozen other photographers out there that night; I'm pretty confident none of them got a shot that looked like this.

5. Always have a camera with you!

At 10:00 PM after a good day of driving we checked into the hotel and went downstairs to have dinner. When I saw this rainbow outside shortly thereafter there was no time to run back to the room and grab my camera (which was charging at the time); so I whipped out my trusty RX-100 V and got two pretty awesome establishing shots. This is why God created the RX-100. :-)

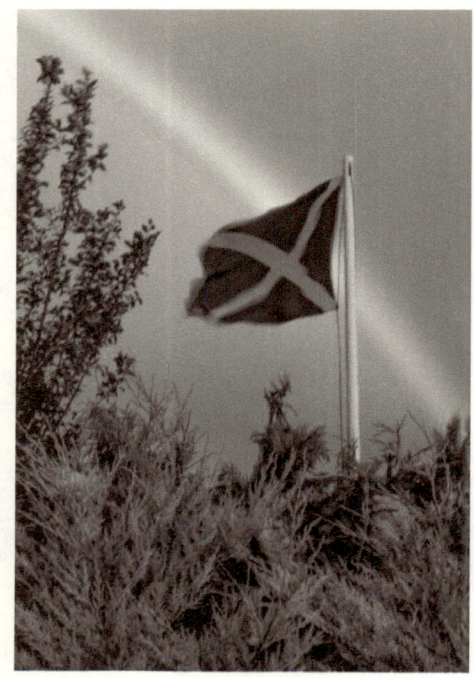

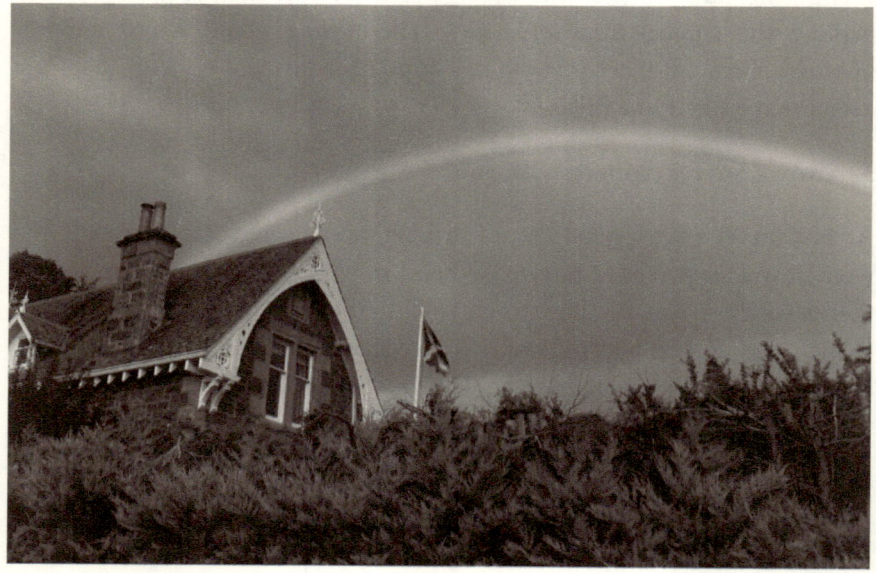

More Selected Shots

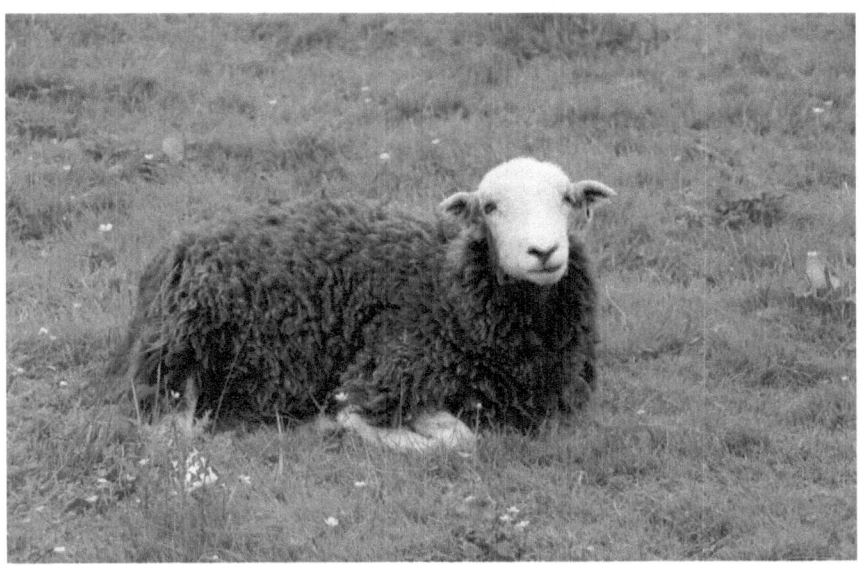

The UK was hit by radioactive rain after the Chernobyl meltdown back in 1986; producing contaminated grass that the sheep grazed upon. I am told that the sheep simply will not graze anywhere else, and it is estimated to take about 30 years for the radioactivity to dissipate. In the meantime, the sheep are being bred and systematically killed until such time as they can once again be used for food. More info here: https://www.theguardian.com/uk/2009/dec/29/sheep-farmers-chernobyl-meat-restricted .

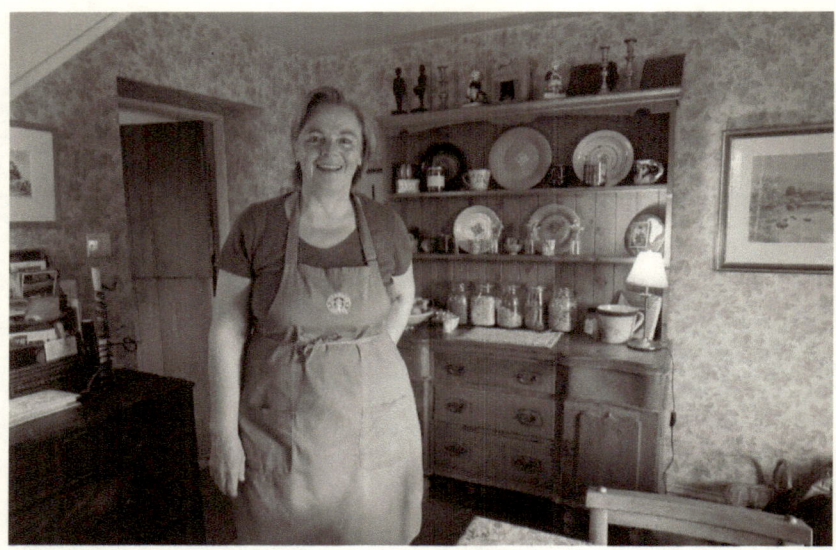

The fantasy of running your own Bed and Breakfast...

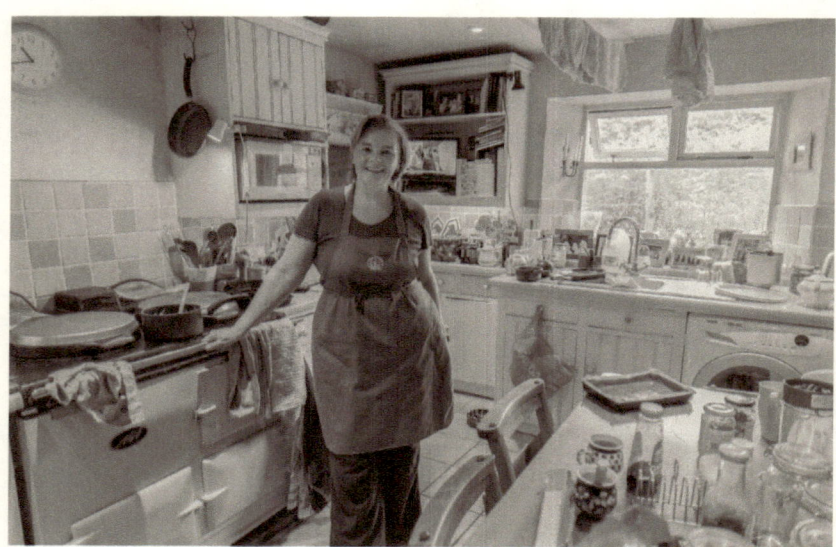

... and the reality.

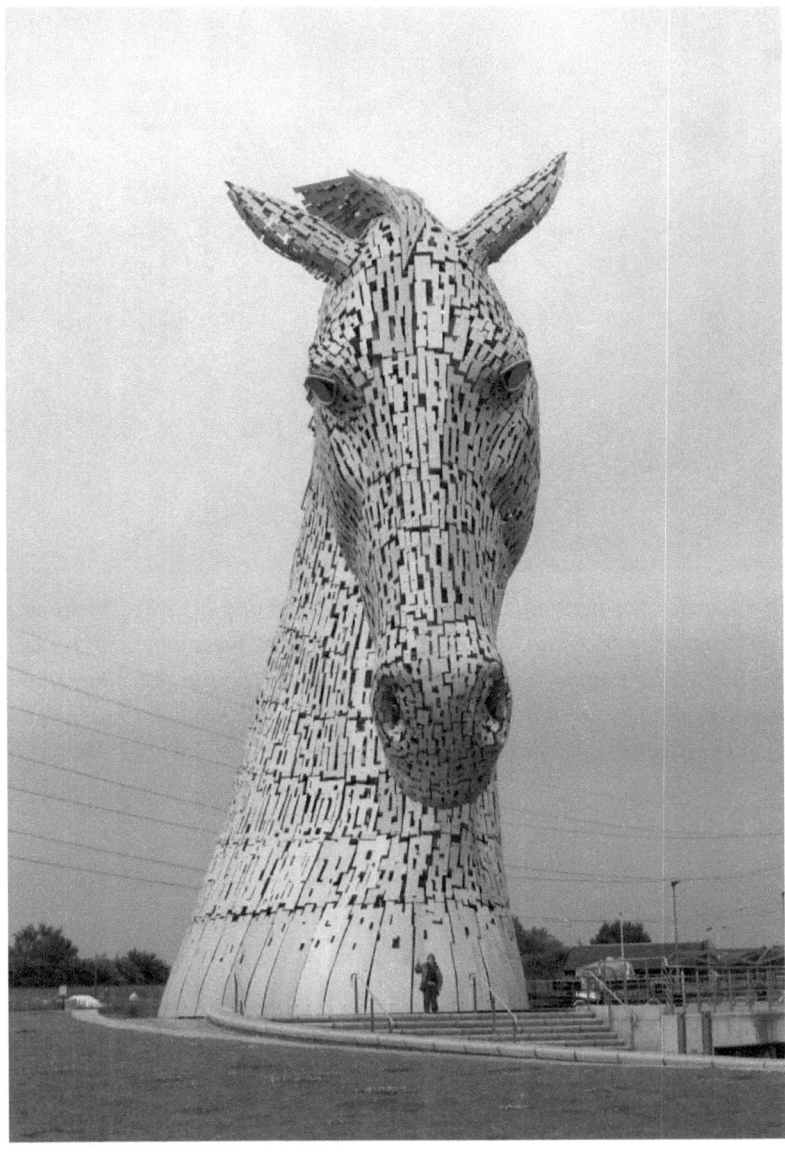

This is how big the Kelpies sculptures are. Carol is standing at the base, wearing a pink jacket.

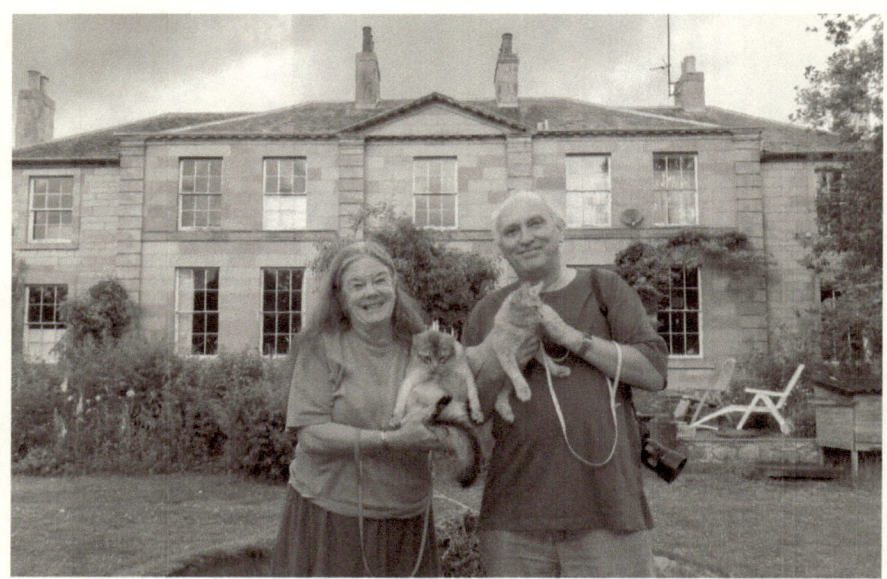

David Kilpatrick (Cameracraft editor and publisher) and his wife Shirley in front of their "castle" in Scotland. Carol and I slept in the west wing. :-) He used to run his publishing empire from the office spaces on the top floor; but thanks to modern technology a laptop is all you need to produce award-winning magazines nowadays.

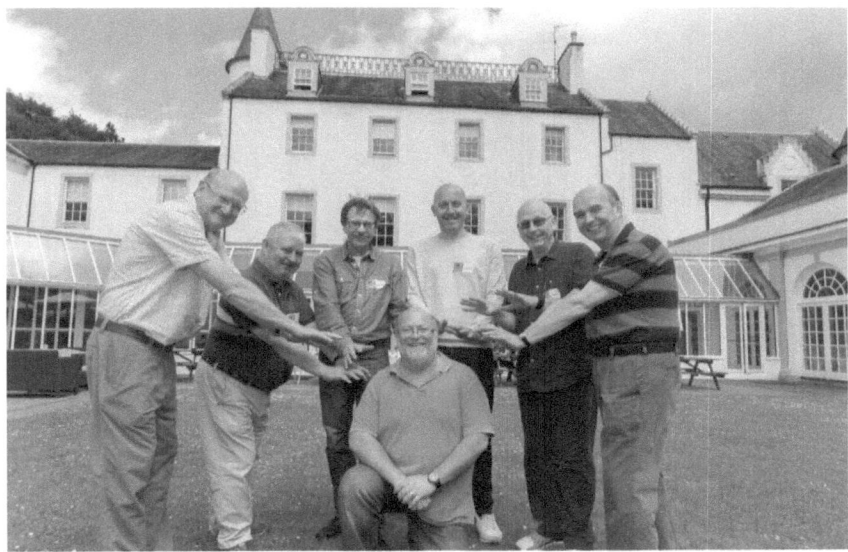

Some of the Seminar attendees having fun. The Scotland seminar was held in a 1400's-era castle.

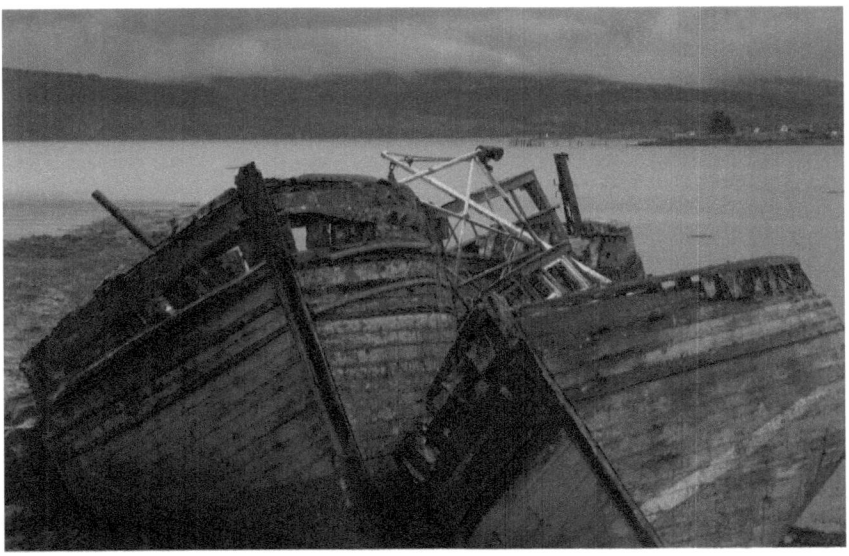

Shipwrecks on the Isle of Mull

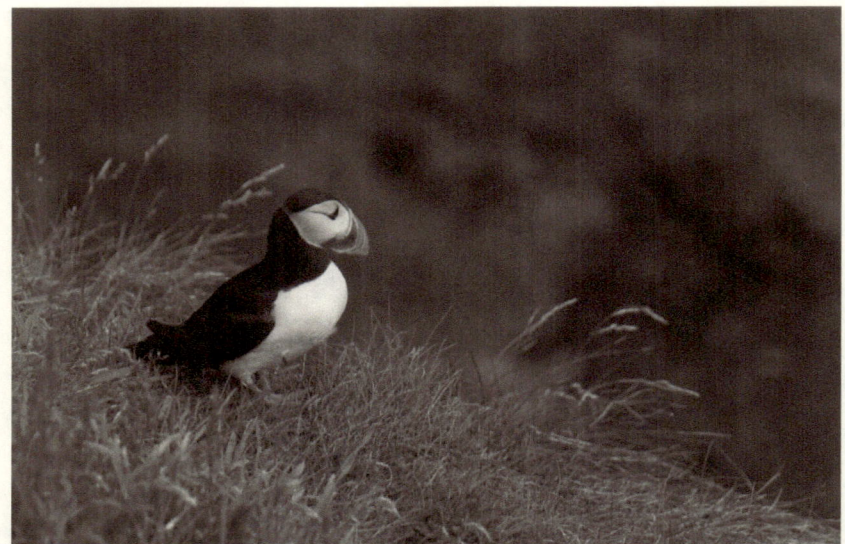

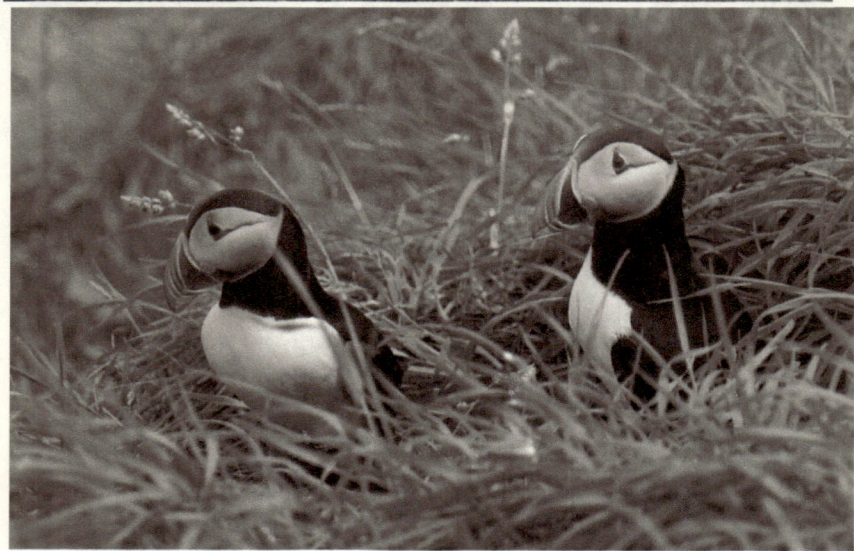

On the uninhabited island of Staffa, in the Inner Hebrides of Scotland, reside hundreds of Puffins. Here are just two shots.

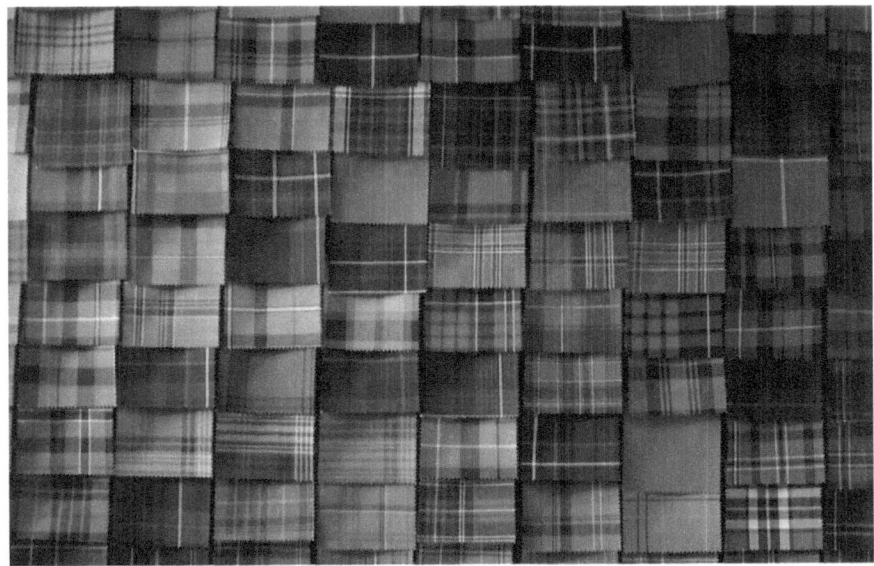

It's a myth that the Scottish tartan pattern represented a particular clan; it actually varied depending upon the region in which they were made (which determined what colors of dyes were available). David Kilpatrick adds: "Only a myth before the banning of the tartan after 1745. George IV broke the ban by visiting Edinburgh and asking the clan chiefs to wear their clan tartans, his own very large figure dressed in full Highland array. It was a publicity coup for Sir Walter Scott, who orchestrated the clan display, ceremonies, dances, dinners. Tartan was permitted, suddenly all the vague connections and historic uses became a goldmine. Tartans linked to names and clans were sold all over the world. A whole mythology of Scotland was created and Queen Victoria embraced it in a big way. But the clan/name connections are all perfectly genuine, as are 'original', 'ancient' and modern researched tartans created on the basis of fragments surviving from hundreds of years ago. I use the 'ancient' version of my tartan (softer colours, more natural) and some of the 'natural dye' very faded re-creations are popular (my ancient really isn't ancient at all)."

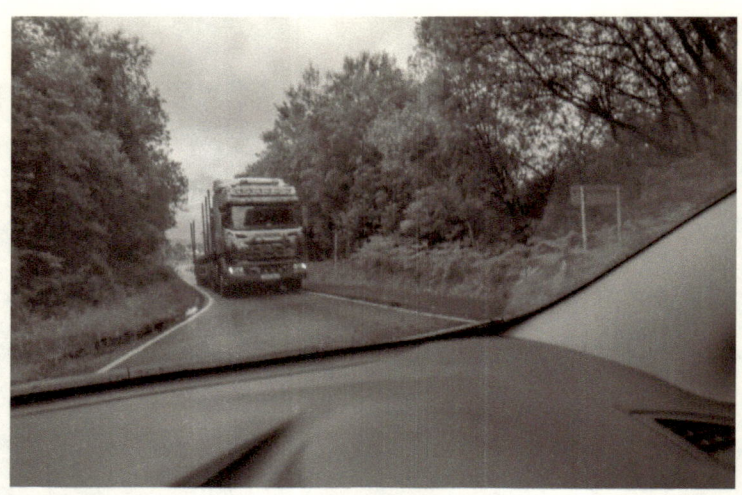

The countryside is beautiful, but it's frustrating to drive. The 2-way roads are barely wide enough for 1.1 vehicles, and if you see a beautiful landscape, there's rarely a place to pull over. A lorry (large truck) and several busses came at me while going down these roads.

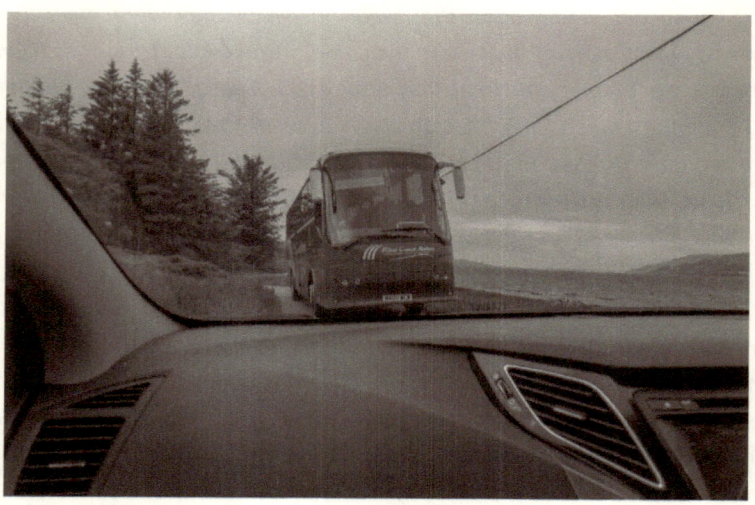

It happened a lot.

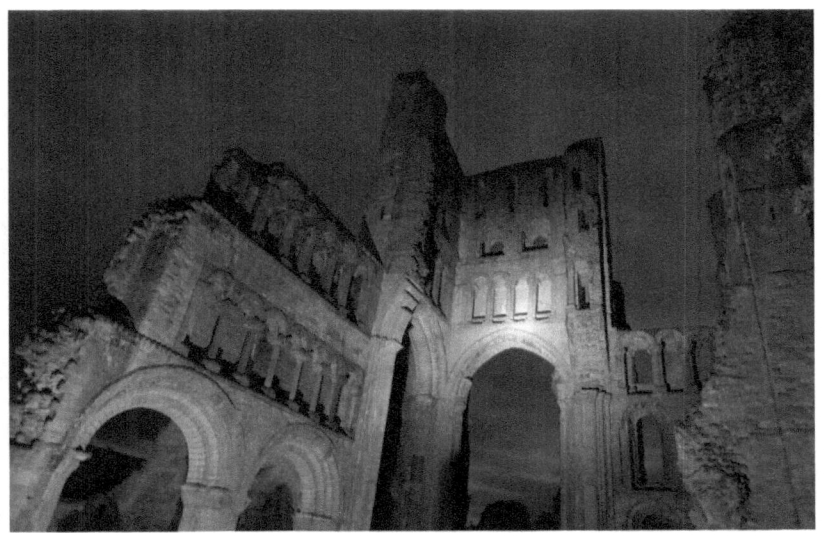

The Kelso Abbey, founded in the 12th century.

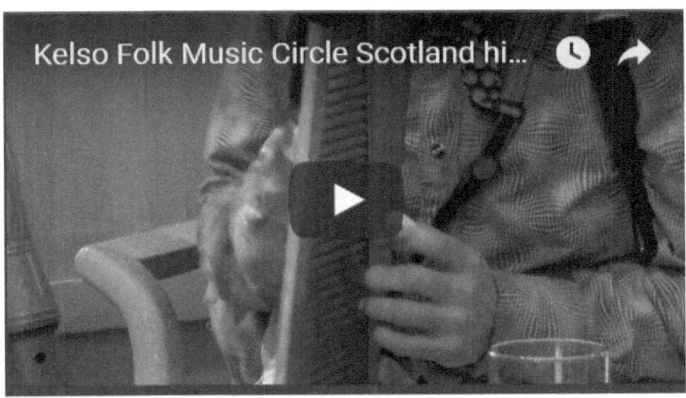

This is a youtube video of my most memorable evening in Scotland - enjoying real folk music made by a circle of friends (not some tourist performance). I promised a compilation of the music, and here it is -- shot in 4K no less with my trusty RX-100. David Kilpatrick sings and plays at the end.
https://youtu.be/gzr-2NhFhRM

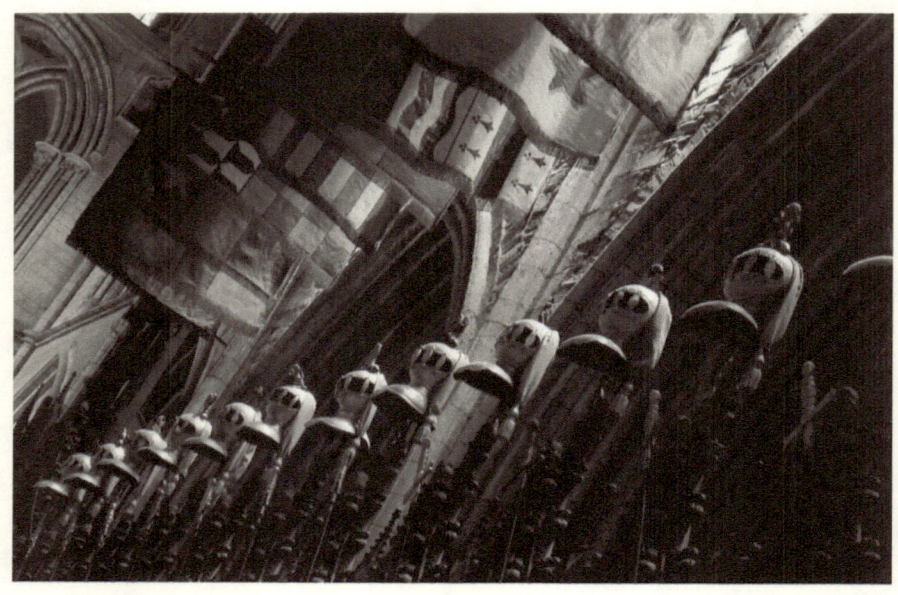

St. Patrick's Cathedral in Dublin

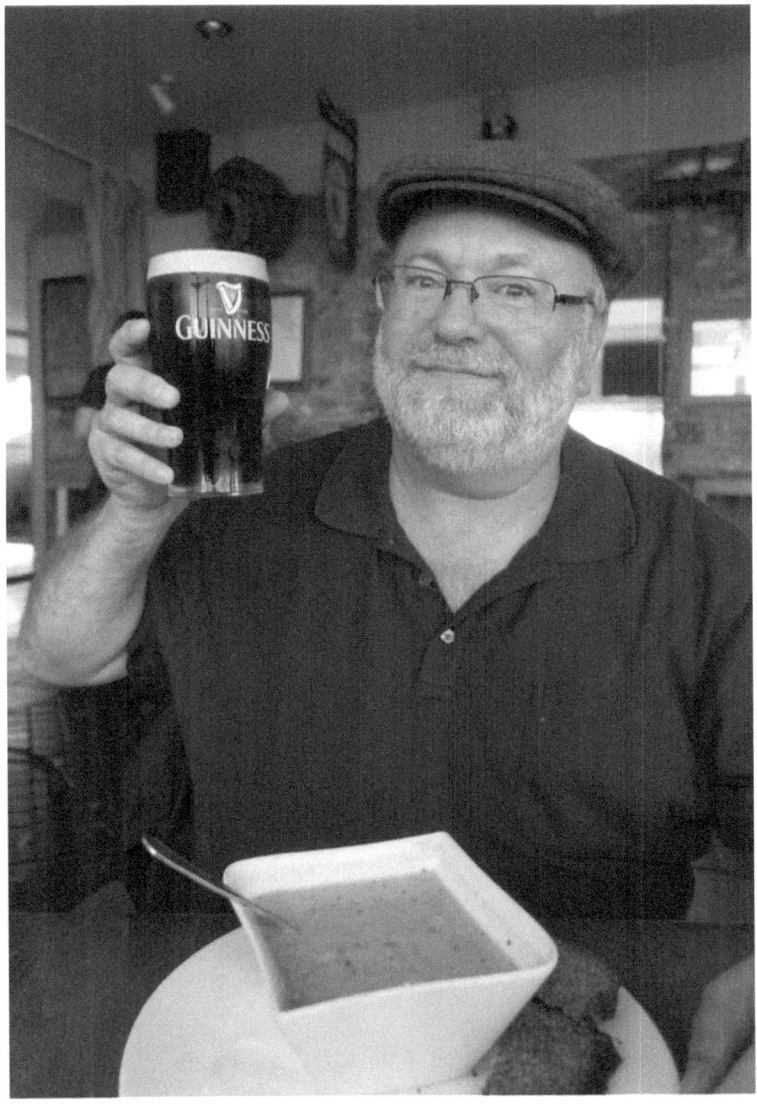

So I went to the Guinness plant in Dublin and said, "I'm in the Guinness Book of World Records - I created the world's smallest phone when I was in college. I'd like a free pint for that achievement!". They really didn't care. So I had a pint at a local pub in Kinsale instead.

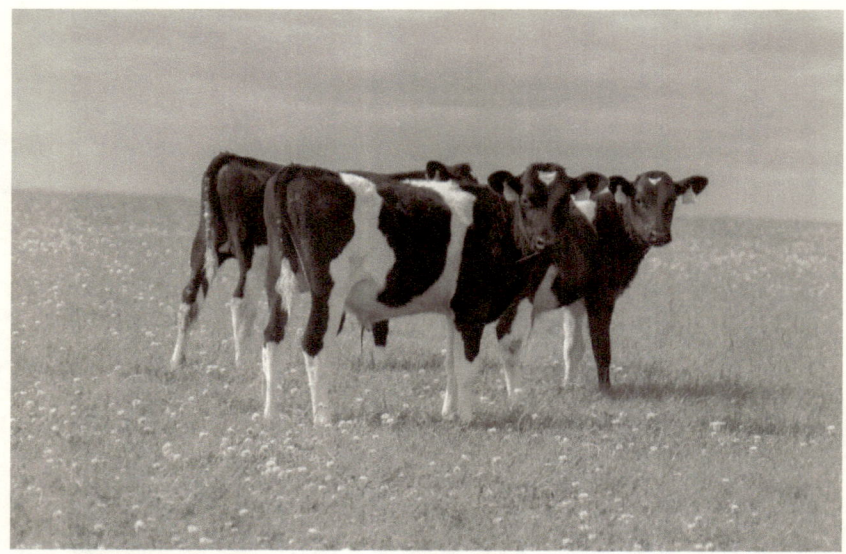

Happy cows come from Ireland.

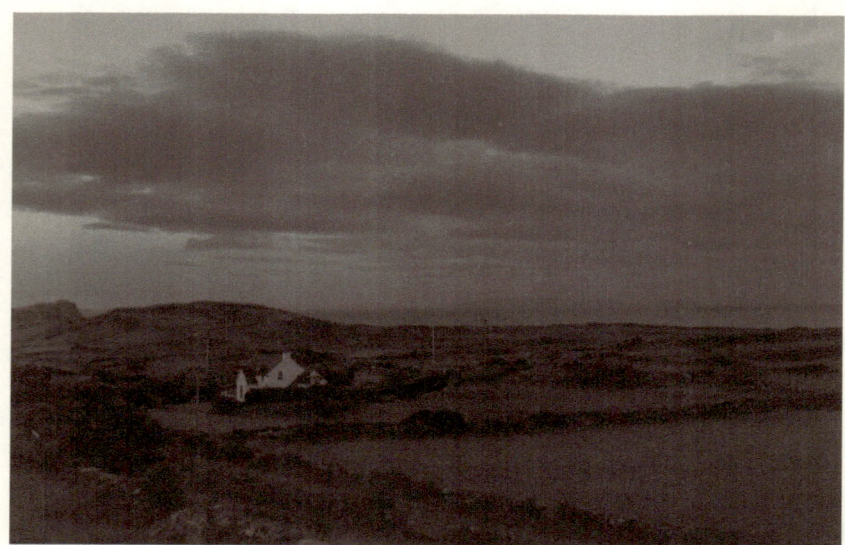

Subtle Irish sunset.

SECTION 2   LIGHTING INSIGHTS

2.1   CLASSICAL ENVIRONMENTAL PORTRAITS

First published January 25, 2015

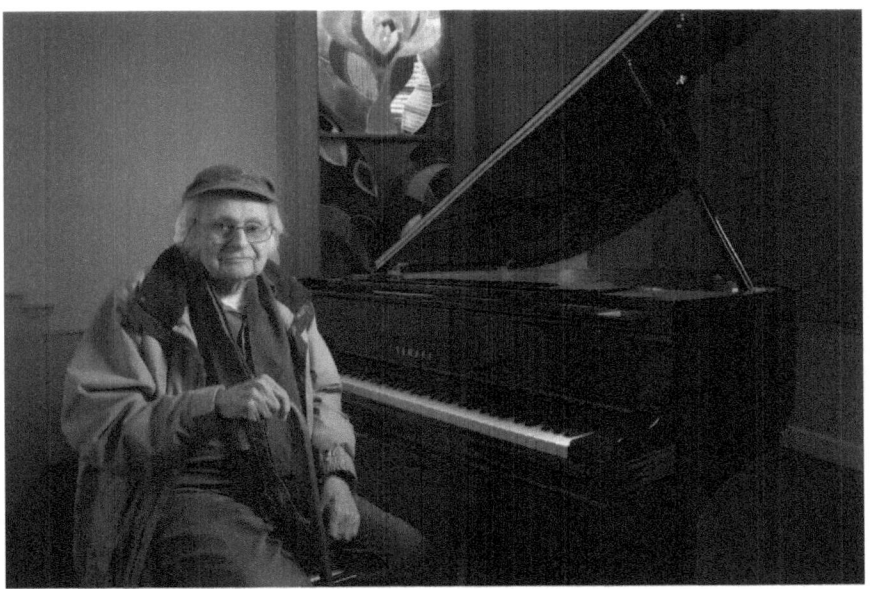

Leon Levitch's life revolved around the piano. He passed away last November.

A "classical" portrait is little more than a headshot, with the eyes placed roughly in the upper third of the vertical frame. An "Environmental Portrait" is a portrait of a person in the environment in which they thrive - it tells the story of a person and who they are in one shot.

So what is a "Classical Environmental Portrait", then?

It's an environmental portrait with classical lighting. The shot above is of pianist Leon Levitch, who had a remarkable history (starting with his escape from the Nazis when he was 15). To take this shot I used just one flash and one softbox, placed in "Rembrandt Lighting Position" (45 degrees to the right, 45 degrees up from the subject. See the setup below, and click on any image to make it larger.)

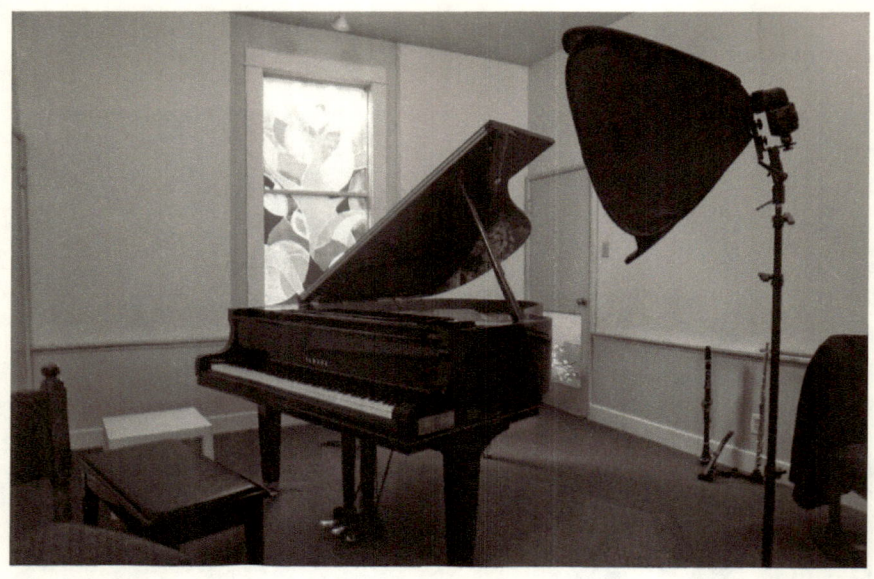

Specs: Sony A7r, Zeiss 24-70 f/2.8, LA-EA4 adapter, Minolta 5600 flash, F20 flash used as a trigger, Lastolite EZYBOX softbox (designed to be used with speedlights).

Probably the most striking thing about this setup is the "before" and "after" look. Here is a similar portrait taken the same day with pianist Danny Brodsley from the Joy of Music (https://www.gigmasters.com/variety-trio/joy-of-music) ensemble:

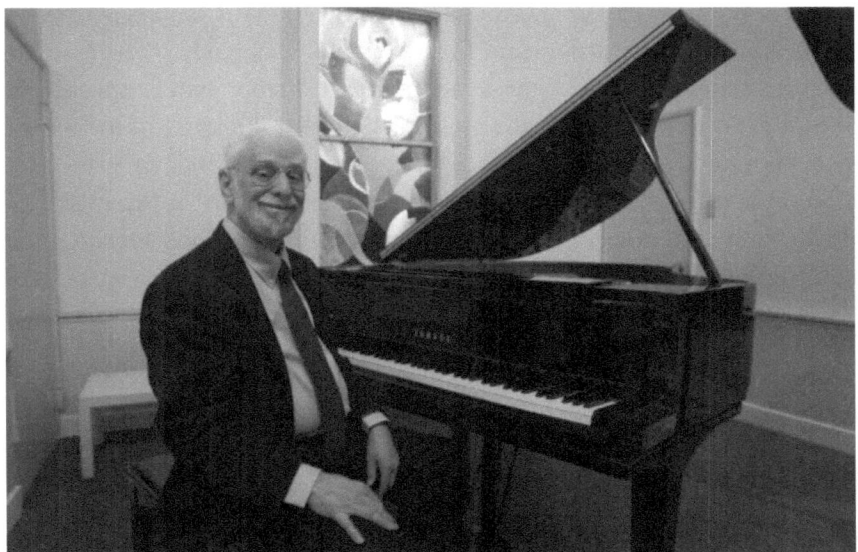

Before: Ambient Light only; 1/6th of a second, f/2.8, ISO 100

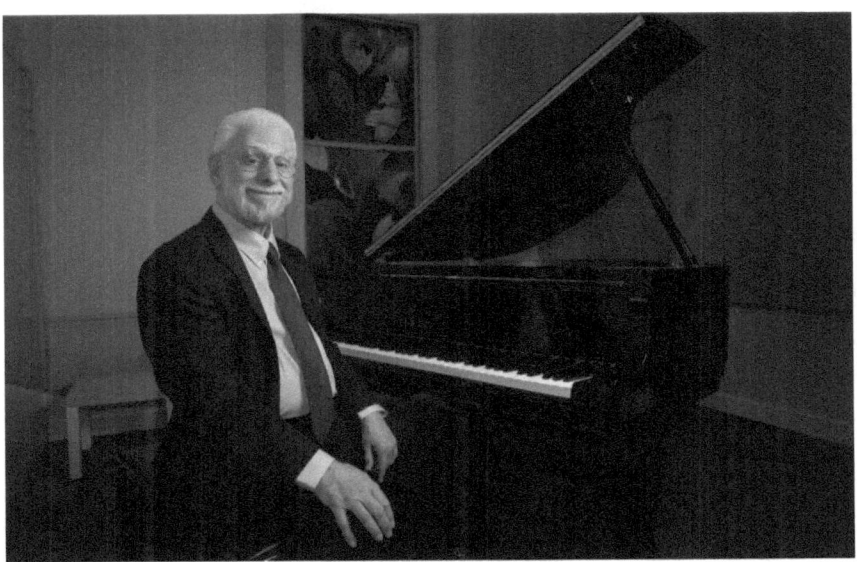

After: Light with wireless flash: 1/80th of a second, f/8, ISO 100. Flash on manual output; 1/2 power. What do you think of him now? :-)

Notice how much darker the room looks - wouldn't it be brighter since you're adding light from the flash to what's already there?   The unintuitive answer is NO - the combination of f/stop, shutter speed, and ISO let in so little light that the ambient light just didn't register. So the flash became the brightest light in the room. (The stained glass is a different story - it should have been a little brighter as in the image of Mr. Levitch, however a truck pulled in just before the shot, blocking the light from the window.)

And for some perspective, here's the same setup but with the flash mounted on top of the camera, universally known as the worst kind of light you can give your pictures in a dark room:

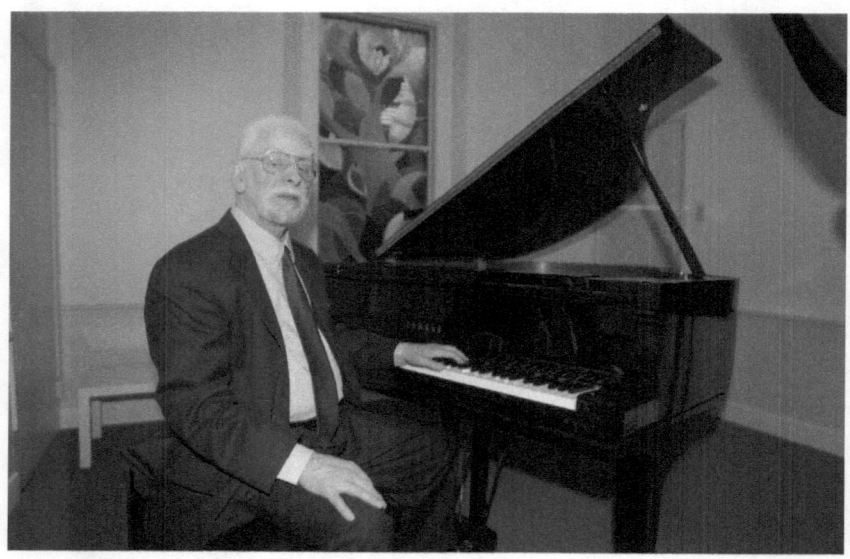

(Scholarly comment: "Yuk!")

If this demonstration of how to completely transform the mood and emotion of your image doesn't get you excited to go out and learn to use wireless flash (http://friedmanarchives.com/WWWF/index.htm), I don't know what will!

2.2   A GIFT FOR MY WIFE

First published October 14, 2015

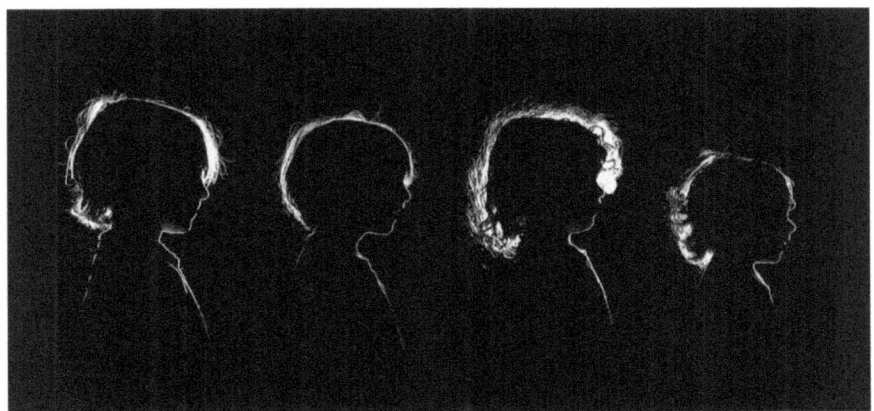

I took these profiles of the grandkids (at the top of this post) in secret as a surprise for my wife. And I did it with just ONE unmodified wireless flash. You can do this too. How, you ask?

In the past, I would create this outline effect by using a single wireless flash placed behind the subject's head, with a homemade grid in front to control the light spill if I were shooting in a confined space. But this time I used a plain flash with no light modifiers at all. I just shot in an open room (no adjacent walls or furniture) and zoomed in to 200mm so I only captured the light around the subject.

The final image was a composite of 4 different shots (surely you didn't think I could get all 4 grandkids to hold still all at once, did you? :-)) Below is a sample of one shot, right out of the camera:

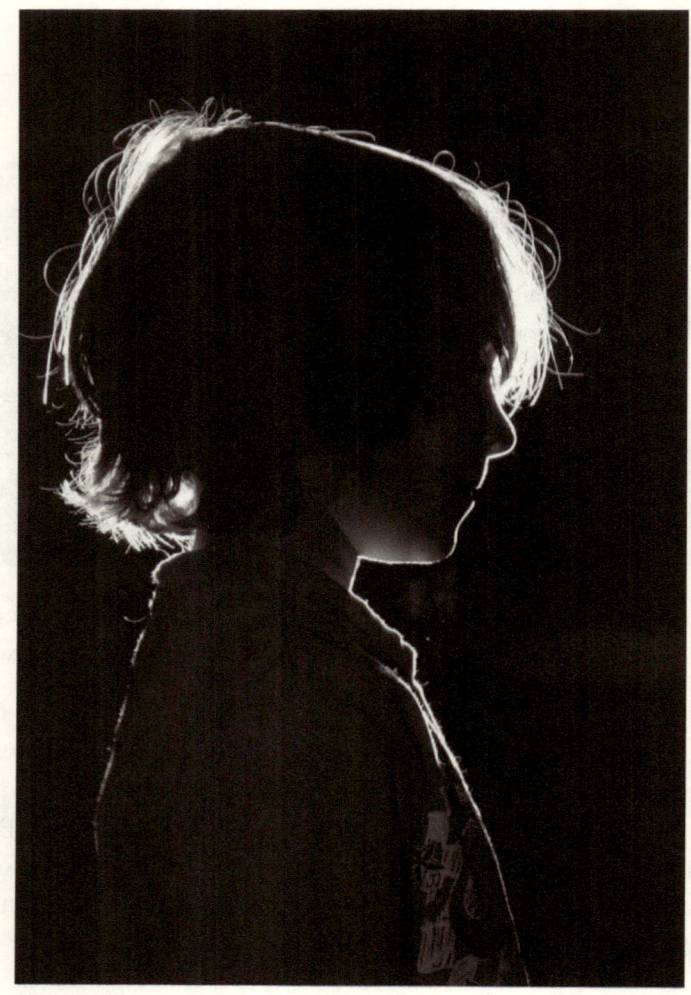

Tech details: 1/400th, ƒ/2.8, ISO 100, RX-10 II. Flash set to manual output at 1/2 power; flash's zoom head was set to "all the way" (in this case, 105mm)

That's pretty close to what I had in mind. Then I went to photoshop and used the Curves tool to make everything black except for the white of the outline:

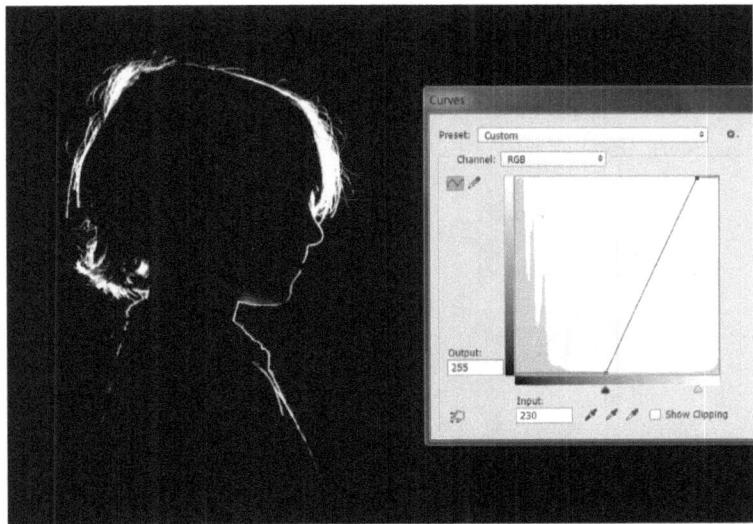

Then I combined four of these images into one, wide, really-expensive-to-enlarge image.

Of all the images I've taken of the kids, this composite probably has the most impact and will have a permanent place in our family's home.

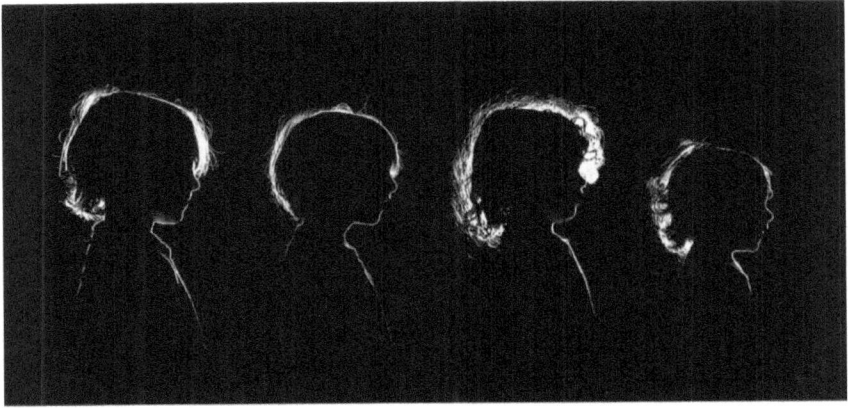

The hardest part was getting the 1-year-old to stay still and look in one direction. What you can't see is the pair of hands that's holding him in place and the distraction we placed in front of him. :-)

2.3   PRODUCT LIGHTING

First published April, 2017

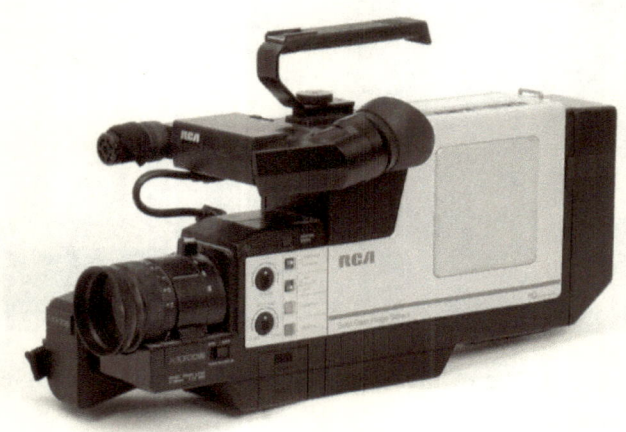

So here I am adding to my Old Technology section of the Friedman
Archives Website (http://friedmanarchives.com/Old_Technology). I
came across two ancient camcorders (one more ancient than the other) so
I photographed and posted them. Old technology seems to appreciate in
value over time.

I used to photograph them on a nice blue background, but learned that
even though it may look nicer, people like to remove the background and
past them into their own contexts. And so I now shoot on white to make
them more marketable.

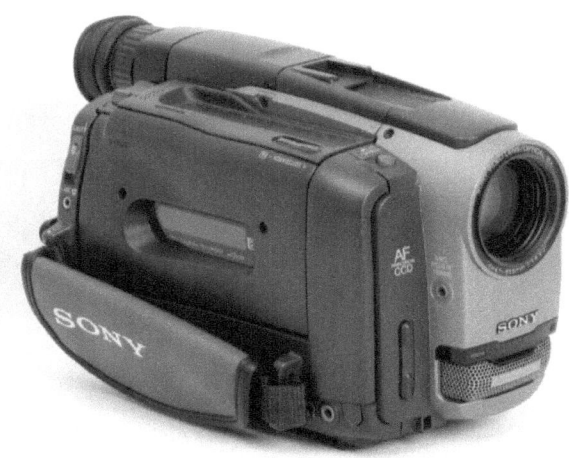

So how is the lighting done? I use two strobes; one with a softbox and one pointed at the white ceiling for a diffused fill. (You can do this with wireless flashes, too.) And a pull-down window shade from Ikea as a seamless backdrop.

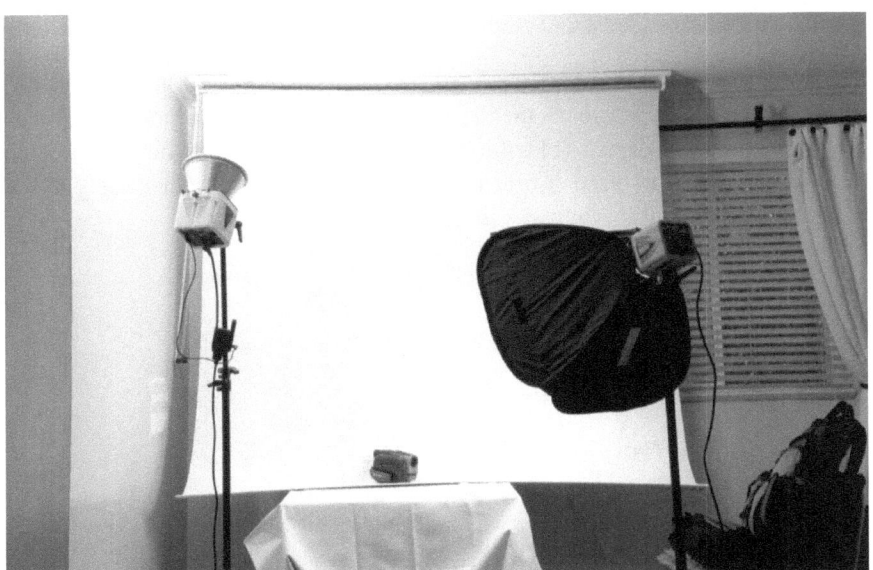

2.4   HOW I LIT THIS CHILD PRODIGY

First published May 17, 2015

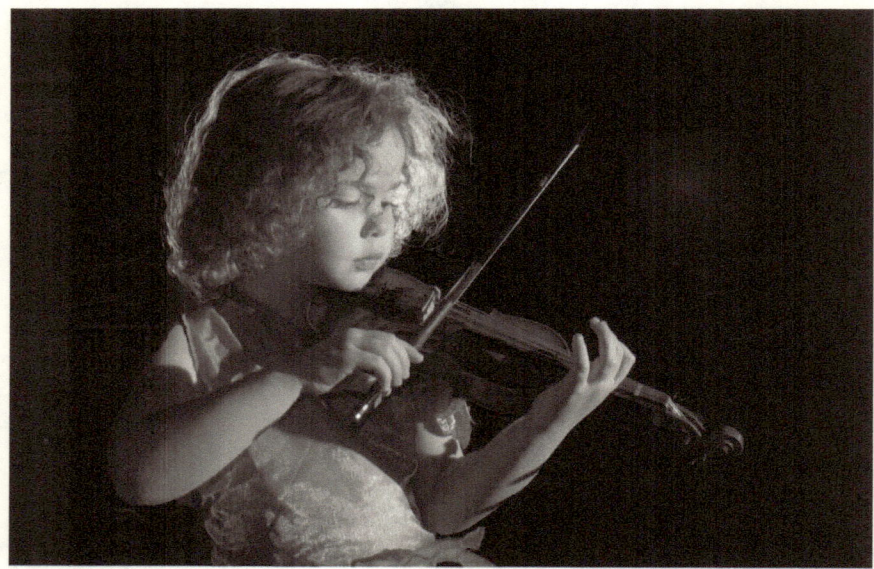

I took the shot above in a very confined space and so it was essential to have as little "light spill" as possible - that is, light only the subject and try to minimize any of the adjacent objects (like the bookshelf and chair behind her) from being lit as well. And so I used two grids - one on the front of each flash - on the front, to keep the rays of light as parallel as possible.

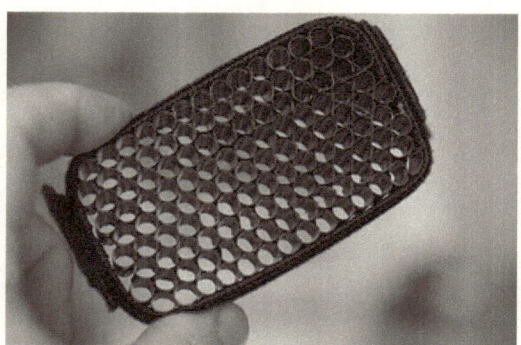

The first flash went behind the subject just to illuminate her entropy-laden hair.

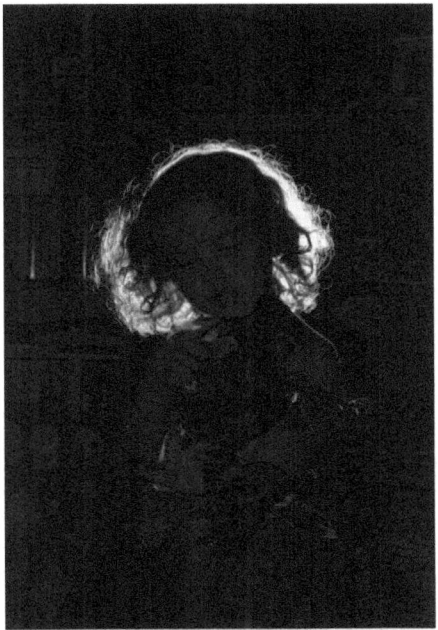

To make sure there was no ambient light showing up in the shot, I put the A77 II and kit lens into manual mode, chose as high a shutter speed as I could without going to HSS to ensure maximum distance of the flash, and I shot at about f/8 both to reduce ambient light some more, and also so I would hit the lens' sweet spot in terms of sharpness.

Then I placed a 2nd flash (also with a grid) to the subject's left:

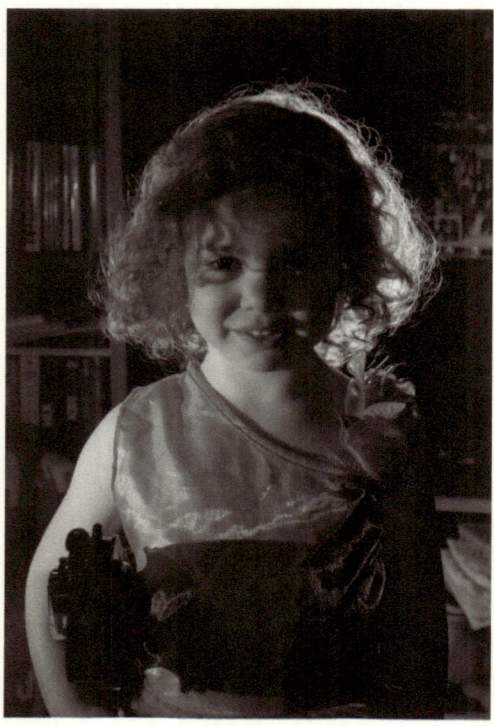

Yuk! Bad aim and too-strong shadows. Plus, once she started playing violin I realized her face would be pointing in the opposite direction. So I quickly moved the light and got this:

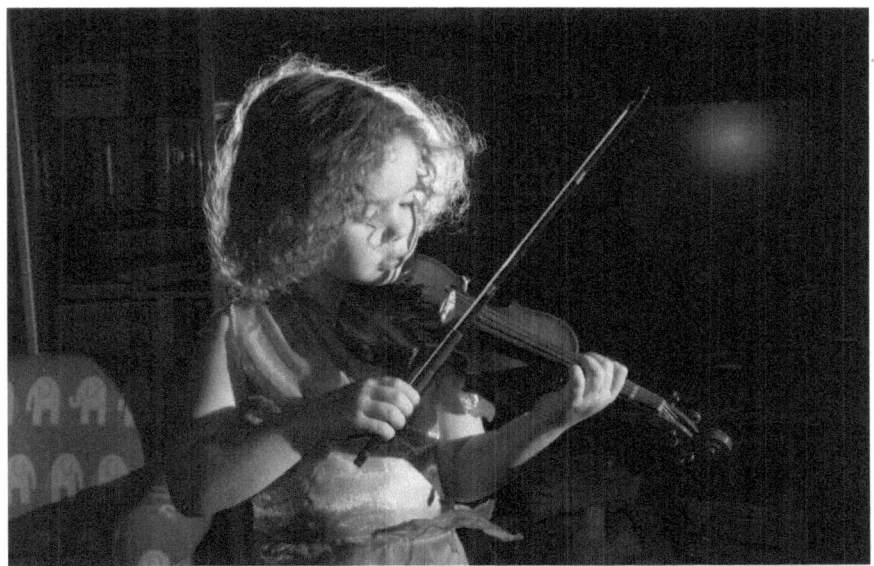

Better! Still some light spill (especially with the green chair in the lower left corner), but I can attenuate that in Photoshop later.

So that was the easy part. Now to overcome the variables I couldn't control:

- If she moves even a few inches in any direction, her hair is no longer well-lit and the flash shines directly into the camera, ruining the shot. (She's 4 1/2 years old. She can't sit still at all.)
- There were many shots where the bow would create a harsh shadow on her face (like in the example above).

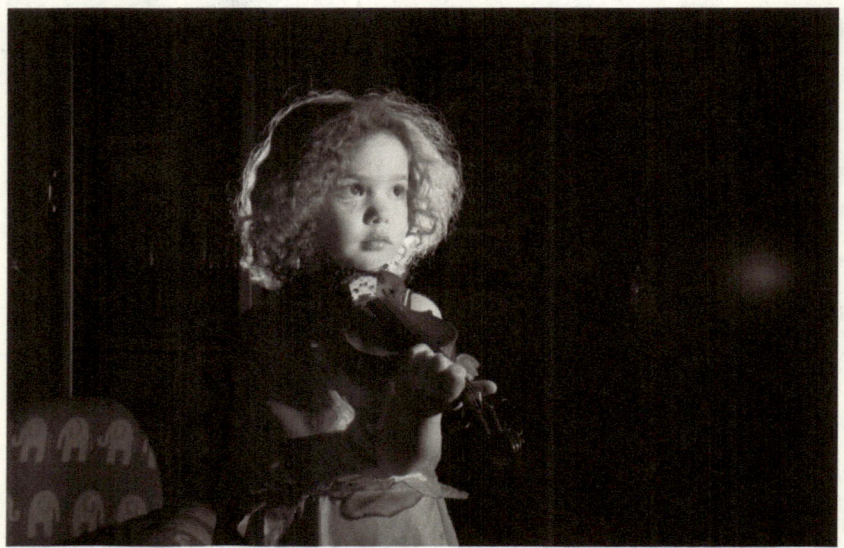

Great expression but there's no bow.

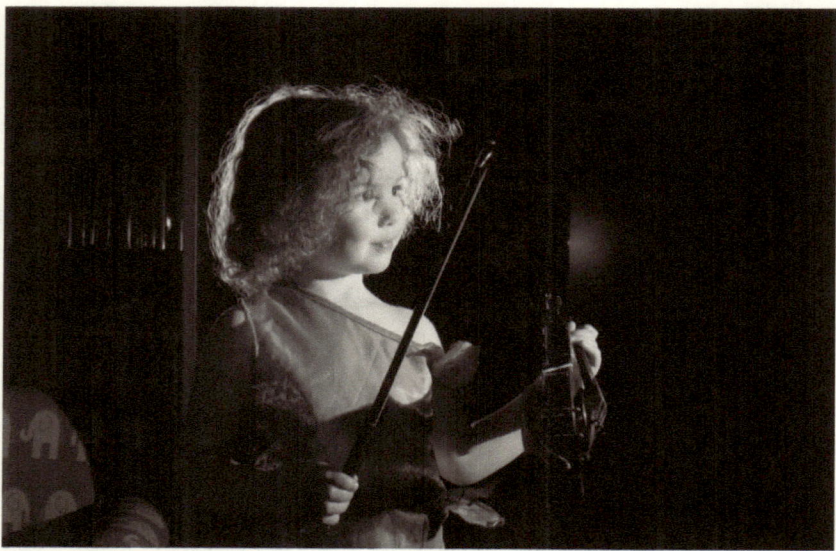

Perfect expression but she's not playing and you can hardly see the violin.

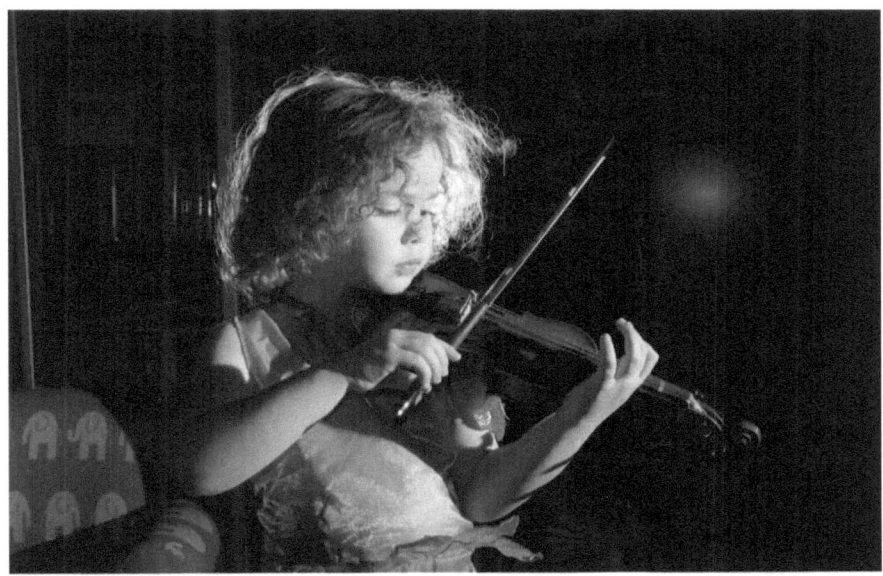

Aha! Now to soften the highlights and darken the background in post-processing:

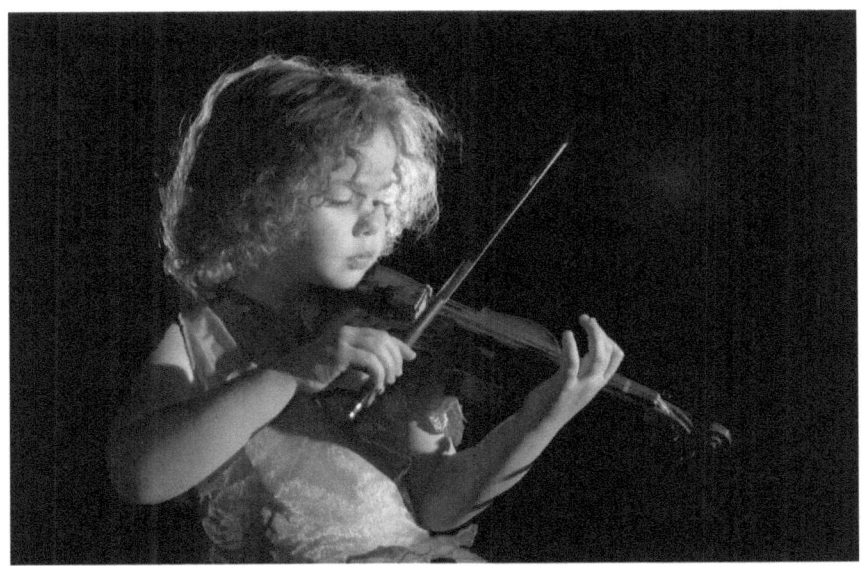

I took a total of about 45 pictures before getting this winner. Not bad for having control over so few variables.

Below is a decidedly un-glamorous behind-the-scenes picture of how the lighting was done. The two flashes are circled in yellow:

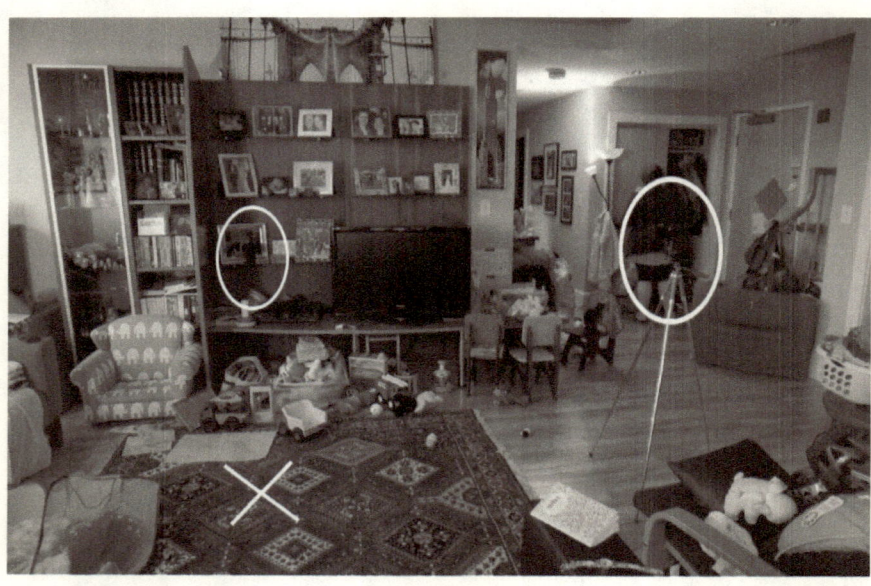

This shot would have been much easier had there not been such close quarters - doing it outdoors at night, for example, wouldn't have required any Photoshop afterwards.

(Shameless plug: Want to get your feet wet with wireless flash? My ebooklet walks you through everything you need using a decidedly non-technical approach. http://friedmanarchives.com/WWWF)

2.5   BETTER   PICTURES   USING   YOUR   SMARTPHONE

First published June, 2015

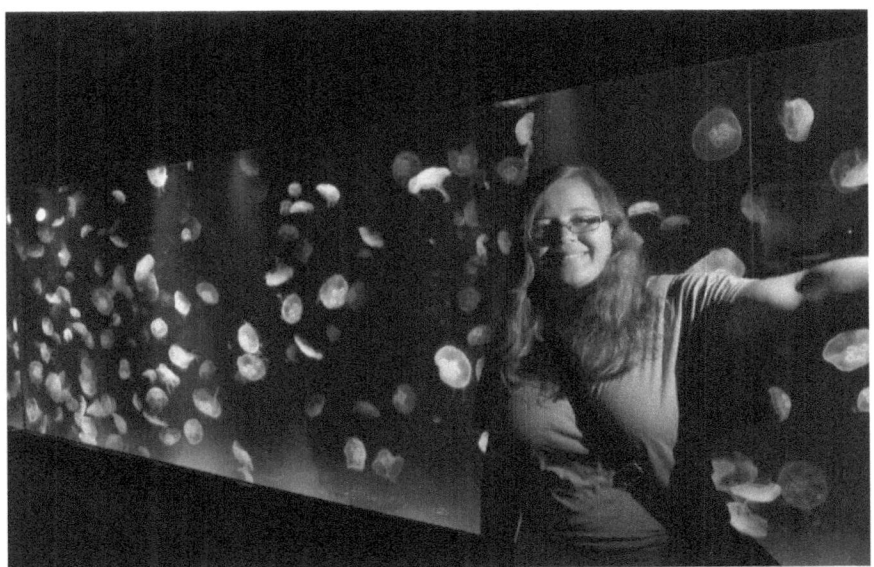

I take family snapshots as much as the next guy. And yet I cringe whenever I see the hallmark of a snapshot: a flash picture taken in a dark room, with the camera's built-in flash as the sole source of light. This is the universally acknowledged, Guinness-book-of-world-records worst way to light a shot.

Want an example?   Here's a picture of my wife (she took me to Disneyland for my birthday). The first picture was taken in front of the world-famous castle with the RX-100 III using the pop-up flash in Program mode:

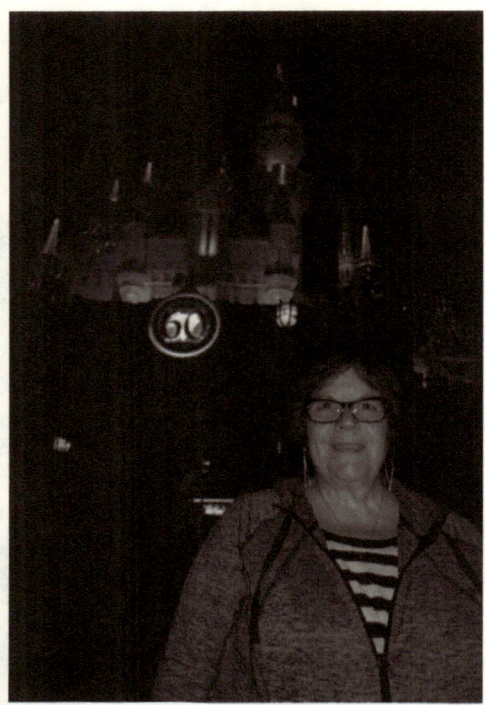

Point-and-shoot mode. Even great cameras can take bad pictures.

Yuk, right?

Right after this my wife Carol, who has listened to me lecture about the benefits of wireless flash for nearly a decade, had a great idea. She reached into her purse, pulled out her smartphone, invoked the "Flashlight" app (which turns on a bright LED on the back of her phone), and held it at arm's length. The results were "wireless flash without the wireless flash":

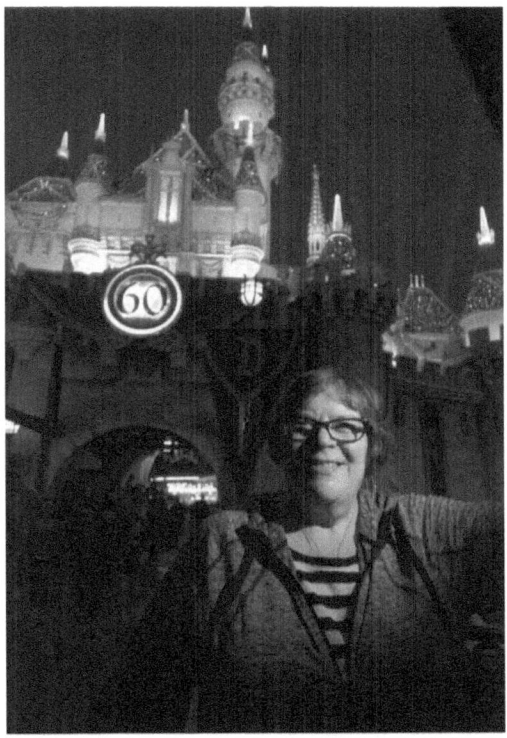

And since the camera didn't think a flash was being used, it exposed for the background properly without me having to dial anything in.

Here's another example, taken at the Chattanooga Aquarium in Tennessee. Now in this instance the background was mostly black and so the camera's automatic exposure was going to get it wrong. And so I did this shot in two steps:

Step 1) without a flashlight, put the camera into manual mode and adjusted the exposure so the background looked the way I wanted it to look (see below):

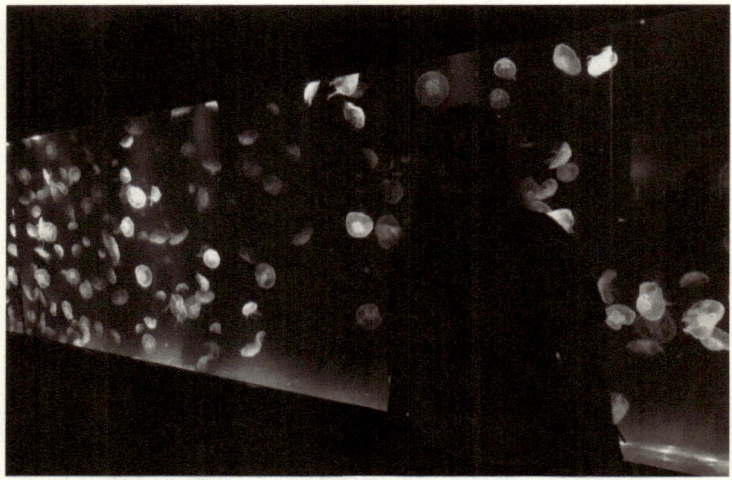

First, set your exposure so the background looks the way you want.

Step 2) Turned on the smartphone's flashlight, handed it to the subject, and had her hold it in "Rembrandt position" – 45 degrees up, 45 degrees to one side:

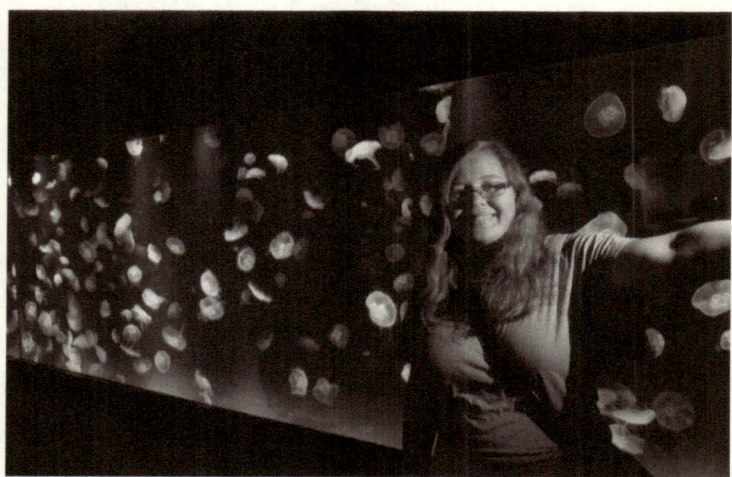

Then, turn on the flashlight on your mobile phone and hold it at arm's length. Dramatic light!

Voila!

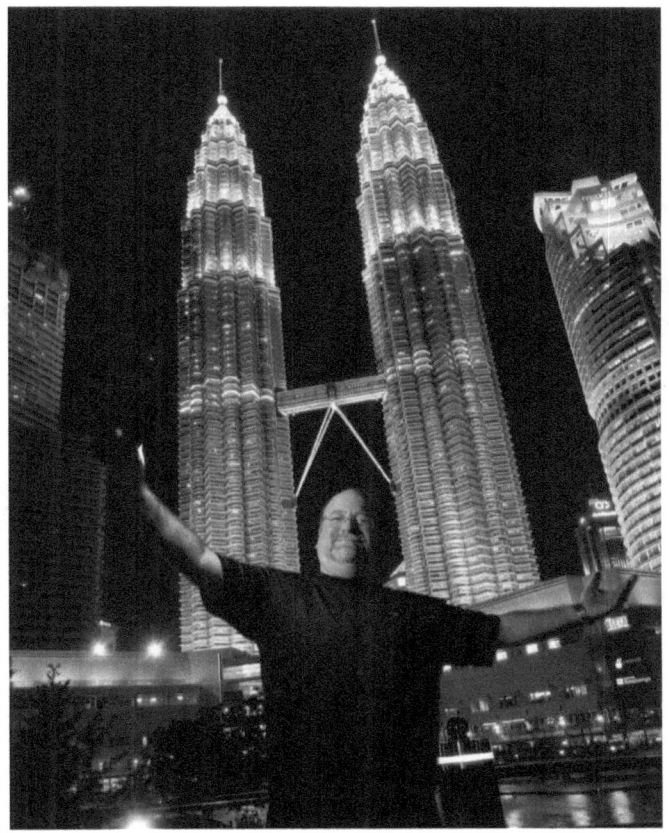

This is a lot handier than carrying a wireless flash with you everywhere like I used to do! :-) (The wireless flash is in my right hand.)

2.6   HOW TO SHOOT A BHARATANATYAM ARANGETRAM

First published September, 2016

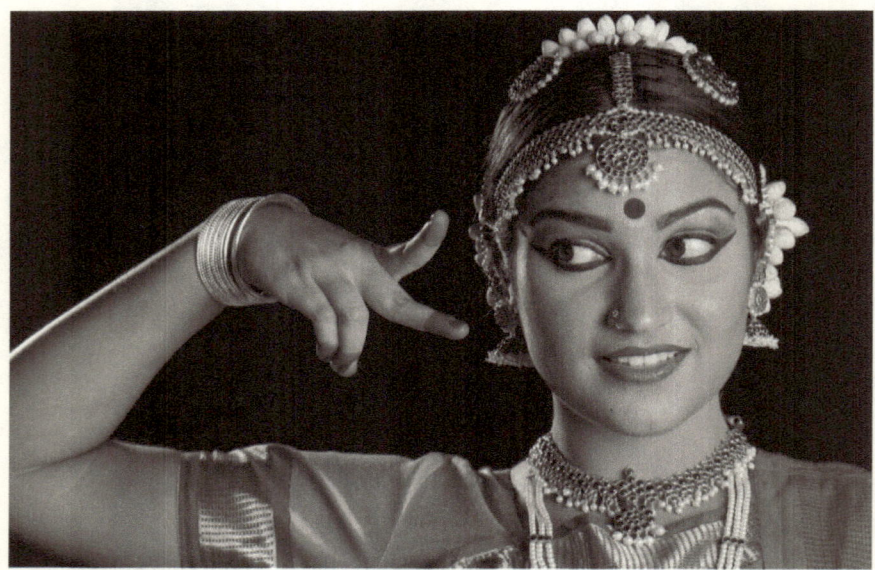

There is a traditional classical dance in India called the Bharatanatyam. It takes years of study to perfect it (11 years in this case), working with an accomplished guru. Every dance tells an epic story, and every movement has significance. When the guru feels the student is ready, the first "coming out" performance called an Arangetram ensues. I was hired to take the invitational and "publicity" shots for this event.

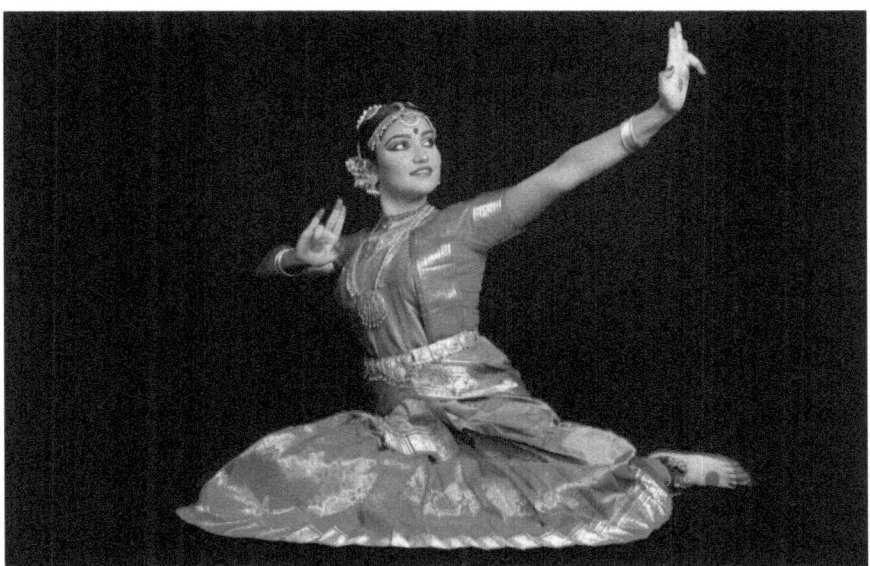

Normally this wouldn't be worth blogging about, since these look just like ordinary shots taken in a studio. But they weren't - I took these shots outdoors, on the front porch, in the daytime. Here's the setup I used:

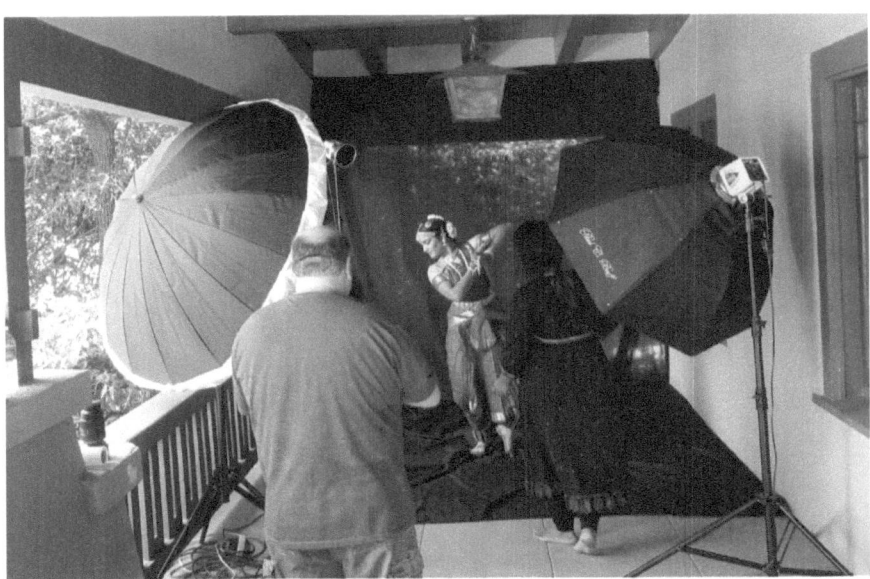

This is a basic 3-light setup: The strongest light (the "key light") is on the right, on the left is a "fill" light set for half of the key light. There's also a 3rd light next to the backdrop called a "hair light", pointing to the back of the dancer's head. Finally, a thin black cloth was hung to provide a dark background.

Notice that the final results look nothing like what the eye sees, either in the above shot or in the behind-the-scenes video posted below. This is because I had the camera set to manual exposure, set my shutter speed to 1/160th (the highest flash sync speed for strobes with this camera), f/stop to f/9, and ISO to 100 to ensure that, without the strobes, the ambient light would not register in the exposure.

And it worked! All of the shots below are .jpgs straight out of the camera:

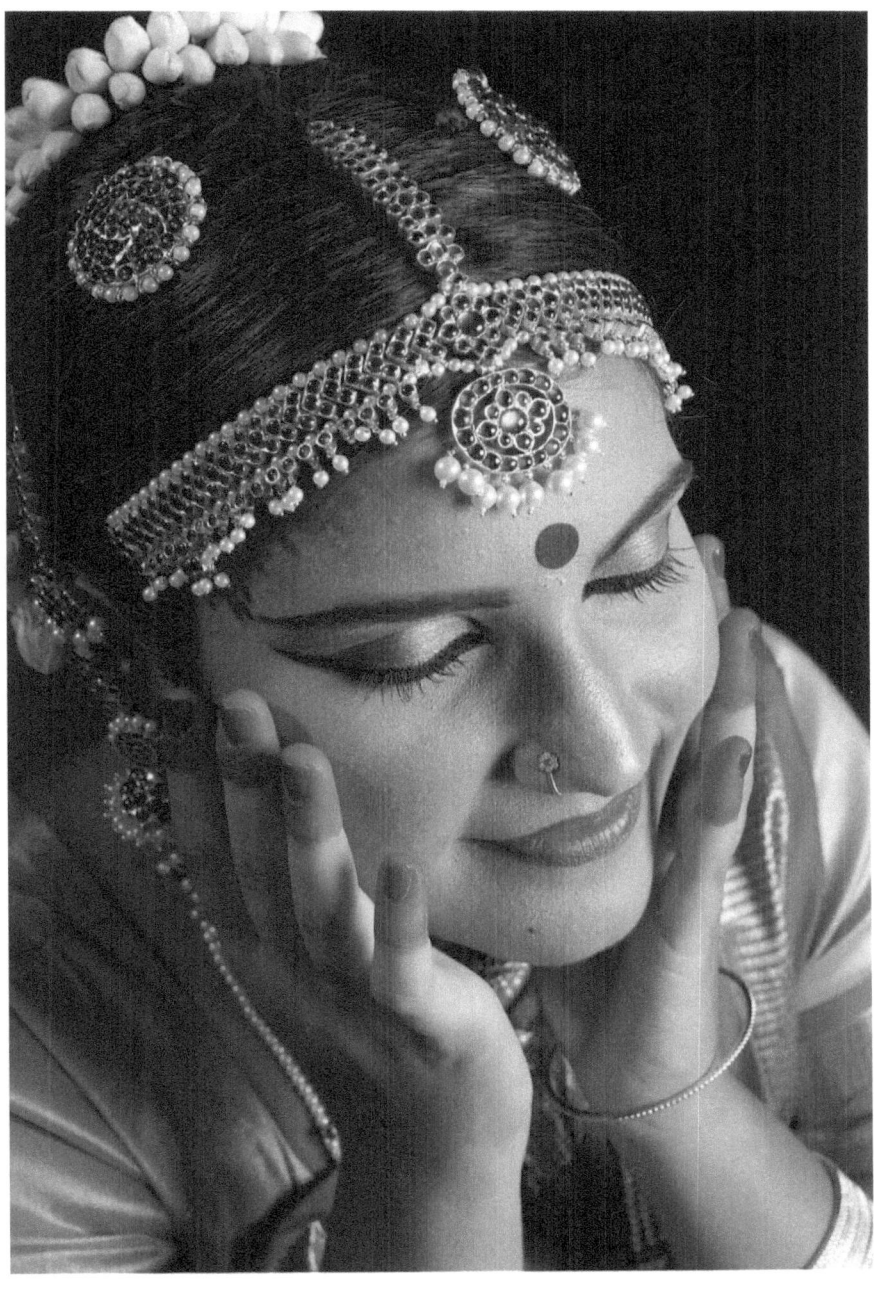

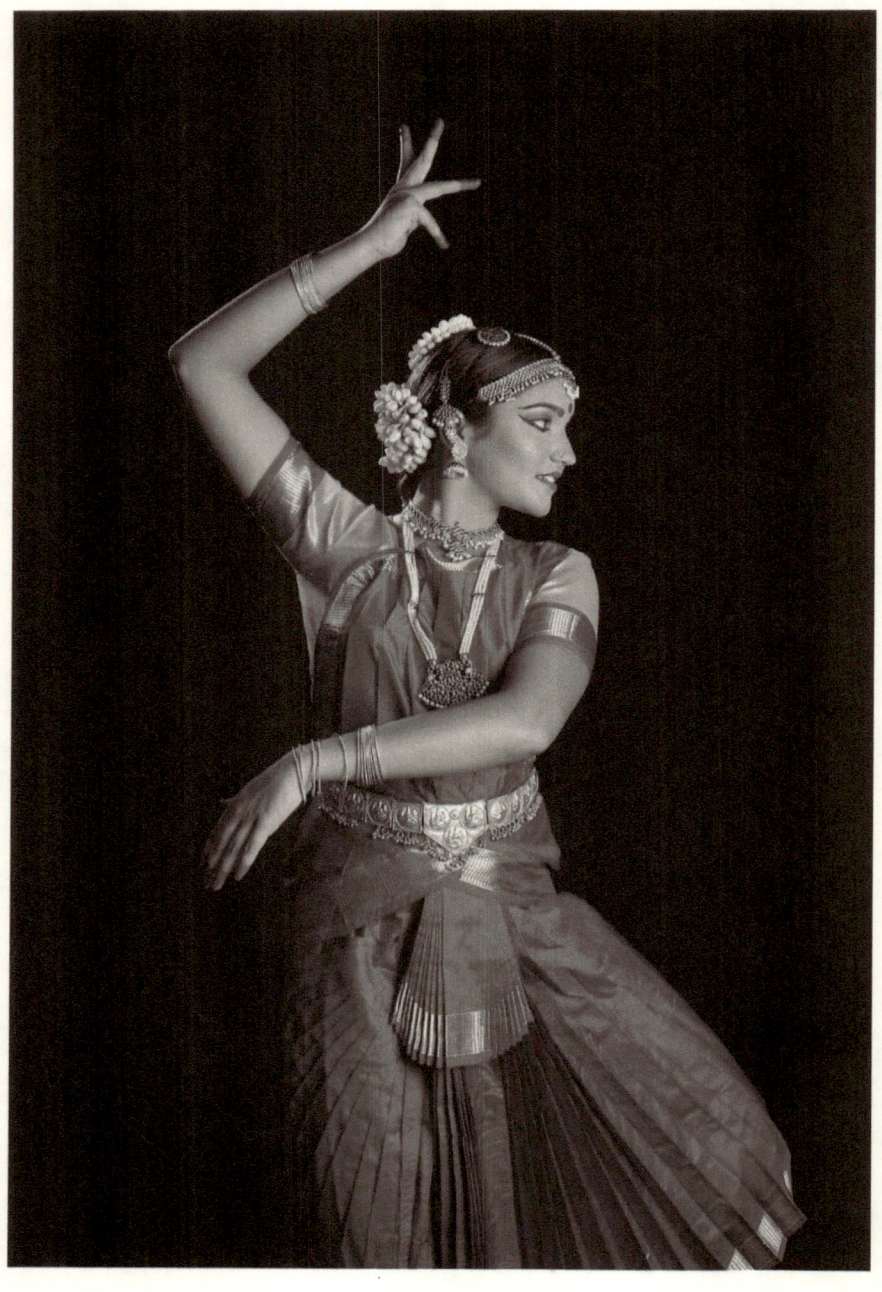

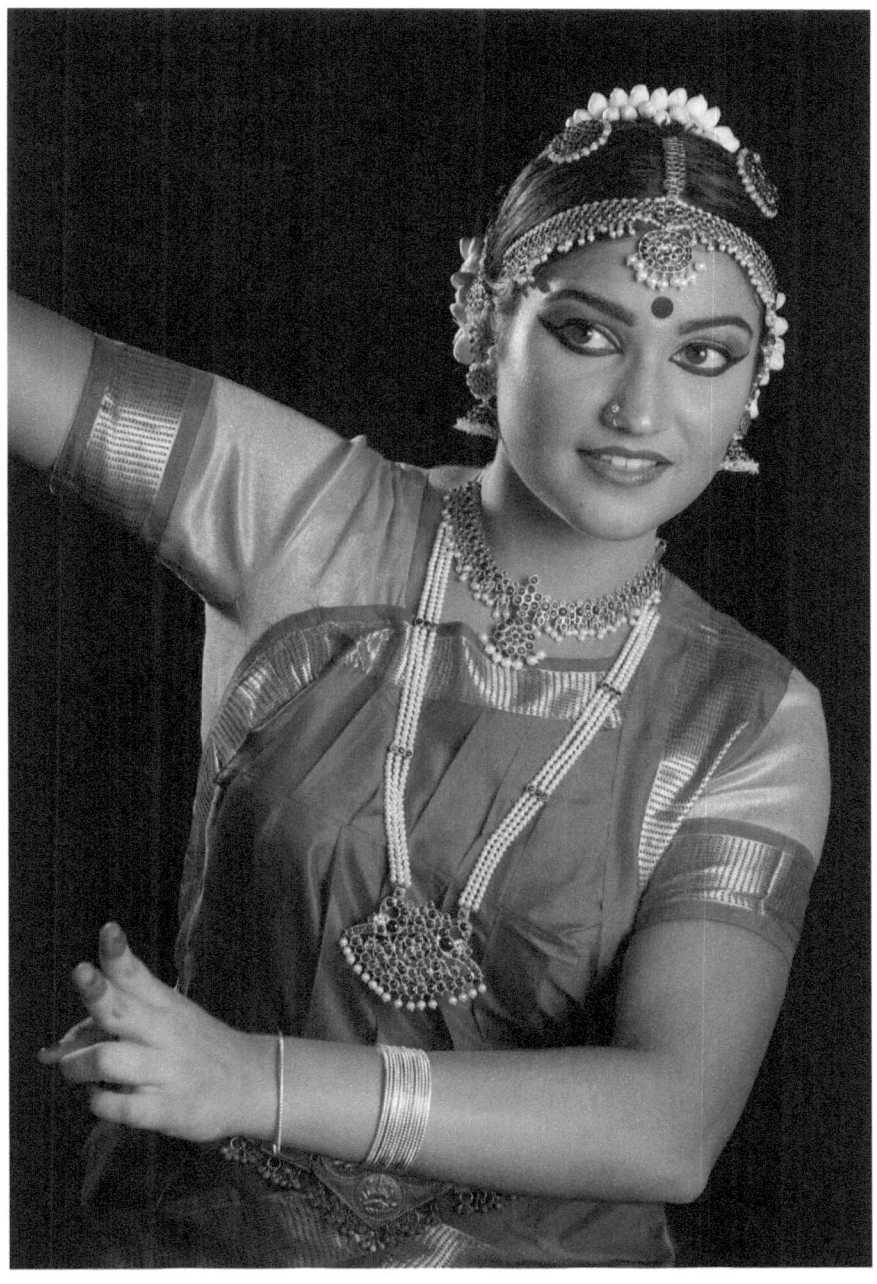

The manual exposure settings were also responsible for you not being able to see the trees showing through the thin backdrop - because the strobes were much more powerful than the ambient light, and it was the strobe lights I had exposed for.

The only time I needed to Photoshop anything was when it came time to take full-body poses. Because the space was so small, lightstands and walls started showing up in the shot.

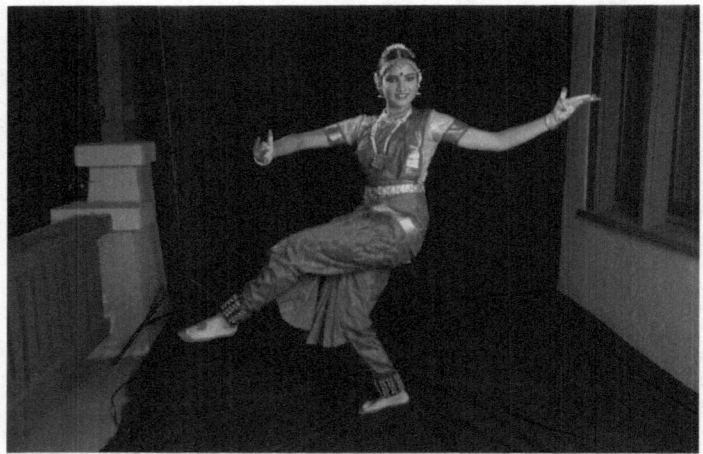

In cases like these, photoshop is your friend:

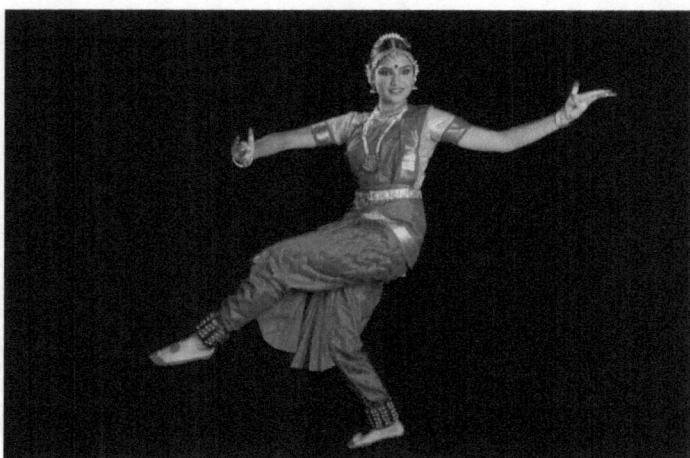

Behind the Scenes

Here's a quick BTS video, taken by one of the parents: https://www.youtube.com/watch?v=j0LAYllWfdA

How to Make a Great Lens Shine

For this session, I was using the Sony A7R II, the new G-Master 24-70 lens, and the Zeiss 135mm f/1.8 lens with the LA-EA4 adapter. As you would expect, the results were amazingly sharp.

"Gee, Gary, looking at your BTS video, I see that the ambient light from the porch looked ideal - it was soft and directional. Why didn't you make use of that instead of futzing with those expensive strobes?"

The answer is if you're looking for "OMG-That's-Sharp!" imagery, strobes will give it to you. Ambient doesn't always look that way unless you're very careful.

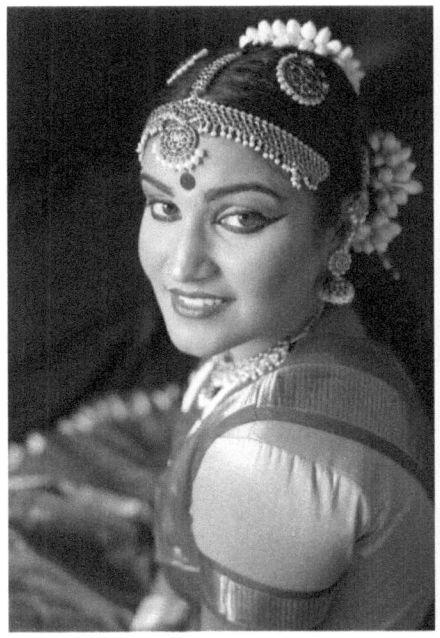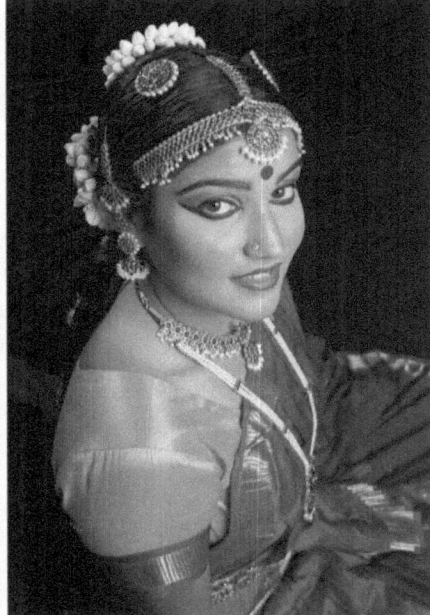

Left: Ambient light. Right: Pure strobes. See a difference?

And to prove that, I took a few shots with the strobes turned off and the camera set to capture the ambient light. (Click on images to see them larger.)

Without pixel peeping, you notice right away that the ambient shot lacks the perceived refinement of the strobe shot. With pixel peeping, you can see a difference in apparent sharpness:

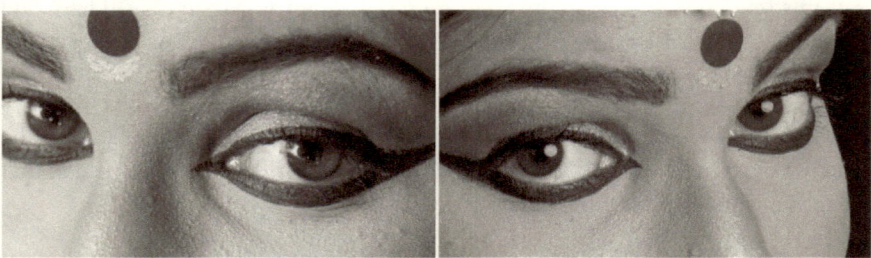

100% crops from above. Notice that in the right shot, Eye AF choose to focus on the right eye. Not the eye I would have chosen had I been using the spot-focus-recompose-shoot method.

People my age won't be shocked by this comparison - every lens has a sweet spot when stopped down, even the new uber-lenses that are supposed to be amazingly sharp wide open (f/2.8 in this case).

The moral to the story: As I've been saying for a long time, good directional light is the key to getting the most out of your lenses - even the super expensive kind. If you think getting a new lens will improve your photography, try concentrating on better light instead if you can. (Or my seminar, which is also a great place to start. :-))

Scholarly notes

1) "Gary, you own studio strobes? I expected this to be done via Wireless Flash!" Yes, I invested in studio strobes during T.E.I.W.S.F.H.T.D.F. (The Era In Which Sony Forgot How To Do Flash), starting with the A77, continuing with the A99's 1/4-second delay, and thankfully ending with the A77 Firmware version 7. (Things are better now.) And studio strobes are a better fit for shooting kids or for outdoor applications like this, since the recycle time is usually less than one second.

2) "Is a G-Master lens really that much better?" The answer is I could have used my existing A-mount Zeiss 24-70 f/2.8 lens with an LA-EA3 adapter instead, and the results would have been just as impressive. (Preemptive strike: the only way to see a difference between those two lenses is to use an optical bench or an electron microscope. Is it that much better to drive a Lamborghini over a Ferrari?) However, the G-Master lens has another, more tangible benefit: the Eye-AF feature only works with native E-mount lenses[1], and in situations like this I find that feature to be extremely handy.

---

[1] Well, that was true as of this writing. Newer cameras and adapters can now work with a wider variety of lenses.

2.7   NEWBORN PHOTOGRAPHY SECRETS

First published March, 2016

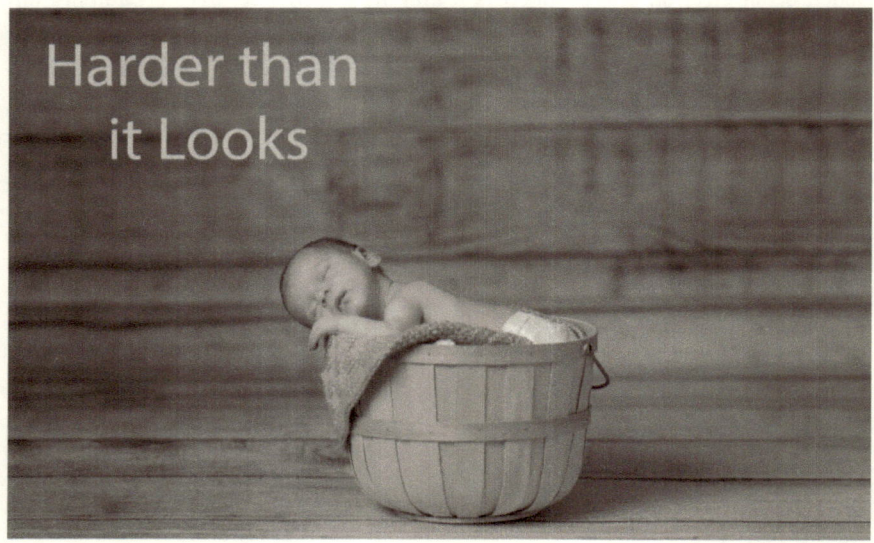

Ever since Anne Geddes raised the bar on the newborn photography genre, an entire legion of people shooting newborns in this style has arisen. And this seemingly simple style of photography is considerably harder than it looks. Not only do you have fussy subjects, narrow windows in which to get the shot, uncooperative siblings (for family shots), and un-photogenic skin, but you also have extremely high expectations from your clients. Unlike traditional portrait photography, you can't always guarantee that perfect photo.

I've been doing newborn photography for awhile, but for this latest session I wanted to up my game and duplicate the kind of uber-processed newborn photography fad that's sweeping the world. Here's what I did to address each of these classic problems of newborn photography.

Problem #1: Dark, reddish / purplish skin.

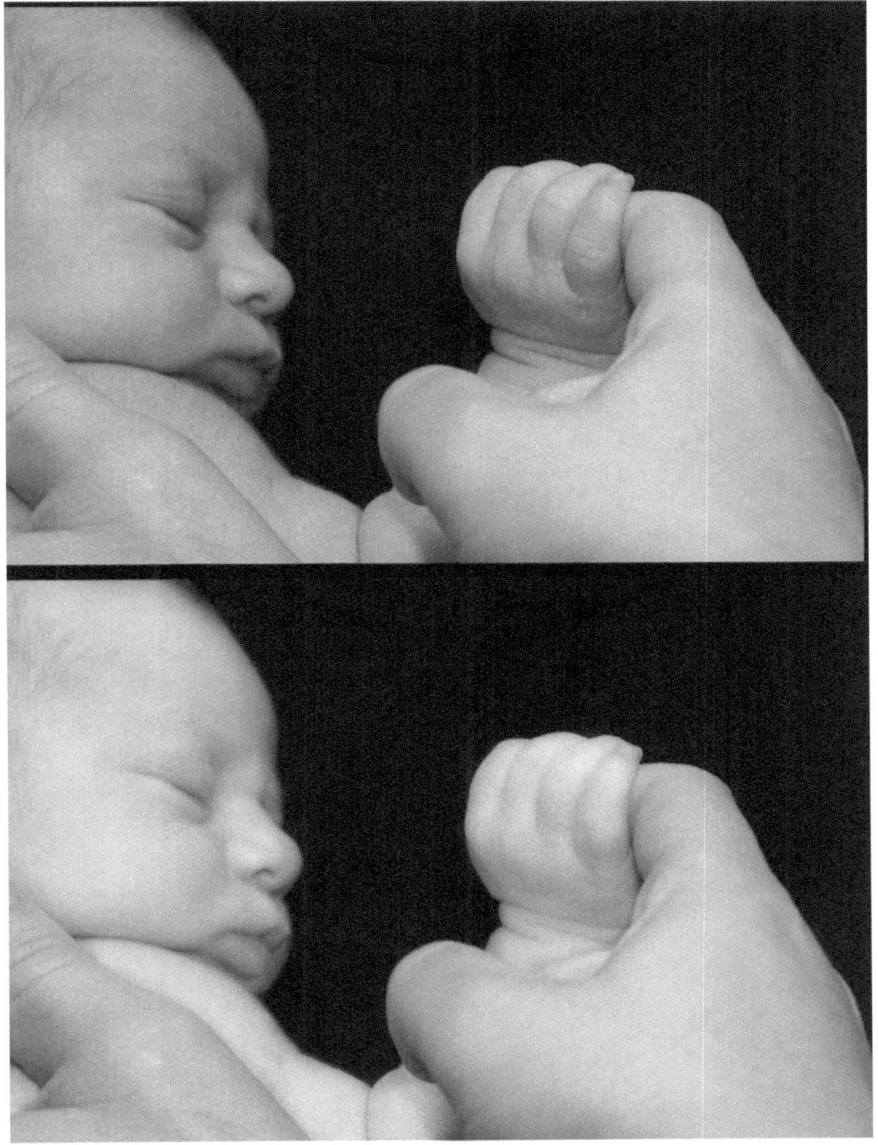

Problem #2: Splotchy red rashes

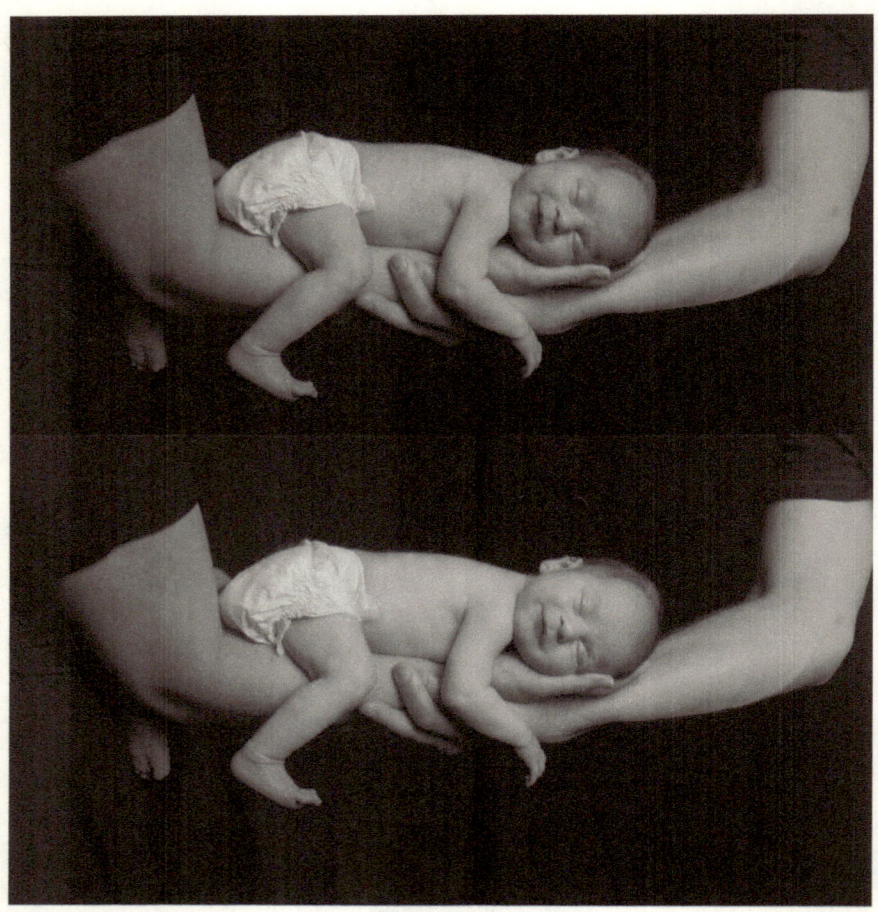

Problem #3: Rough Skin

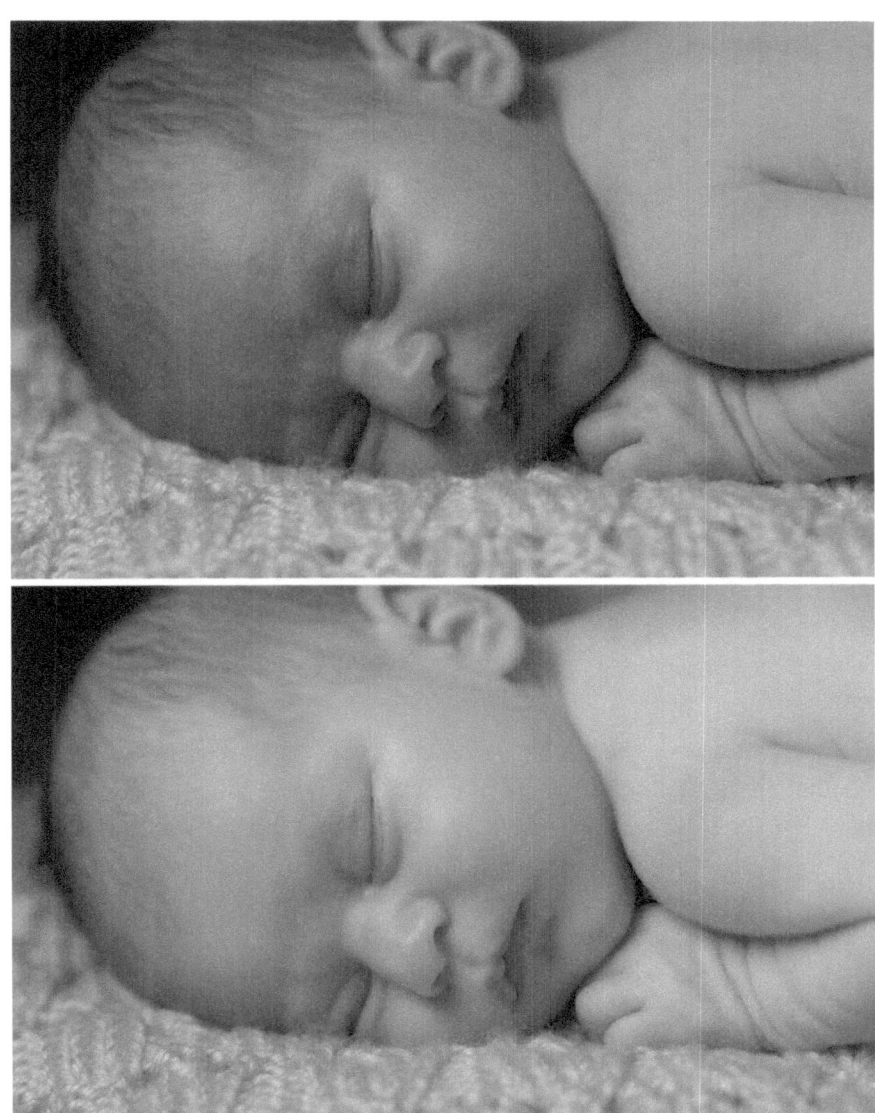

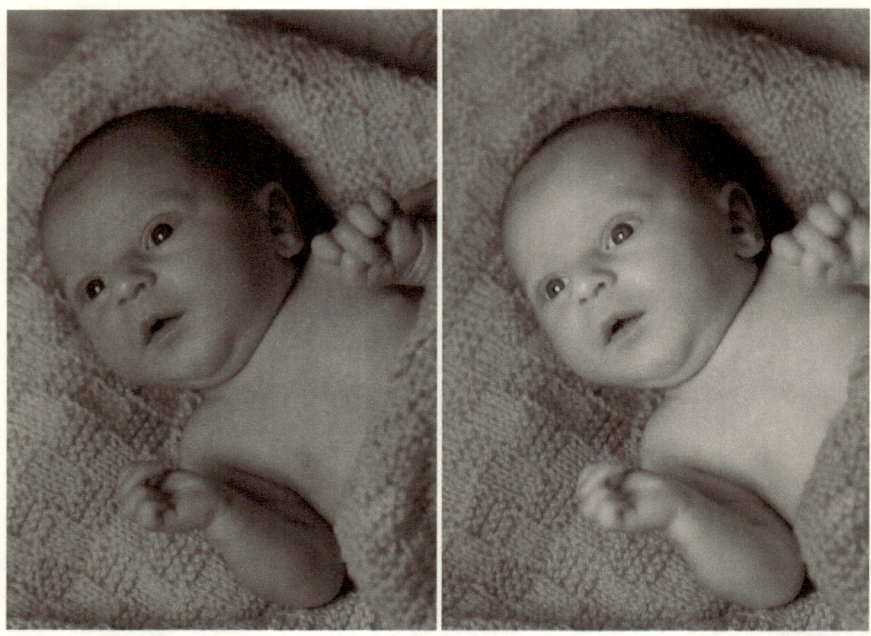

Before Photoshop, the problems of unphotographable skin was usually handled by shooting in black and white. When shooting Caucasian babies, a red filter was often added to make the skin look whiter.

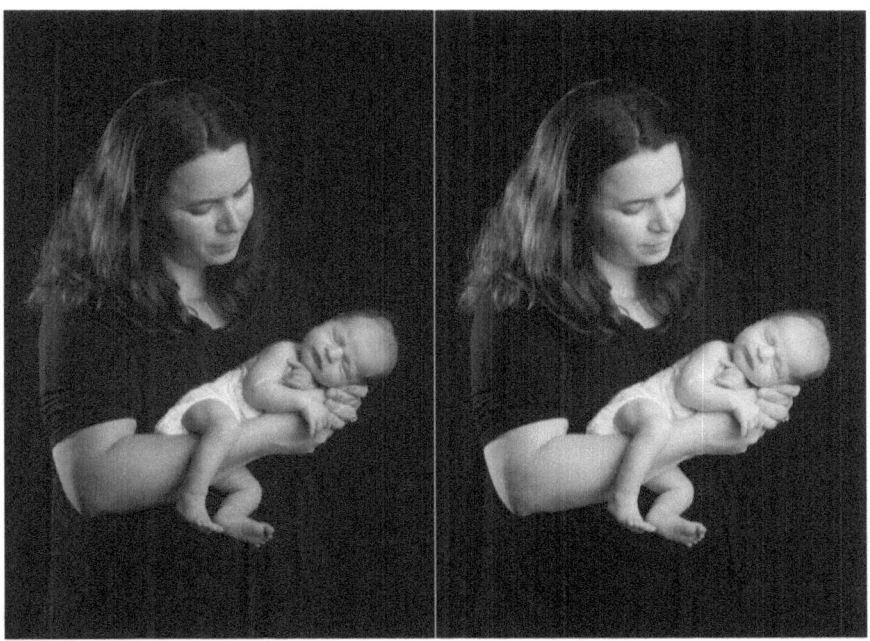

Today this same red filter effect can be emulated in Photoshop. When using the Image --> Adjustments --> Black & White... feature, move the red and yellow sliders to the right a little to get this classic Hollywood "look".

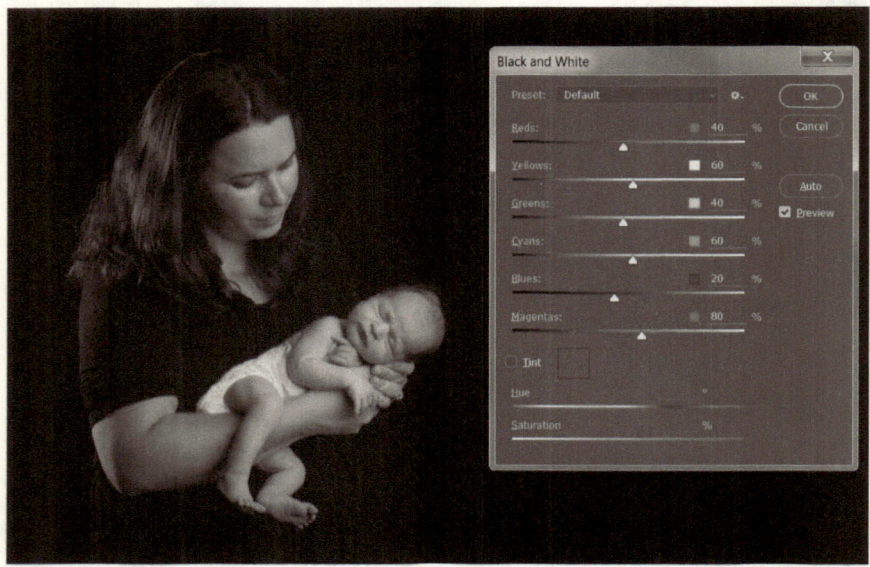

This is your standard black and white conversion. Everything translates into some shade of grey.

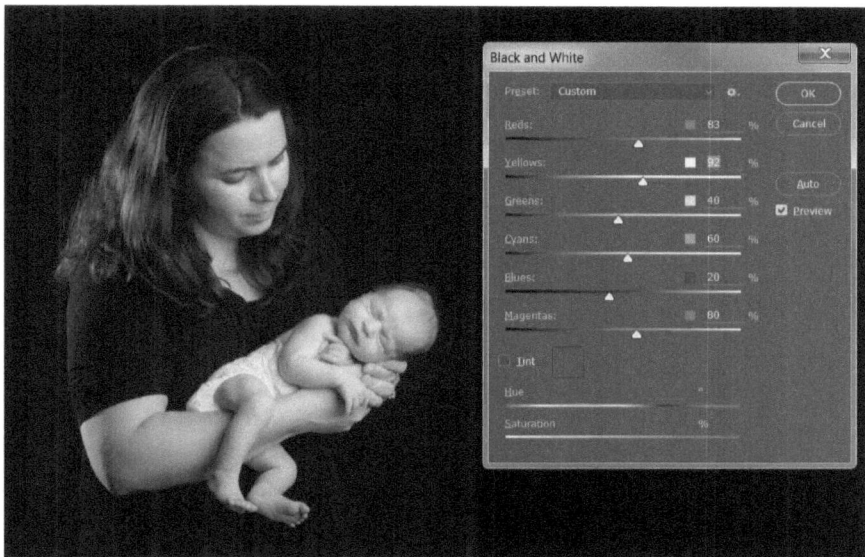

Move the red and orange sliders to the right a little to make the skin look whiter:

So that's one way. But if you want color photos, you can either spend tens of minutes tweaking each image in Photoshop or Lightroom (after having learned how to do it), or you can spring for some commercial-off-the-shelf tools that can help you achieve the same effect while spending considerably less time. I'm going to recommend two such tools below that are actually useful (and one of them is free!).

The Free Option

There's a photoblogger named Rita who runs TheCoffeeShopBlog.com from her home in Texas. One of her claims to fame are the free photoshop actions she creates. I found one of them very useful for cleaning up the skin of newborns: The "Coffeeshop Baby PowderRoom" collection, which you can download from here:

http://www.thecoffeeshopblog.com/2009/11/coffeeshop-baby-powderroom-free-pspse.html (Instructions are provided as well. She has many other actions available too; browse around!)

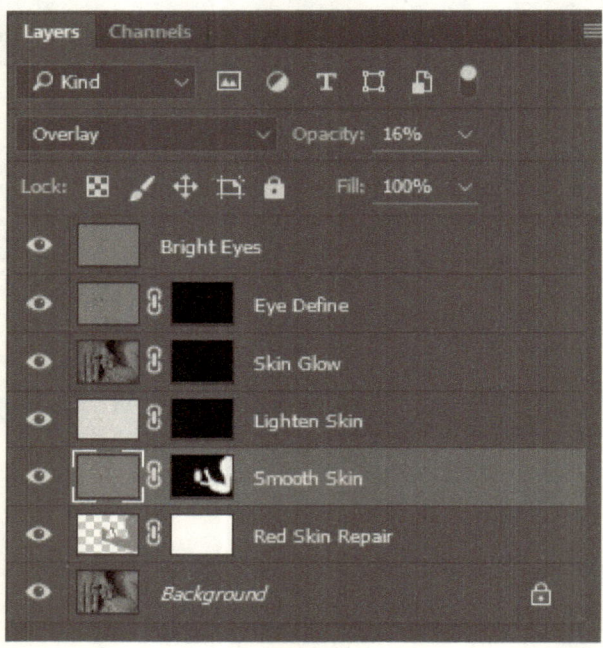

Basically, when you open your file and run the action, it creates 6 new adjustment layers on top of the background layer. You then use the brush tool on the mask to "paint" in the desired effect on your image; then adjust the layer's transparency to taste. It works wonderfully, taking the process down to about 3 minutes per image. I processed all of the above examples using this tool.

If you're doing this for a living, you might want to go for something that might speed up the workflow even more. And "Speeding up workflow" is what Lightroom is all about, but do NOT make the mistake of just installing 1,300 baby photo presets and pray that one of them will work on the image that you have. The problem with presets is you can't selectively apply an effect to part of an image; it gets applied to the whole thing. What you need to look for instead are presets that can be applied via the adjustment brush so you can, for example, only smooth the skin on parts that don't include the eyes or mouth. Here is such a package; it allows you to do skin softening, lightening, and red (rash) removal all via the adjustment brush. And for a scant USD $50, it's quite a bargain:

https://cc.colesclassroom.com/newborn-lightroom-presets

Lighting for Newborns

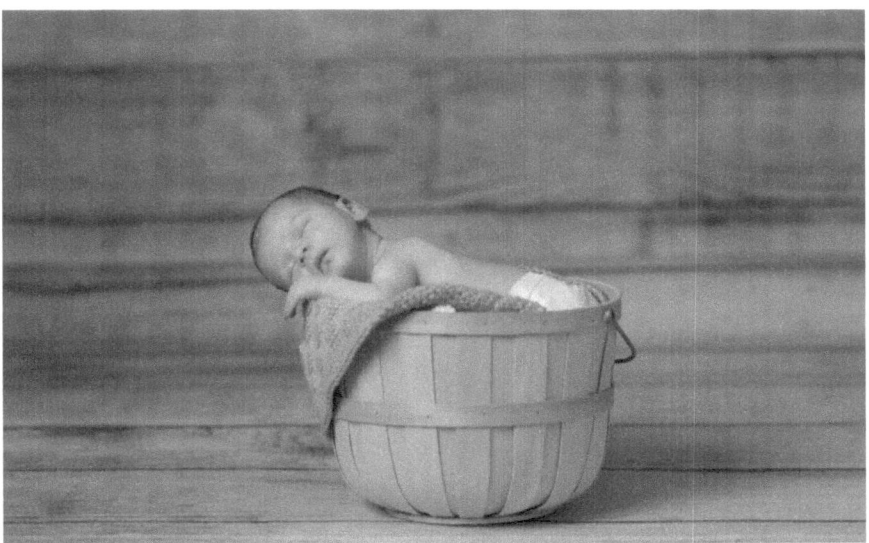

Now, then, the hardest part. Lighting for shots like the above is not obvious. The earlier shots on this page were done with one softbox and a black background, and for most portraiture the rule is that the larger the softbox (and the closer to the subject), the softer the light.

But for newborns, that doesn't work as well as you'd think. The light, as well as the shadows, are still strong and it has to be softened yet further. So you need to start with a large light source, and then *light the newborn using the very edge of the light*. Not only does this provide softer light, but also less light, great for those photographers who like to show off shallow depth-of-field with their f/1.4 lens.

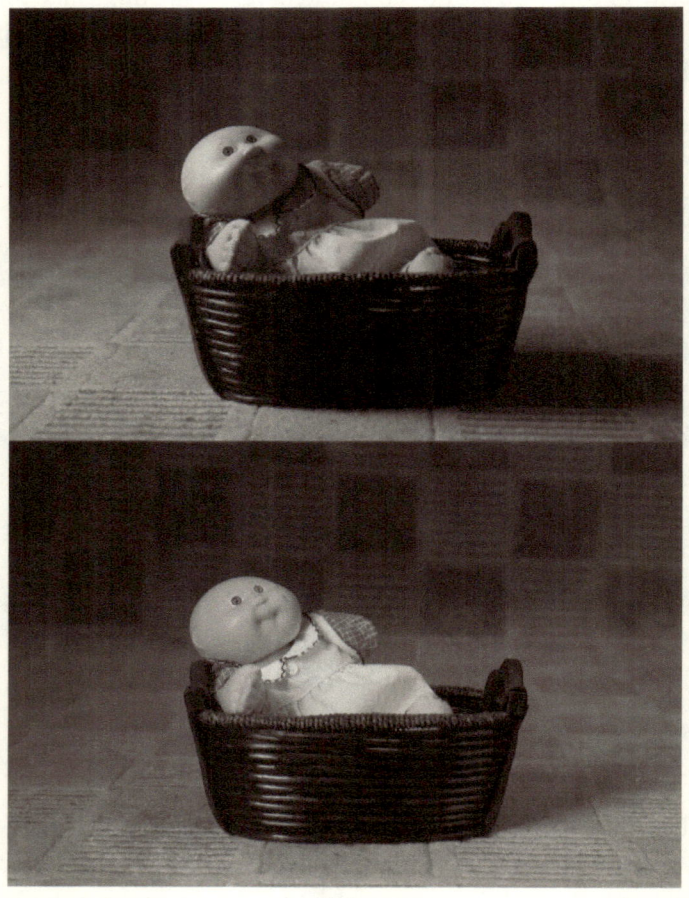

Top photo is a plain softbox with the subject in the center. Bottom is softbox' edge, with a fill reflector. Much softer!

This technique is called feathering, and yes, it requires that you waste 99.9% of the light from your expensive softbox. That's why large reflecting surfaces are required as well, to bounce back some of the wasted light and fill in the shadows. Below are some test shots, plus a wide shot showing the light setup. The large softbox is actually 3 feet in front of the newborn, so only the edge of the light is hitting him.

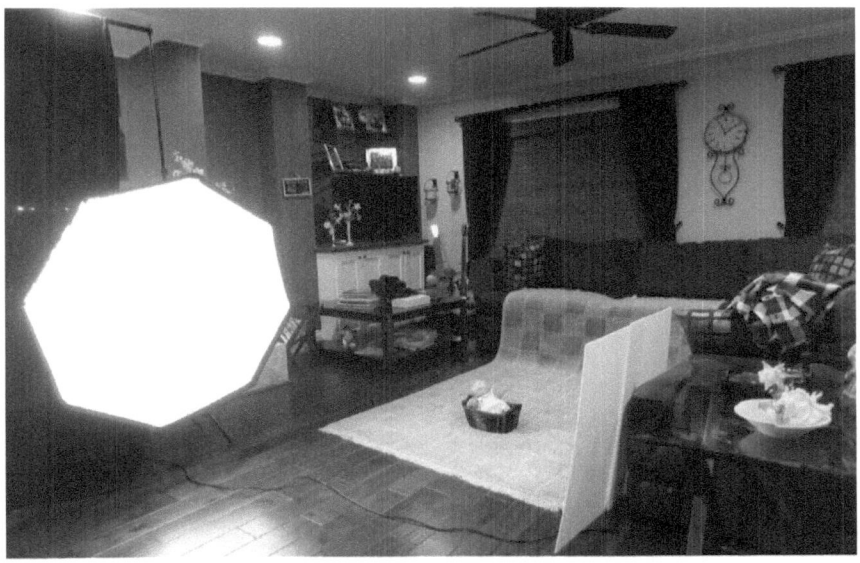

Behind-the-scenes of the test shot..

2.8   5 Types of Outdoor Portrait Lighting

First published April, 2017

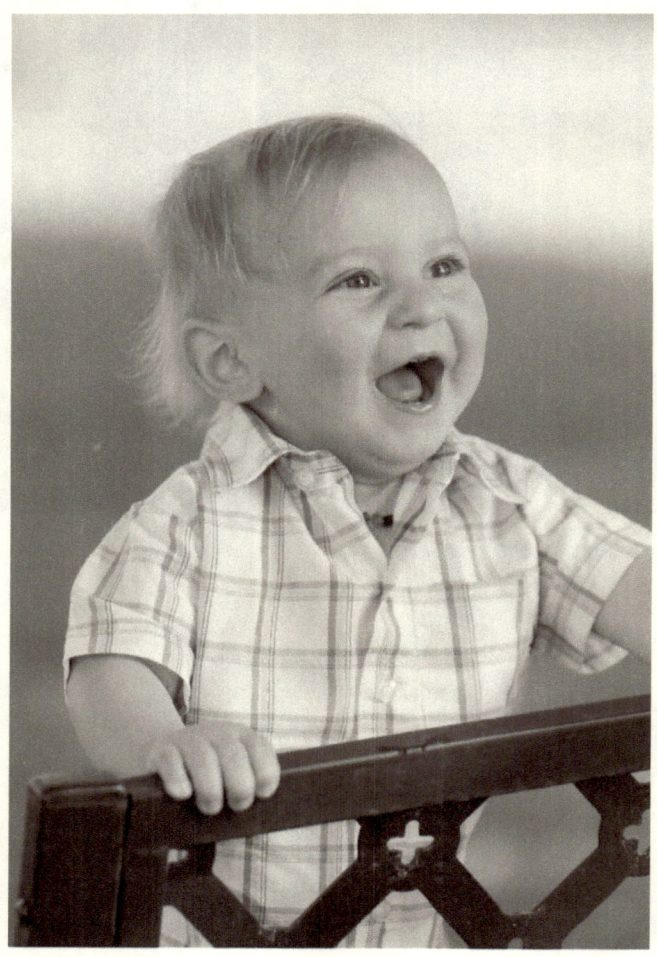

Today I'm taking pictures of a 1-year-old.   And just to add to the unpredictability, I'm going to light him 5 different ways.

1) Outdoors, in the sun.

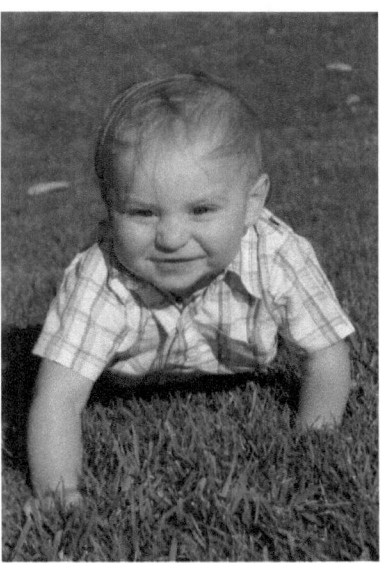

Nothing wrong with this; but any iphone could have taken it. If you want unique results, you need to experiment with better kinds of lighting.

2) Open Shade

Shade is better than direct sunlight, as it doesn't cause harsh shadows which look OK to your eye but can really stand out on the camera. But open shade can look kind of bluish (your automatic white balance doesn't always work very well in these conditions). You could set your white balance to "Shade" (adding yellow to the subject to compensate), but that's not as good as the next suggestion.

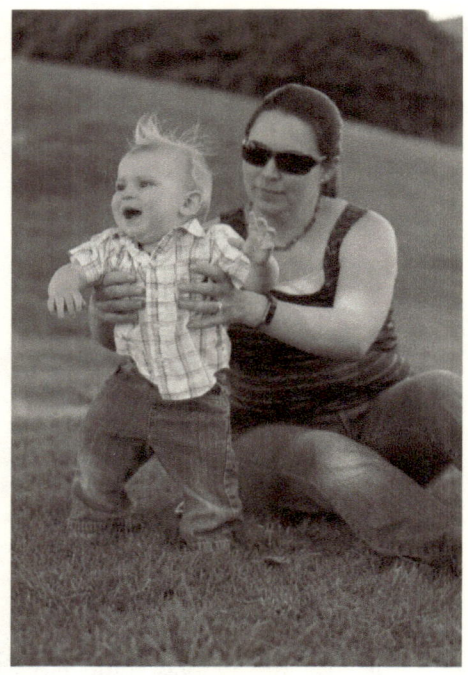

3) Shade with Fill flash

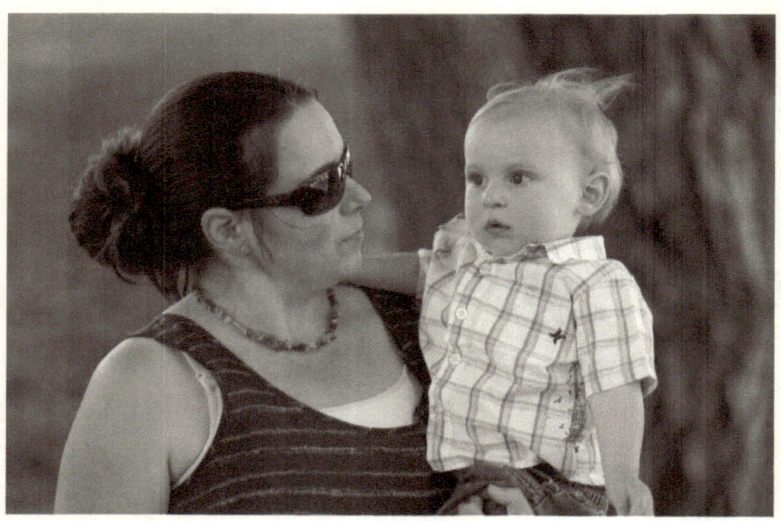

That's right - add some light! Notice that none of these images look like I used a flash. To achieve that look I usually set my flash compensation to either -1 or -1.7 (your mileage may vary; as every camera will produce different results here. Experiment with the equipment you have.)

To get the blurry background I used a 70-200 f/2.8 lens and set the f/stop wide open.

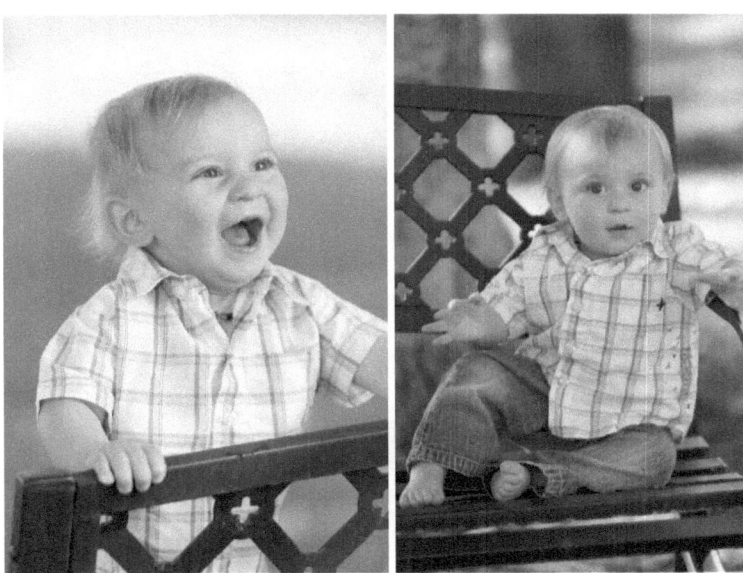

You've heard me say before that the worst place to have your flash is on top of the camera. The only exception to this is when you're using for fill flash, augmenting existing light to lighten the shadows. As you can see it works quite well. Can we make it better?

4) Shade with off-camera wireless flash

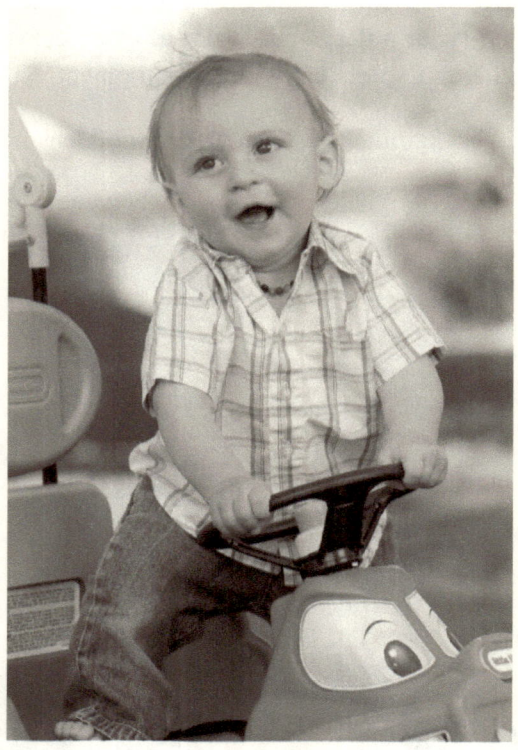

Can moving the flash off-camera make things look better? For most cameras the answer is certainly "yes"; however for Sony (what I'm shooting with today) I have to make an additional adjustment.

You see, when left to its own devices, the modern Sonys will tend to overexpose the background when your subject is in shade and you're using fill. (They've been behaving that way for a long time - http://friedmanarchives.blogspot.com/2009/12/rebuttal-to-all-those-lukewarm-sony.html .) So to make the enhanced drama of the wireless flash stand out, you have to underexpose the background.

5) Shade with off-camera wireless flash with underexposed background

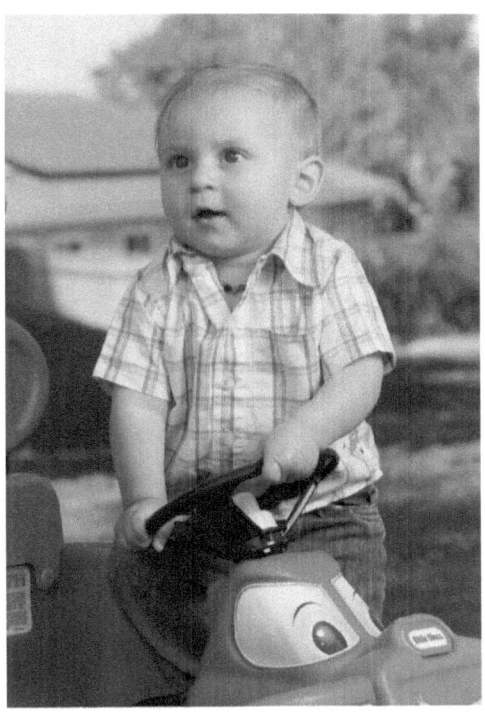

Much better! (Well, to my mind anyway.)

But how can you control just the background intensity and not affect the flash intensity? Here's the answer, an excerpt from the A99 II ebook which was just released:

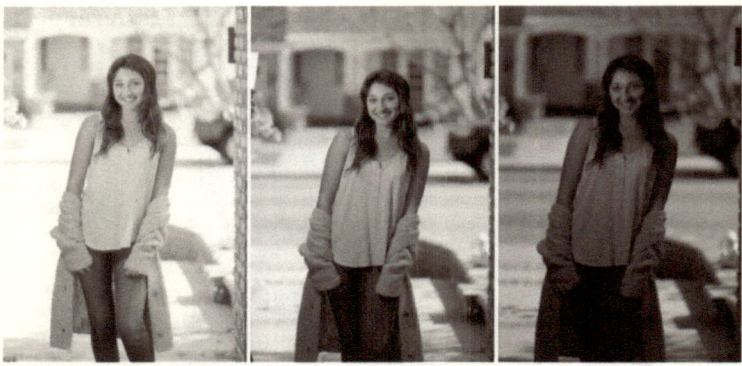

Figure 5-59: *In a fill-flash situation, all recent Sony cameras will tend to overexpose the background (left). To quickly fix this in the field, I just dial down my exposure compensation by 2 stops. When Exp.comp.set is set to "Ambient Only", only the background gets darker (center). When set to "Ambient & Flash", they both get darker (right). Who wants that? You can see why I recommend "Ambient only"; if I want to make the subject brighter or darkr I'll do it separately via the Flash Compnsation function (Section 5.40).*

And here's the setup I used:

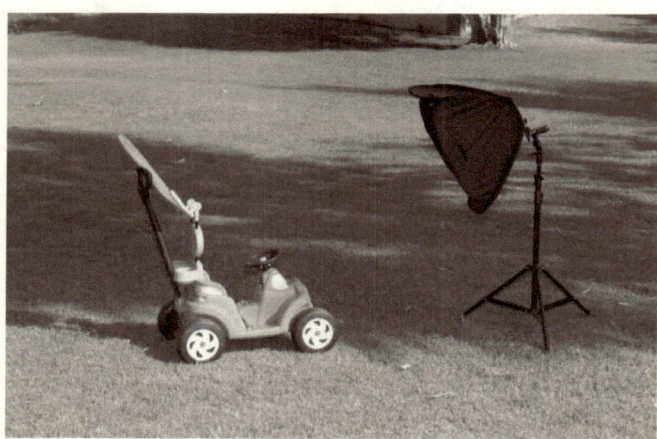

One wireless flash and a softbox. I took this shot as I was packing up. Look closely and you'll see the accessory flash behind the softbox had been put away. :-) I used a radio trigger on this day, but in this configuration optical triggering would have worked as well.

2.9   A TALE OF TWO PORTRAITS

First published February, 2016

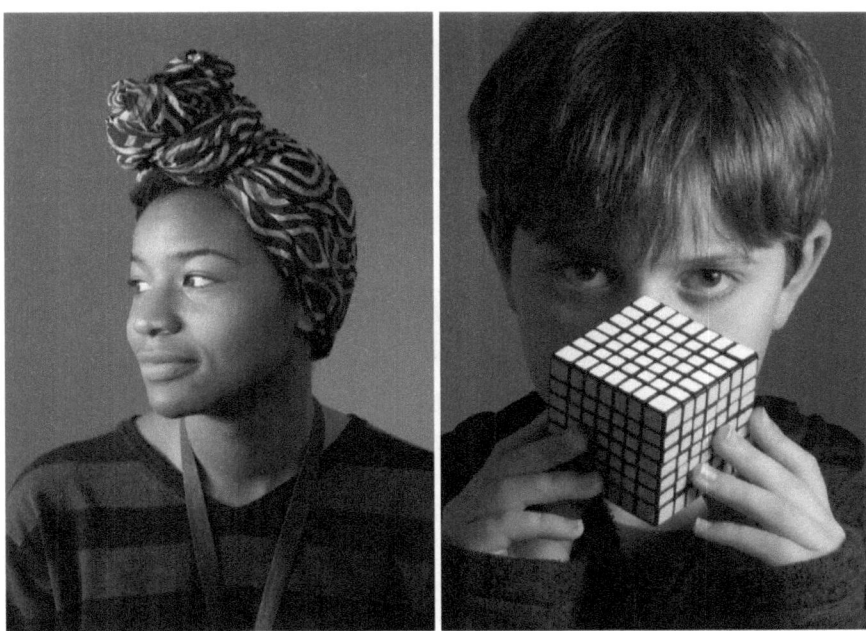

Neither one of these portraits above was done in a studio. The first used natural light (something I'm always on the lookout for), and the other used   The   5   Dollar   Studio (http://friedmanarchives.blogspot.com/2010/07/5-dollar-studio.html   ) which I blogged about a few years ago.

Below you can see the setup for the first shot - there's a large room with large windows. My subject was sitting right there working at her computer. After taking this behind-the-scenes shot, I moved in front of her, zoomed in to about 200mm, and took the portrait. Everything was on Auto.

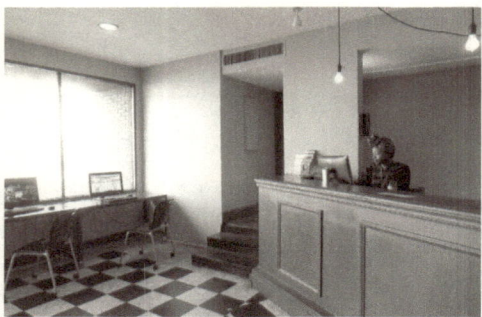

Behind-the-scenes for the first portrait, which used natural light only.

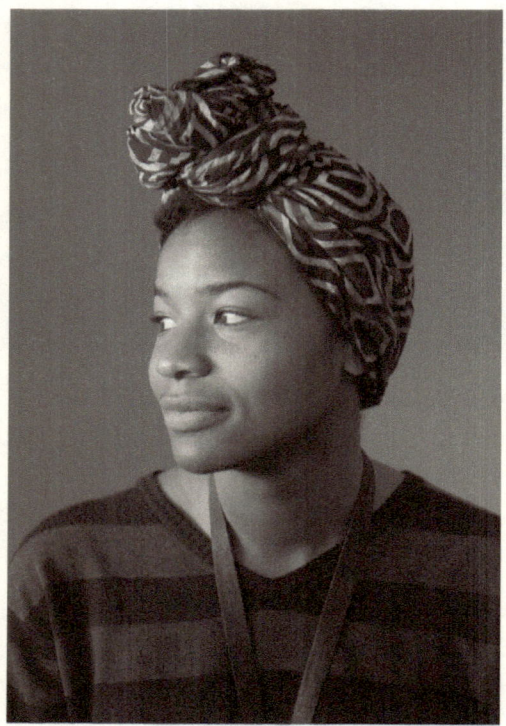

First I recognized the good light, then I used the classic headshot composition: Eyes in the upper third; no distracting background.

Next was a portrait of a Rubik's Cube enthusiast (next page). (And before you ask, yes, that's a real 7x7 cube.) Here I had some volunteers hold a wireless flash and a diffusing cloth to the right of the subject, just out of frame.

Below is the behind-the-scenes shot:

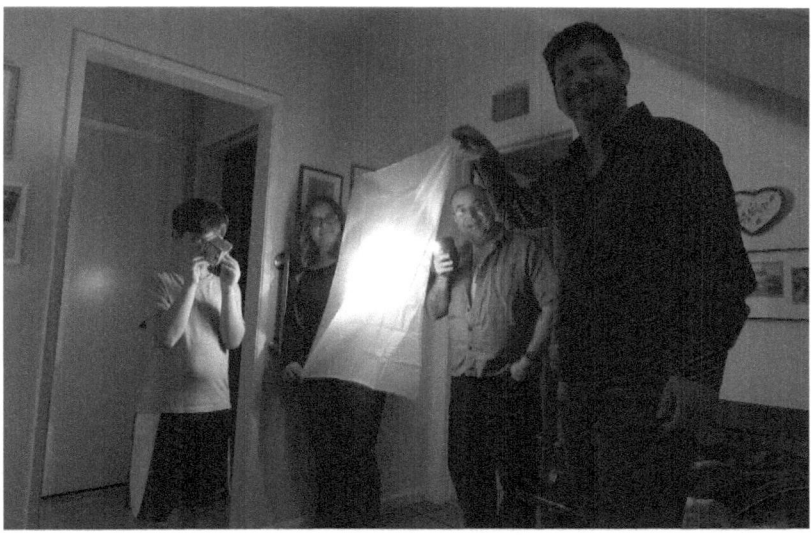

If you don't have a budget for a softbox, it's amazing the results you can get with one flash and a few volunteers. :-)

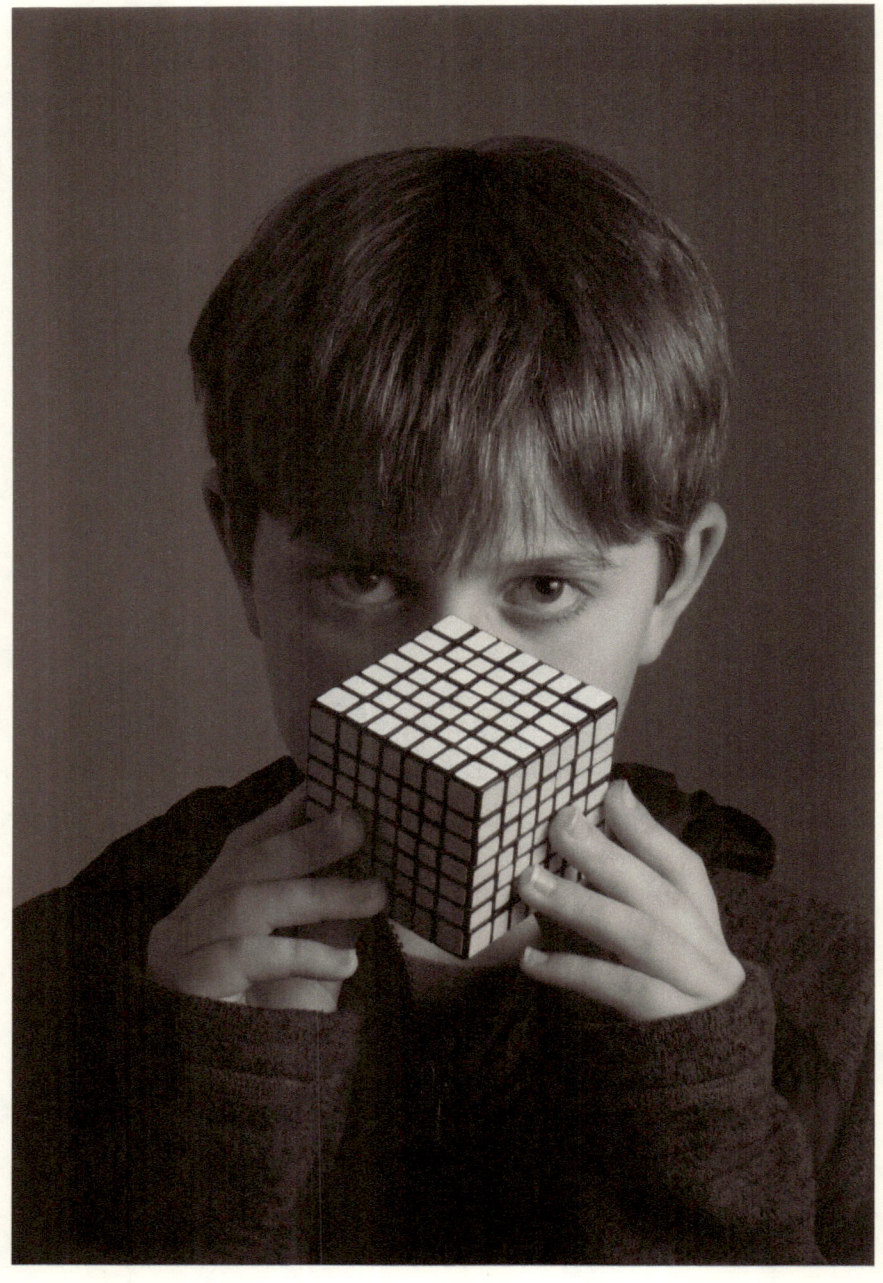

Now compare the previous "good light" shot with a concept shot I did earlier using existing room light:

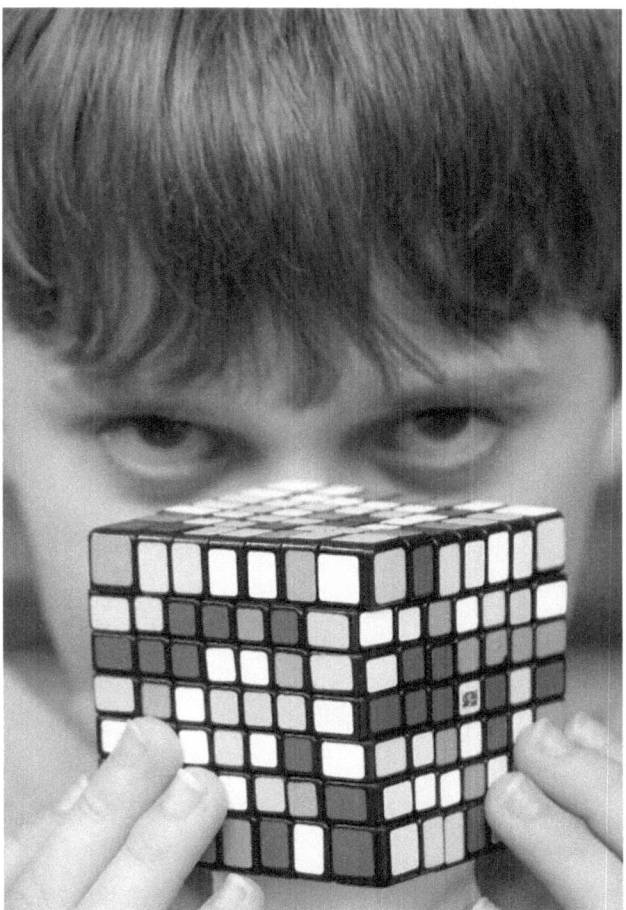

Not nearly as impactful. Good light makes you take things more seriously.

SECTION 3   PHOTOGRAPHIC MISCELLANY

3.1   I FOUND A USE FOR 14-BIT RAW

First published January, 2015 in Cameracraft Magazine

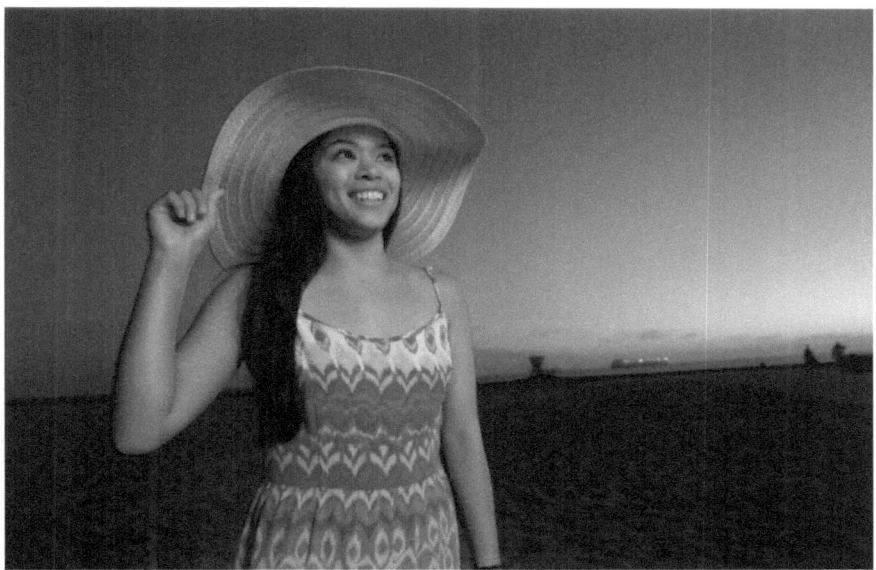

Once upon a time, back in the days of Kodachrome, there was no such thing as Photoshop. If you wanted any kind of special effect, like being able to change the color of the sky but not your subject, you usually had to invest in some fancy filters and do it all in-camera. And although the technique worked moderately well, I've discovered a better technique for doing the same thing using only ONE tiny filter and a digital camera!

First, some background: You know you can put a filter in front of your lens and apply a tint to the entire image. But what if you possessed a MATCHED pair of filters – filters of opposite colors, such as blue and orange? The idea is that you put one filter in front of your lens (such as the orange one) to make a nice sunset, then you put the blue one *in front of your flash* and illuminate your subject with a bluish light designed to cancel out the orange cast of the lens' filter. Your background changes to orange but your subject lit by "correct" light!

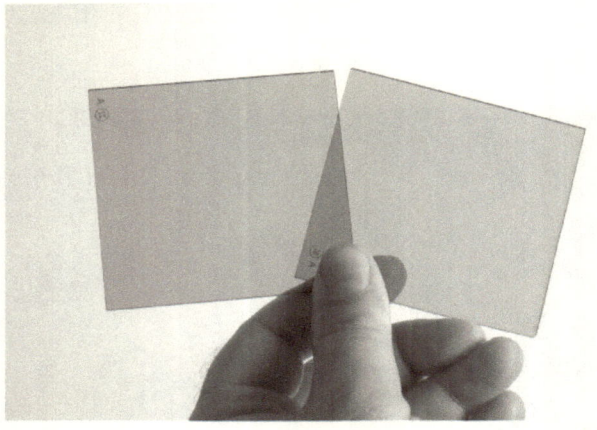

I played around with this technique briefly in the days of film but the results didn't "wow" me enough and so I dropped it. (Right image.)

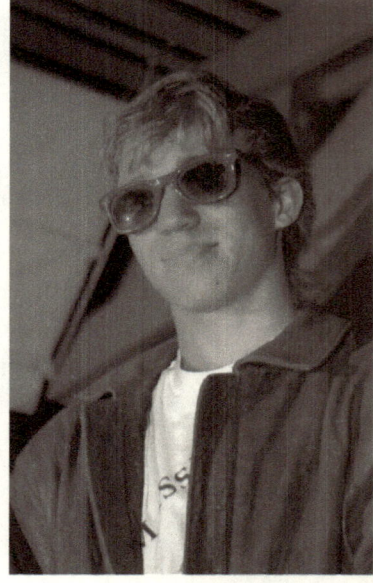

30 years later, I exhumed the very same matched Cokin filters to try it again for this article. In this instance I wanted to turn a blah grey sky into something more appealing, and so I put the blue filter in front of the lens and placed the complimentary orange filter on the flash. Like before, I saw moderate success but nothing like the examples I remember seeing back in the 1970's. (Perhaps I should have shot closer to sunset...) Still nothing to write home about (next page).

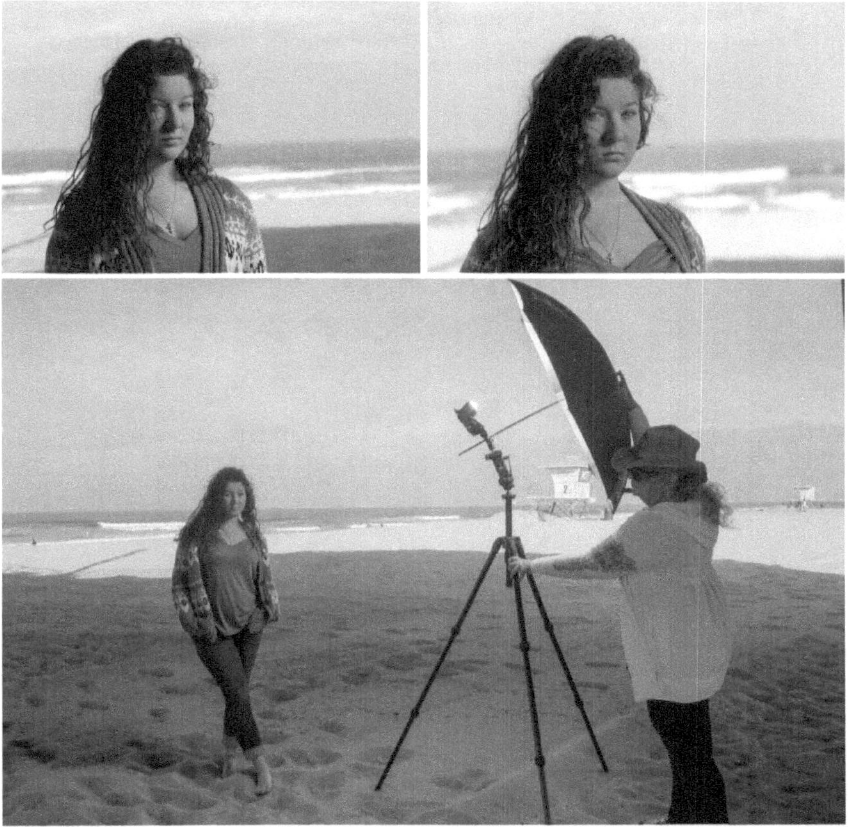

The old filters worked OK; but nothing to write home about.

Can I do this same thing (but easier) using modern technology? Here was my thought: With digital cameras, we no longer have to put color filters in front of lenses to compensate for non-white light like incandescents; we use the White Balance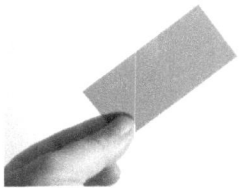

function instead. So why not just put a small filter in front of the flash, and use the camera's custom white balance to act as the lens' filter?

I tried this technique outdoors, turning a blue sky to a nice golden color I'd say that's pretty compelling!

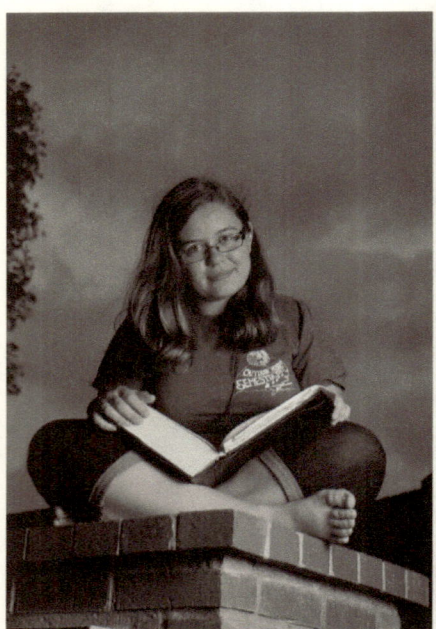 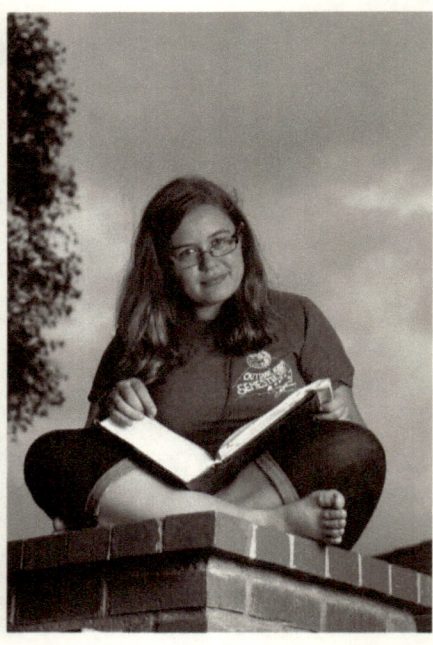

Same idea, newer technology.

Here's how I did another example, step by step:

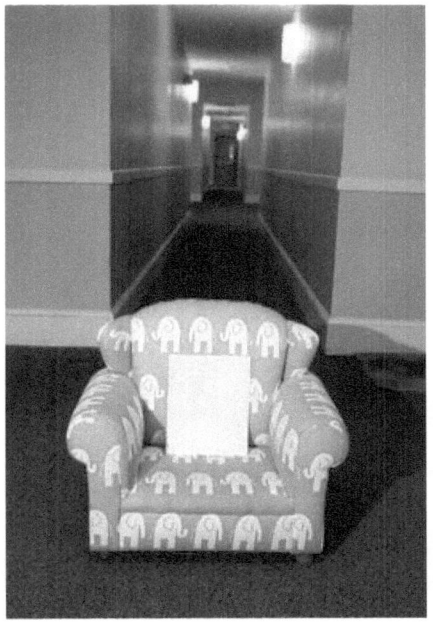 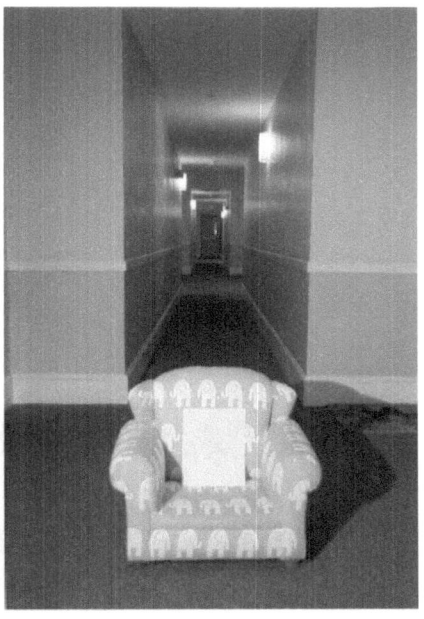

First, I set up my shot, putting a white cardboard in it for calibration.

Then I put a dark green filter in front of the flash and took this intermediate shot.

I took the camera off the tripod, and composed a shot of just the white cardboard. Then I invoked my camera's Custom White Balance function, essentially telling the camera "See that white piece of cardboard in the shot? Add whatever colors you need to add, and subtract whatever colors you need to subtract, in order to make that cardboard look white!".

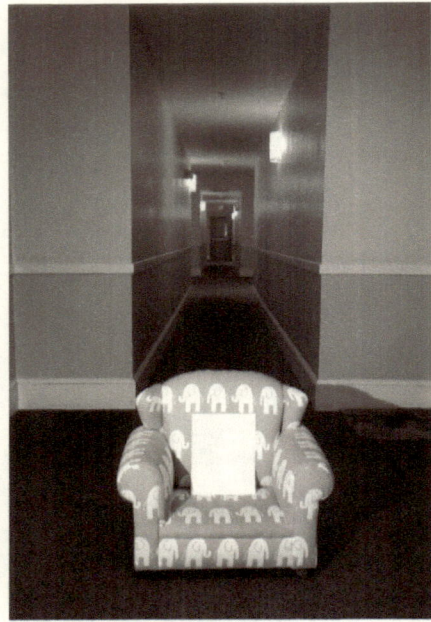 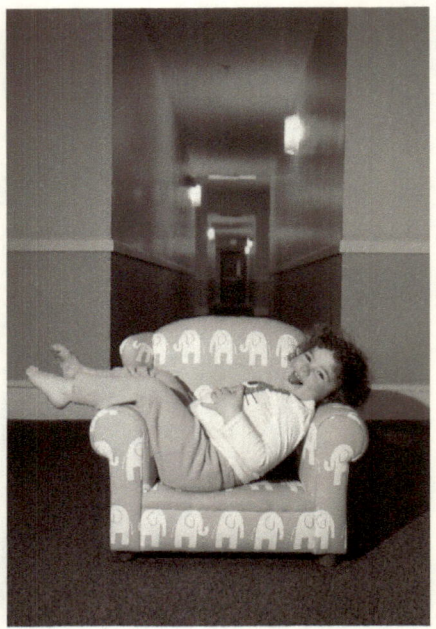

Then I put the camera back on the tripod and shot again, resulting in color correction for the subject and the background turning red.

Then I added an uncooperative subject and shot away!

So this is the essence of the technique – use the camera's custom white balance to match whatever filter you happen to have. There is a downside, in that you actually reduce the overall dynamic range of the image. But if you choose your subject carefully this won't be a limiting factor.

Can I make it better?

The time-honored appeal of this technique was that no Photoshop was necessary to create such special effects – what you see is straight out of the camera. But the technique has its limits – your filters couldn't be too intense otherwise the overlap of the two wouldn't have enough of a full-spectrum to make the subject look normal.

I wanted to push this technique a little just to see how extreme I could go. And so I got the most intense filters I could find AND I used the Sony Alpha 99's 14-bit RAW mode. Ironically, this would necessitate using Photoshop to do the RAW conversion and the color balance, but hey, this is for Science.

I started with a beautiful model near sunset:

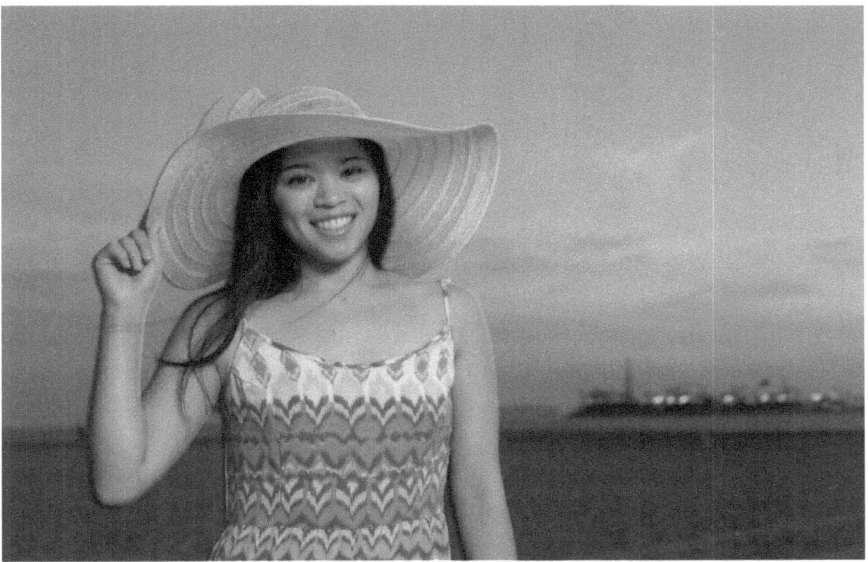

Then I found the most intense magenta filter I could find and added it to the flash. Here, Photoshop *was* required – I had to open the RAW file and color correct for it TWICE since the amount of adjustment needed exceeded the slider limits of the color balance tool.

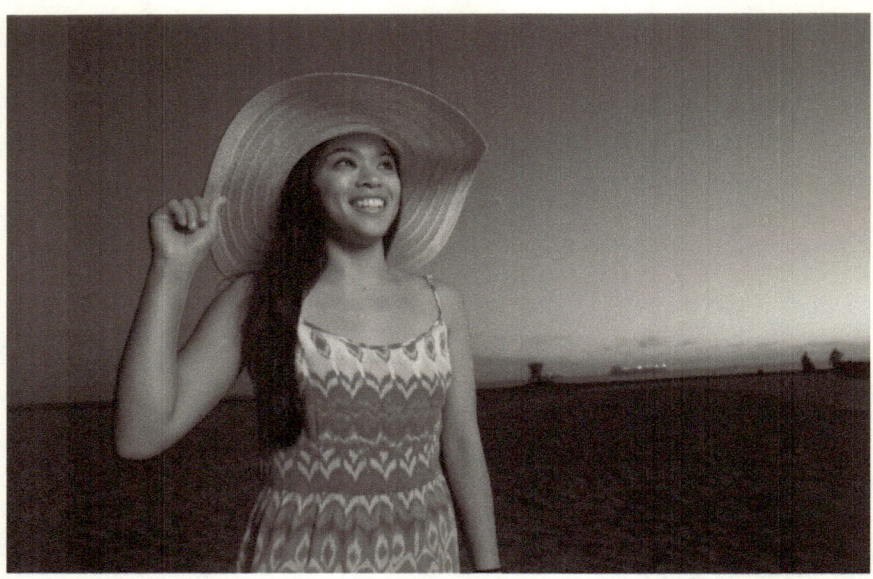

This was the first practical application I found for the 14-bit RAW mode – in my tests, the normal 12-bit RAW mode that exists on any other cameras produces channel clipping when color corrected this intensely.

Another intense Green filter shows just where this technique breaks down – there was insufficient spectrum coming from the flash to make the subject look normal after compensation (next page).

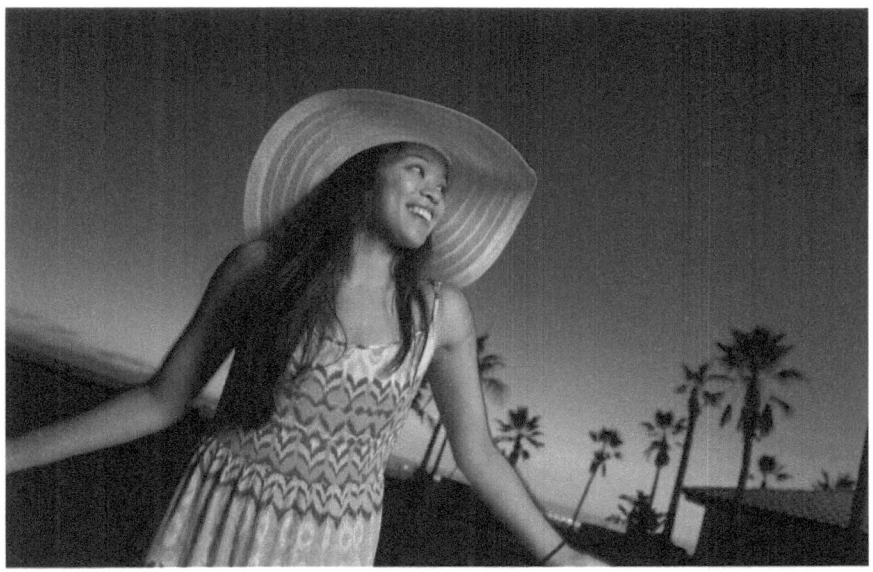

One caveat to know if you're planning on trying this yourself – when mounting the filters to your flash, it's best to use a filter holder rather than just tape the filter to the front of the flash. How do I know this?

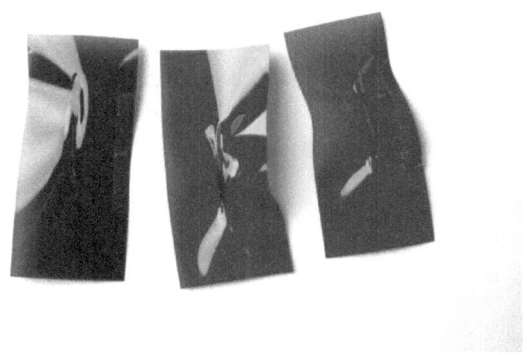

3.2 How High-Megapixels Can Lead to Sharper Pictures

First published November, 2016

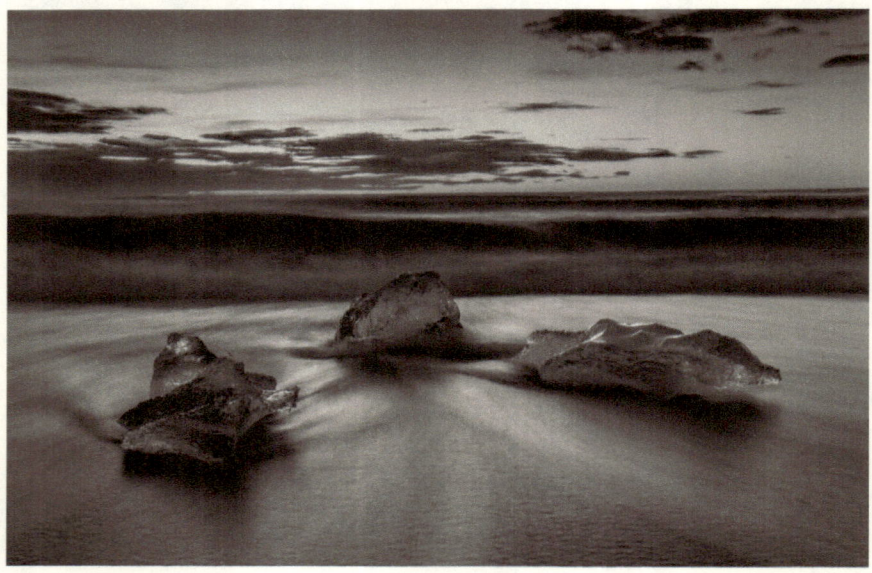

Iceland seems to be the hot place for photographers to go this year. All of the internet photography celebrities have gone there recently, including Scott Kelby. Dpreview.com went there to shoot some test images for the Olympus E-M1 II. And now Carol and I are here as well.

I write about the trip more in the next edition of Cameracraft magazine, but I'll give you the short version here. The weather wasn't that good, but I managed to come home with some licensable shots.

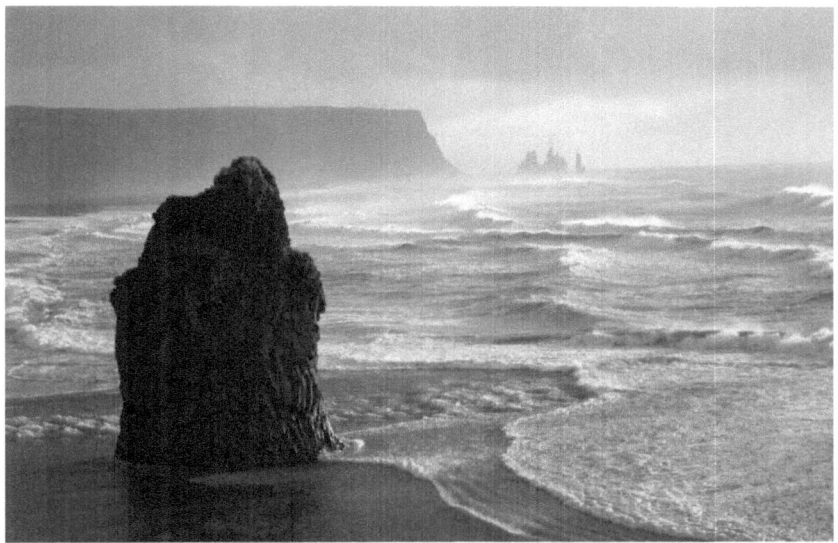

We only had about six minutes of good light. At least this time it didn't start hailing when I got out of the car with my camera.

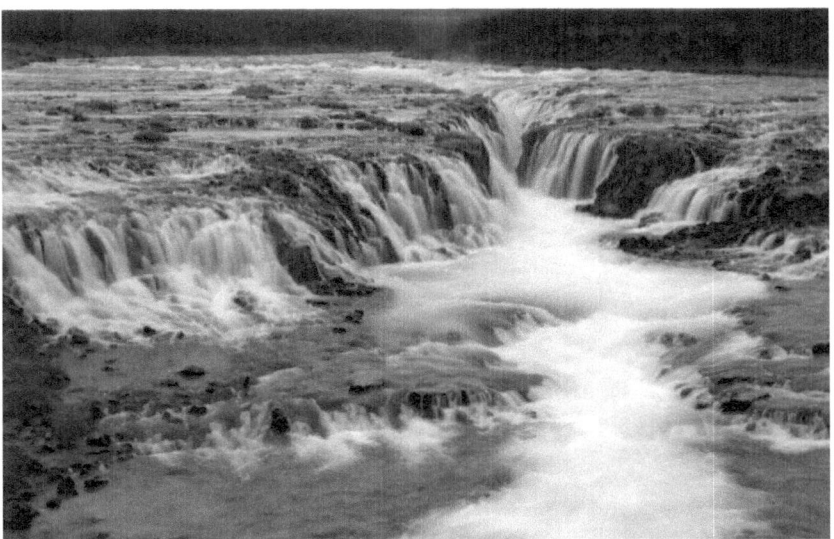

The Brúarfoss Falls were hard to find, requiring a 60-minute walk through mud on private property. Worth it, though!

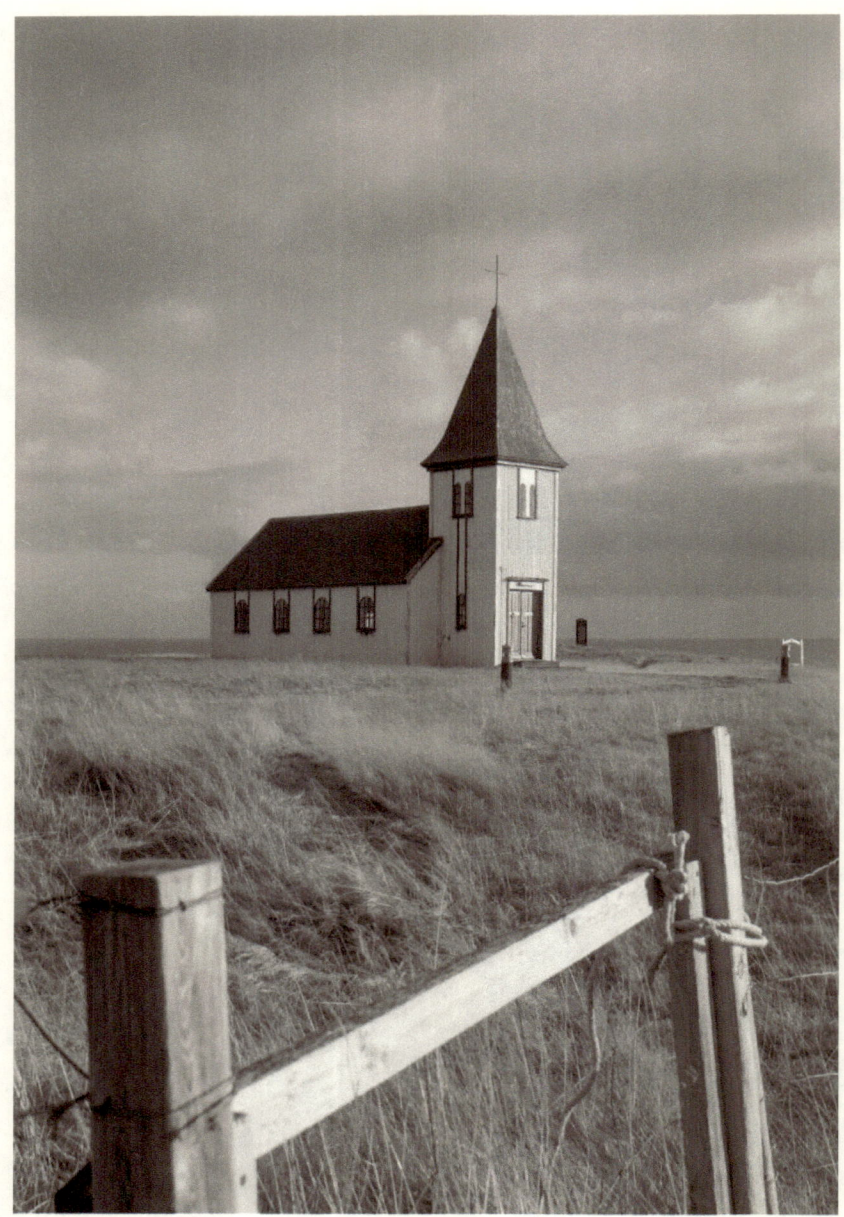

90% of the churches look like this.

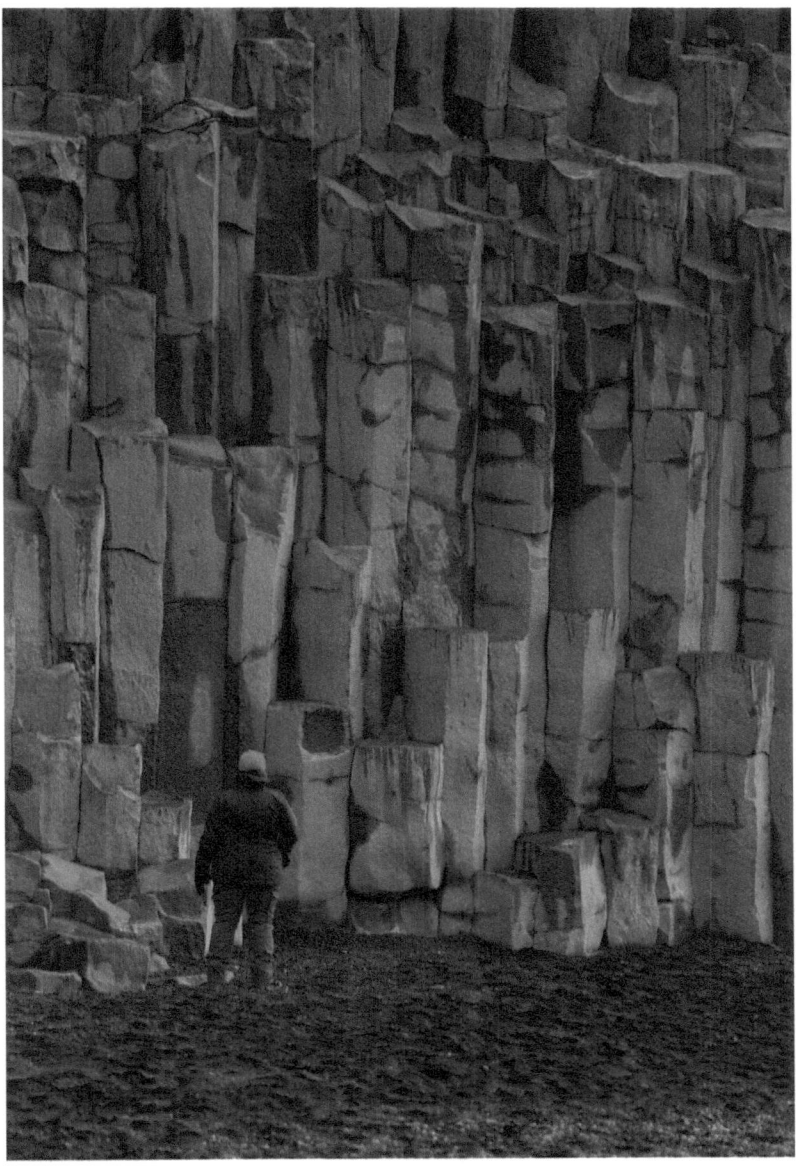

This wasn't photoshopped. Image was underexposed by about -1.7 stops.

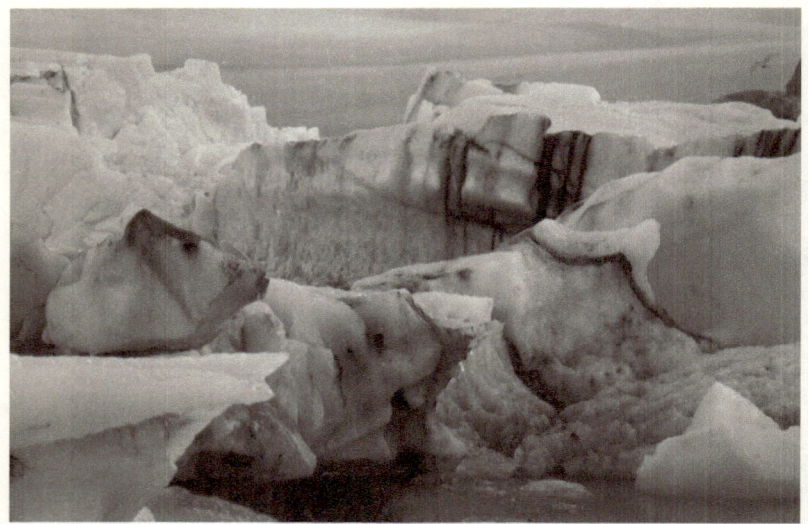

Glacier Lagoon

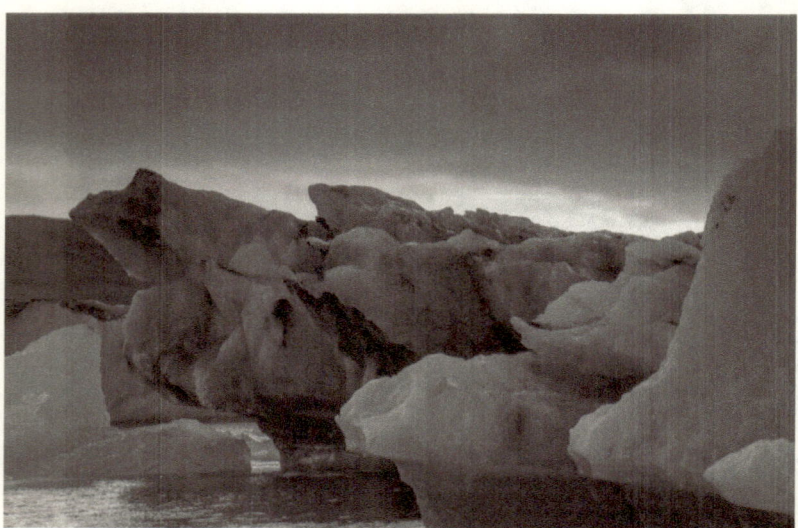

Glacier Lagoon 2

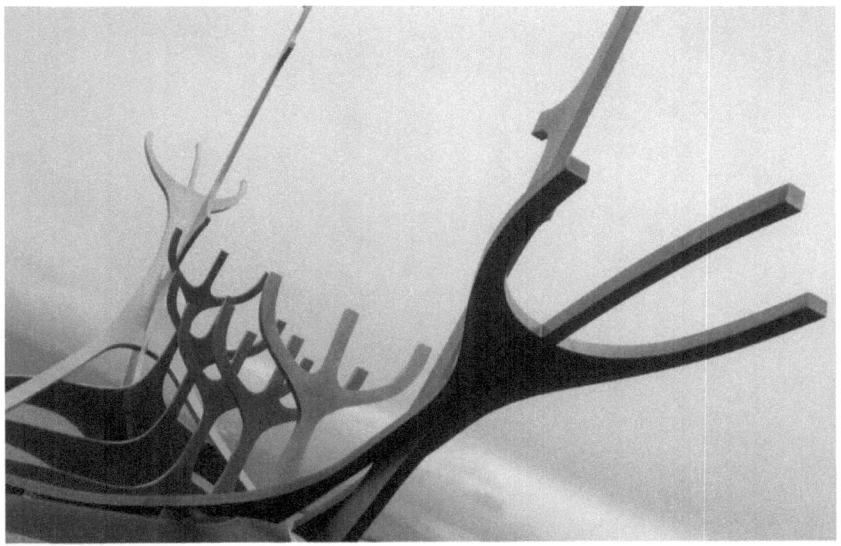

If you have bad light you can sometimes save it by converting to black-and-white.

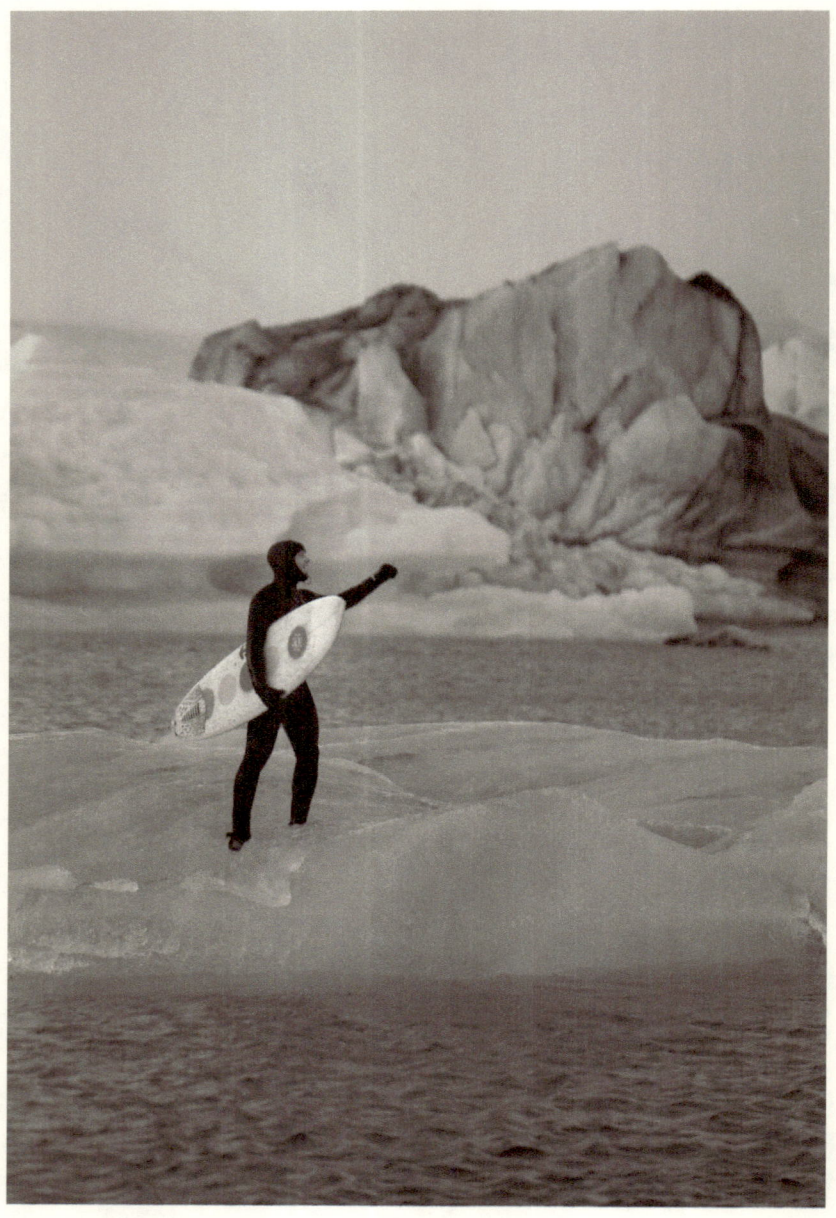

Some surfer dude thought it would be cool to surf in glacial waters. Ah, youth...

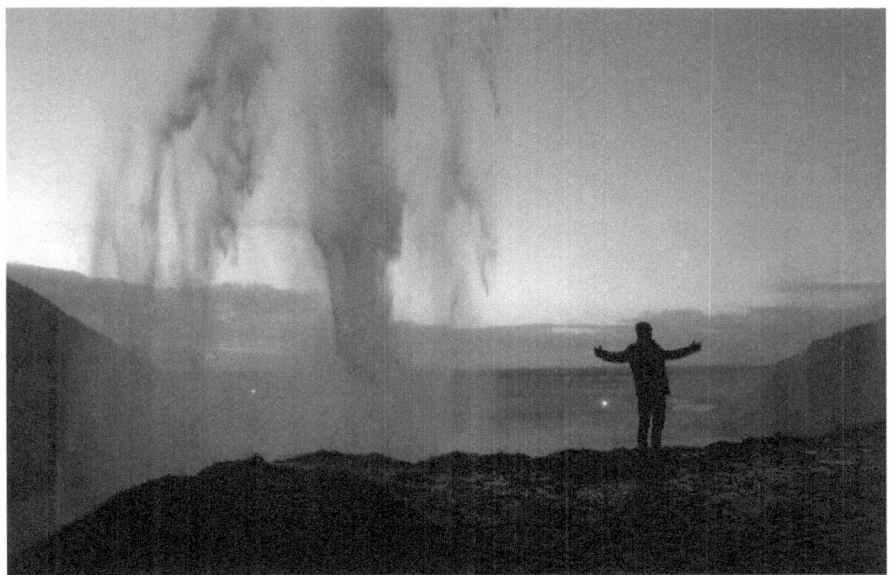

From the back of a waterfall.

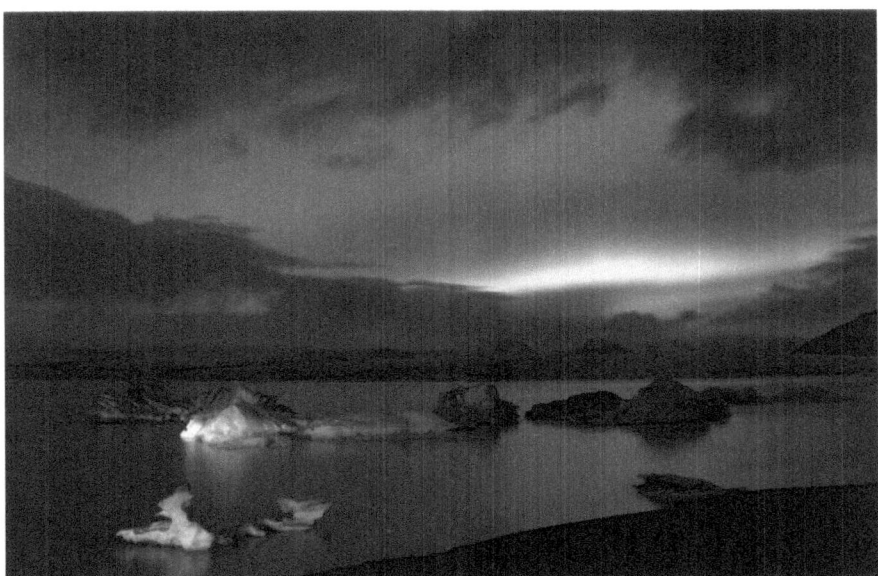

Aurora Borealis and Icebergs.

(You can see more photos from the trip here: http://bit.ly/2zhUtuN .)

Now here's the part that really frustrated me. See those switches on the side of the 70-200 f/4 G lens? They control many things, including the SteadyShot feature. And they are easily moved accidentally when you slip the lens into and out of a tight camera bag several times.

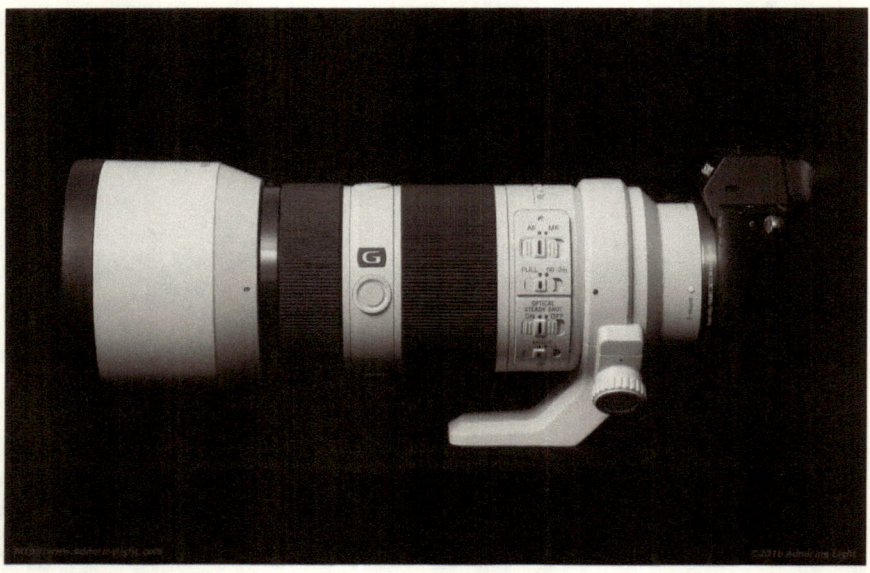

So there were times when I was using the camera handheld in iffy light, thinking SteadyShot would save me. And I got fuzzy pictures when they really should have been OMG-that's-sharp-what-kind-of-camera-do-you-have?-like quality. Can something be done in post production?

Normally there's no substitute for proper focusing, but when I was in China teaching English back in 2003, I stumbled upon a technique that bordered on cheating, but it worked and nobody questioned it. Read about the technique in my blog post from that time: http://bit.ly/2x5leBN . Essentially, the technique involves downsizing the image and applying Photoshop's Unsharp Mask filter to make things appear sharper to the eye.

But the example from 2003 was with a 5 megapixel camera and shrinking it down to less than 1 MP for web viewing. Can the same technique be applied to a 42 megapixel image, and make it appear sharper when printed at, say, 8 x 12 inches?

Below is an example of a fuzzy shot that should have been perfect:

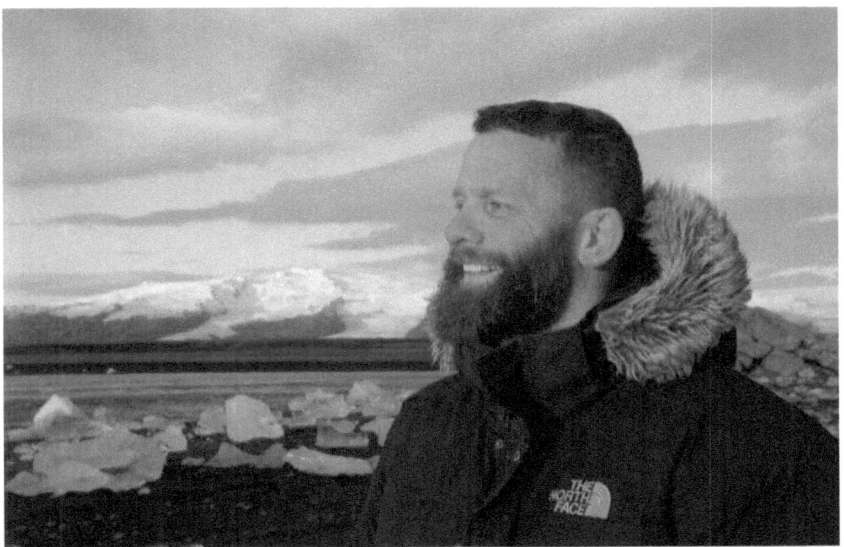

This is Oli, our photo guide from Enroute.is Highly recommended!

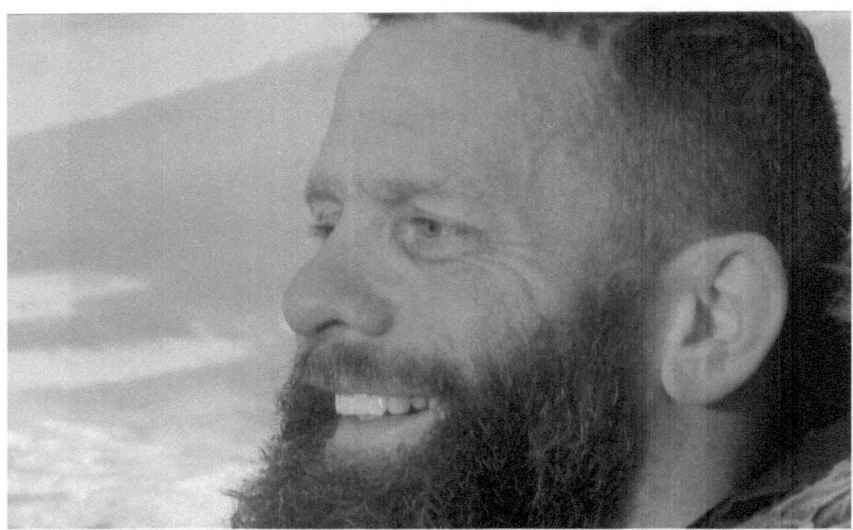

50% crop. Not as sharp as I was hoping. Can it be saved?

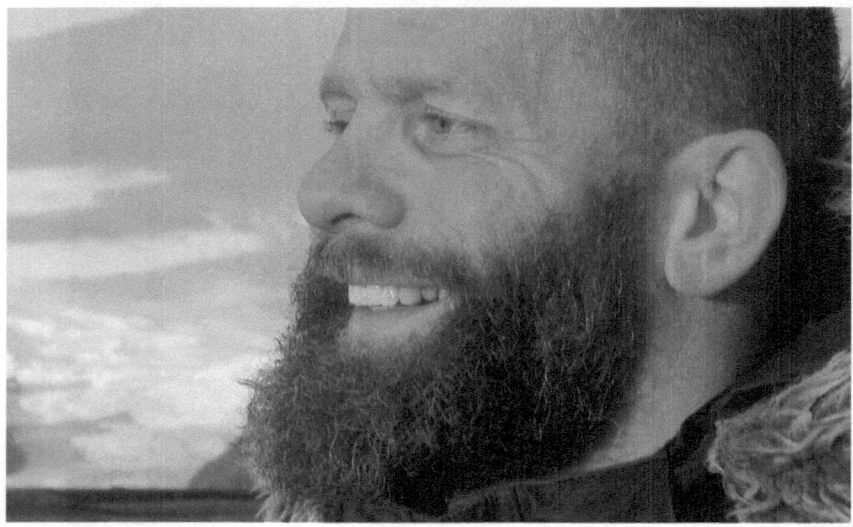

100% crop after image reduced to half size (approx. 8.5 x 12), unsharp mask applied the first time at 100 / 0.9 / 0 and a second time at 500 / 0.2 / 0. Click on both images to examine closely. This technique provides a significant improvement!

So that's another reason why high-megapixel cameras are valuable - they allow you to use this downsize-and-sharpen technique and still have enough megapixels left over for most needs.

3.3 BASEBALL WITH RBS (REALLY BAD SHADOWS)

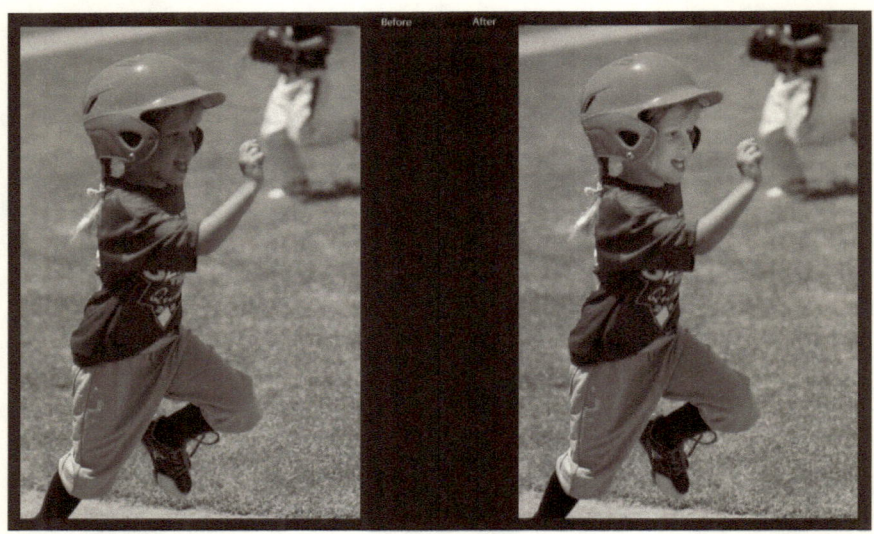

In the states, there is a special kind of baseball game called T-ball which caters to 4-year-olds. Rather than having to hit a ball that is pitched to them, the baseball sits stationary on a stand (a "T") and the kids swing the bat to hit it.

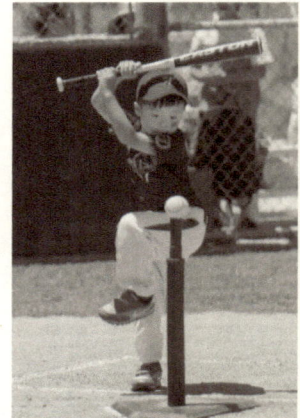

T-ball tournaments are all the rage here, but this month I witnessed what I think is pretty extraordinary. At the end of the season there was a "World Series" playoff, and a whole team of T-ball players from Taiwan flew in to participate!

That's right – a whole bunch of rich parents paid gobs of money to give their kids an international travel experience that they are very

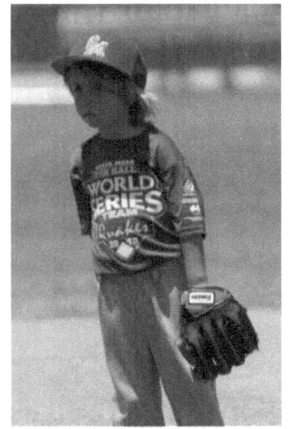

likely too young to appreciate. I had the honor of shooting one of the games in this historic playoff.

To get these shots, I wanted as much of a classic fuzzy background as I could get, so I used my 80-200 f/2.8 and an A77 II set to "A"perture Priority mode at f/2.8. Being a bright day, the camera naturally chose a fast shutter speed, appropos for sports.

Now in sports photography, you're not in control of much. Not your light, not the players, not the action. And I was particularly hampered by the adult-sized hats that the players were wearing, casting giant shadows over their faces that looked dark to my eye and came out entirely too dark to the camera (which doesn't have as much dynamic range as my eye). If I was close I could use fill-flash, but if I wasn't...

Most of you are probably thinking "The shadow problem could be minimized if you shoot RAW and pull out the detail from the shadows later on". Which is true. But it turns out RAW isn't necessary here. I daringly shot 2,000 pictures in .jpg only on "Standard" quality (hey, it's a T-ball game!).

So could I squeeze great pictures out of jpgs that you've always been told couldn't be manipulated very much? Have a look at some of these "before" and "after" shots:

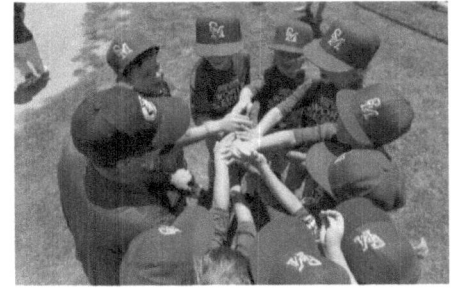

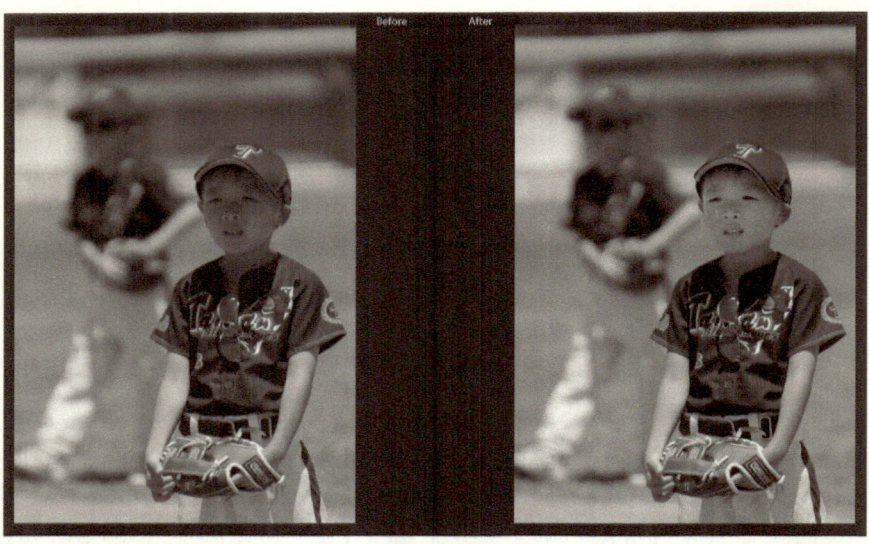

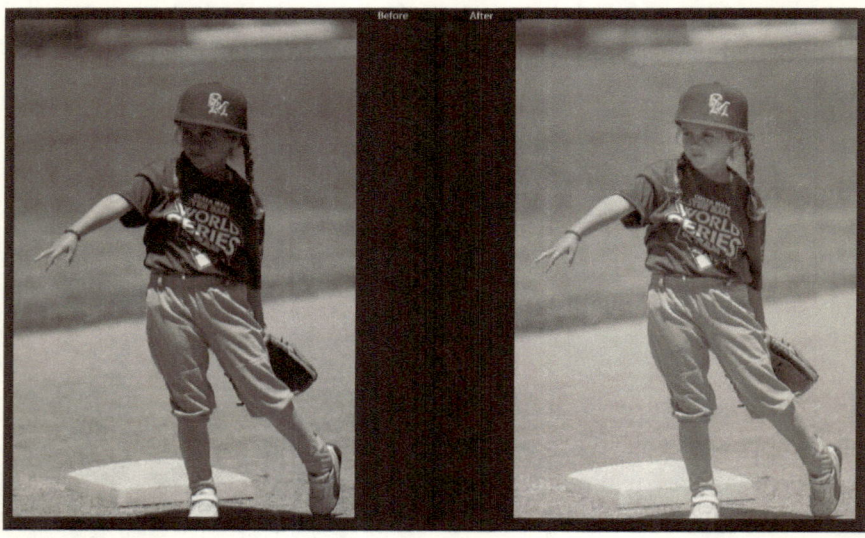

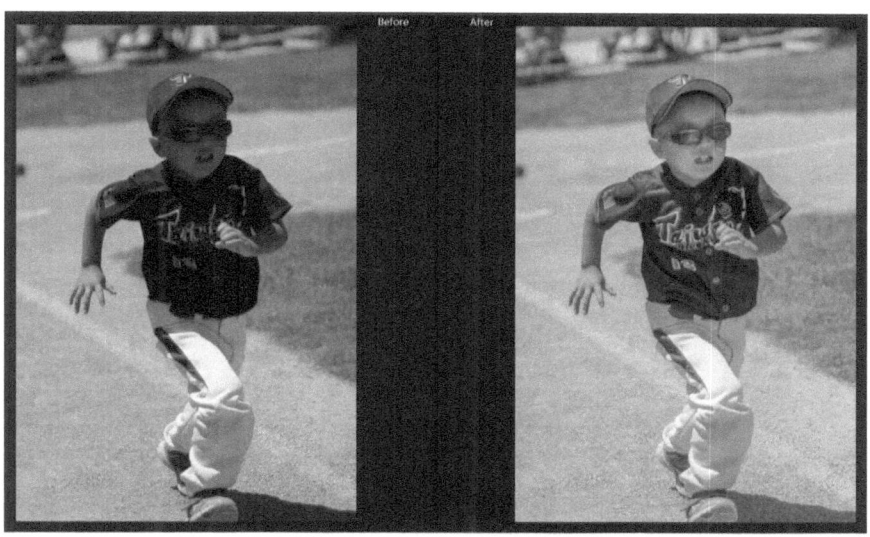

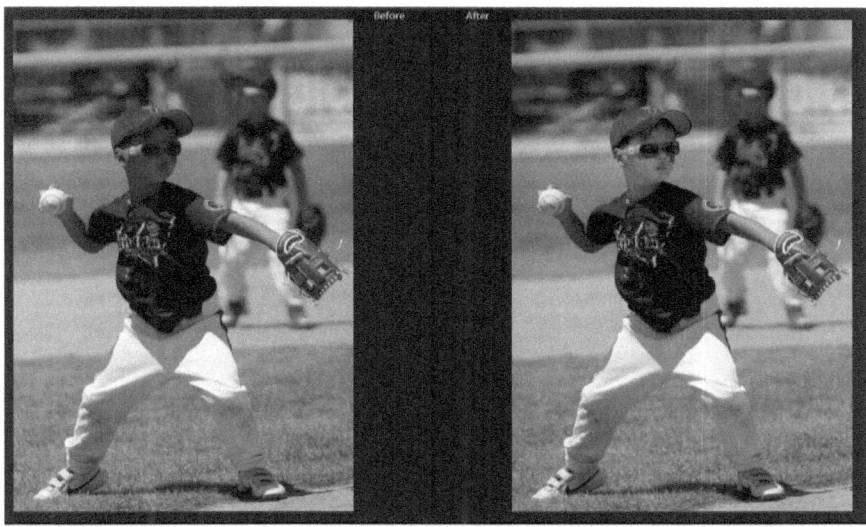

(Mind you, if I had had Face Detection turned on, the camera would have biased the exposure for the face and then the background would have been blown out, so that's not at all preferable.)

To get this effect I used the adjustment brush and the Auto Mask feature in Lightroom and essentially painted the faces lighter. (See Adjustment Brush settings below.) Then I raised the shadow level and in some cases reduced the highlights just a little – doing too much of any of this will make it look post-processed and I definitely didn't want that look for this game.

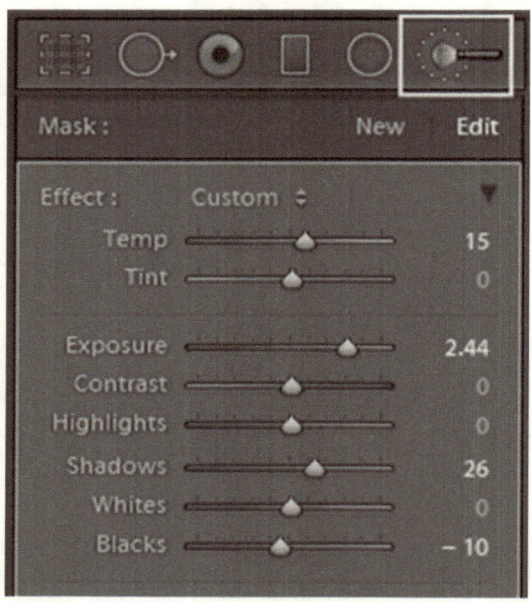

The Adjustment Brush in Lightroom (yellow rectangle), and the settings I used. Then I just painted the face until it looked right.

The team managers had no idea that I had done any of these things – instead they all remarked about how strong my colors were (something I never touch in post-processing). The strong colors were a direct result of strong light.

3.4   AIR SHOW IN RBL (REALLY BAD LIGHT)

First published October, 2017

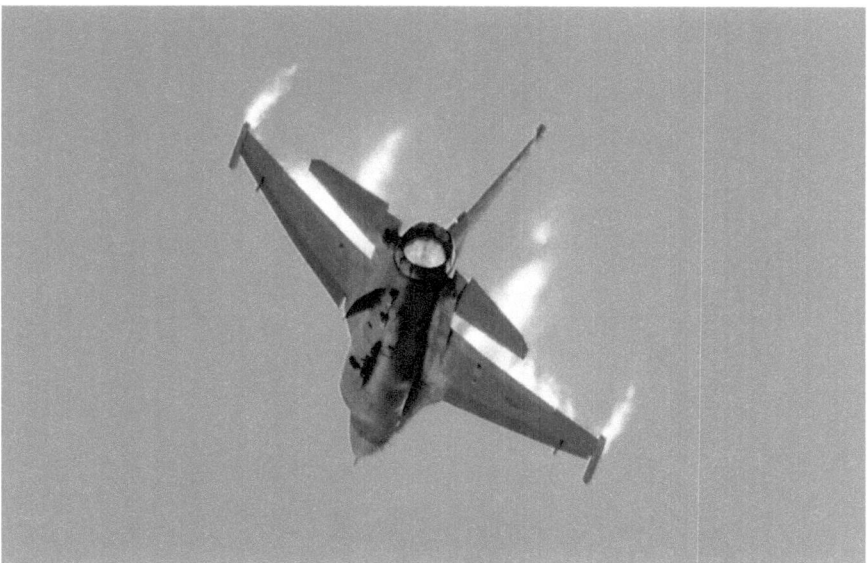

It seems that there's a conspiracy against photographers by people who plan air shows. I'm speaking particularly about the Huntington Beach, California air show in my home town. It's a great tourist event, but they always schedule it at the time of day when you have to look into the sun in order to see the planes. Fine if you're a spectator; awful if you plan on using a camera.

So what did I do? Here's a short laundry list of techniques that, taken together, increased my chances of a usable shot.

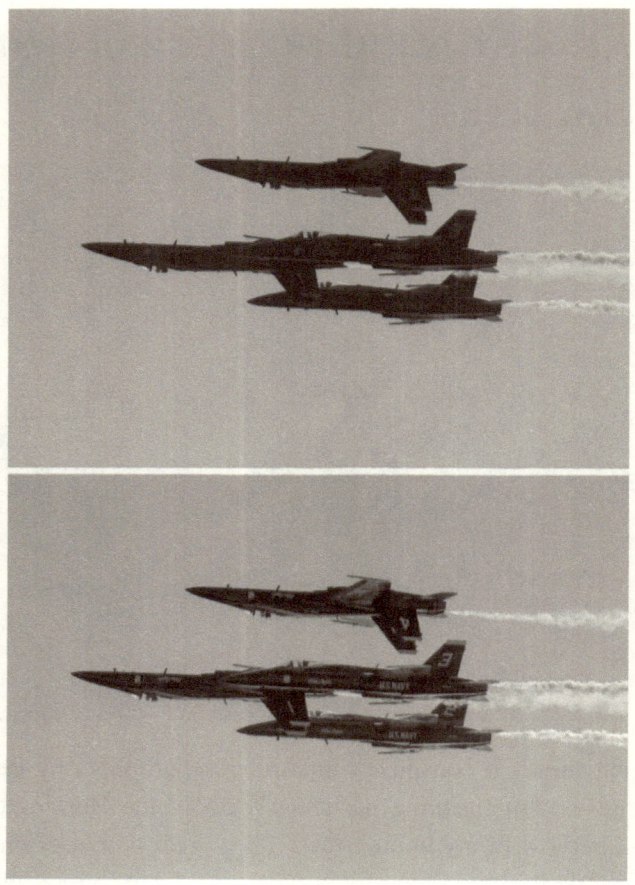

Really hard to do. These guys make it look easy!

First, the gear. The A9's not needed here; as the distance between the camera and subject isn't changing all that much, and 20 fps is simply not needed. My wife and grandkids were with us, and so I brought a lot of cameras that might do the job - all APS-C bodies so I would have the benefit of the 1.5x crop factor when full-frame lenses were attached:

- A6500 with FE 70-200 f/4 (hey, 11 fps is no slouch!)
- RX-10 II with the built-in 24-200 f/2.8 lens (the RX-10 IV with it's 24-600mm lens would have been ideal here, but mine still had not arrived at that time)
- A77 II with Minolta 100-300mm APO
- Sony A700 (!) because my wife had a hard time seeing through the other cameras' EVFs on such a bright day. So I dusted off this DSLR with an optical viewfinder.

All cameras were set to Shutter Priority mode at 1/2000th of a second, the fastest drive mode available, wide-area AF, and Continuous Autofocus (AF-C). "Why not use a center focus point?" I hear you ask. Because there were many occasions when the planes appeared without warning and I needed as much automation as possible to increase the chances of getting a sharp image. Plus, with rare exception there was no distracting background subjects, meaning the AF would not be fooled.

So which one came out with the best results?

Let's start with the RX-10 II. I gave it to one of the grandkids, set it to .jpg only, and enabled Digital Zoom feature, turning it into a 24-800mm lens. Yuk! It could track the planes OK but the results we got from the Digital Zoom feature pretty much validates my recommendation not to use this feature unless you're shooting video.

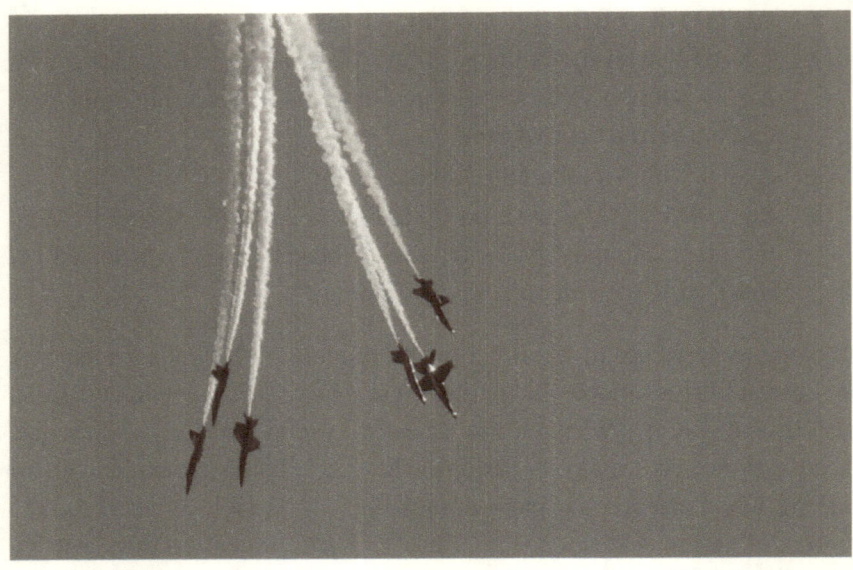

Digital Zoom will essentially crop your image so the subject appears larger within the frame; then it will up-sample it back to 20 MP, making it look worse than a .jpg from 2001. This is from the RX-10 II.

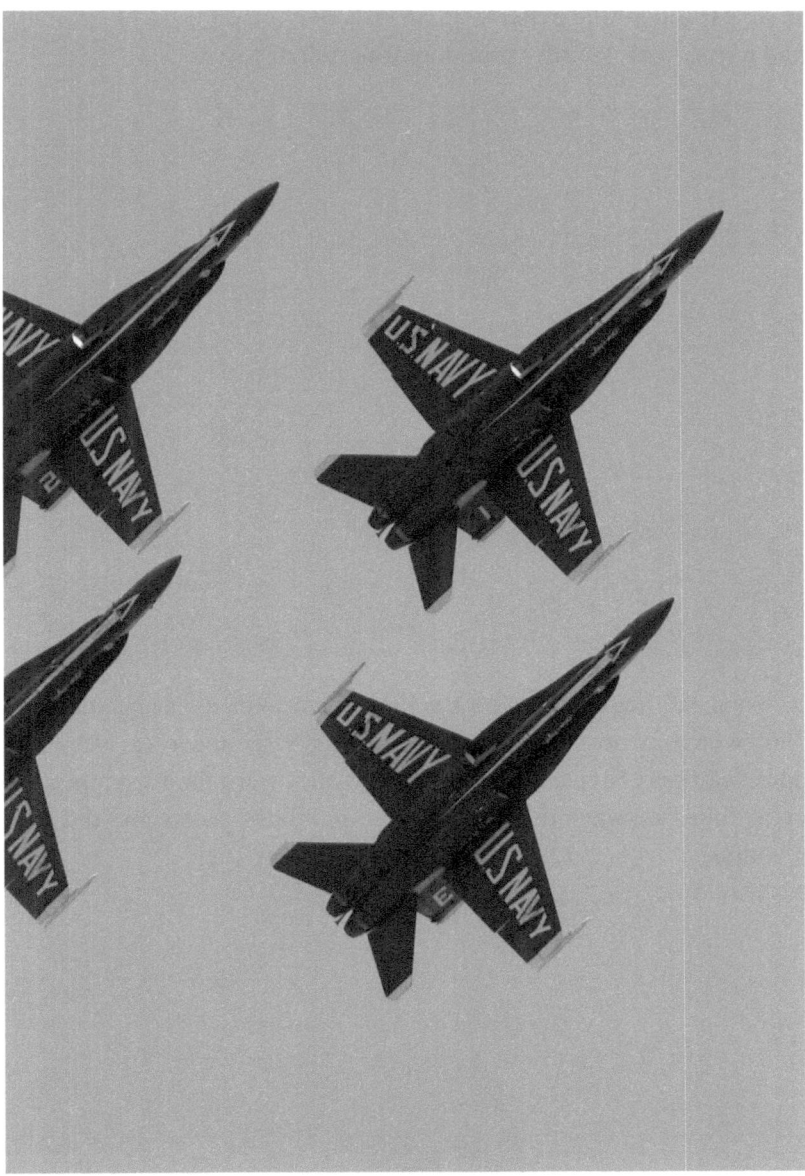

The RX-10 II does exceptionally well with its native lens range, though.
Moral to the story: Don't use the digital zoom feature.

The A77 II did a little better with an effective focal length of 450mm, but it had a (relatively) harder time acquiring initial focus.

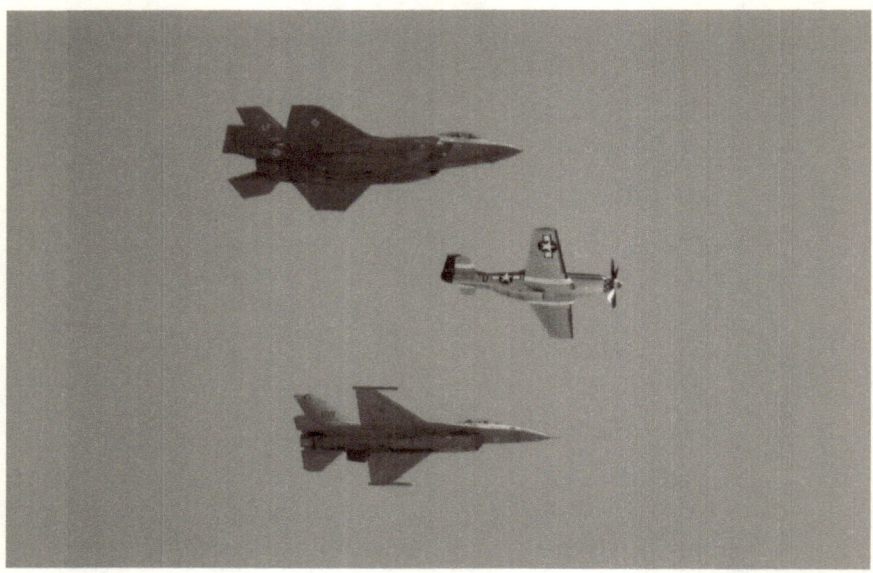

The worst AF acquisition and tracking performance was the decade-old A700, which is no surprise and serves as a reminder of just how far modern cameras have come. When the planes were far away, they would be positioned between the phase-detect autofocus points and the AF just got confused.

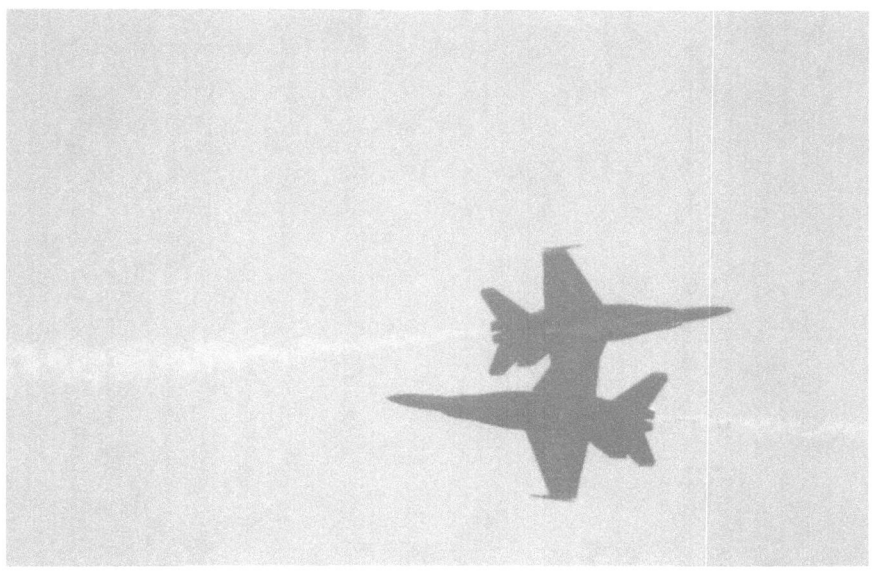

(I TOLD you it was Really Bad Light!) Shooting close to the horizon made it worse, since that's where all the haze was. Not surprisingly, the Alpha 700 had the hardest time acquiring focus. Here I took it off AF and set the lens distance manually so the beginning shooter had a better chance.

The best AF tracking and best image quality (due to that awesome white Sony lens) was the A6500. Even when the planes were far away, it never got between focus points because there are SO MANY baked-in PDAF points that it was impossible to miss the tiny speck. :-)

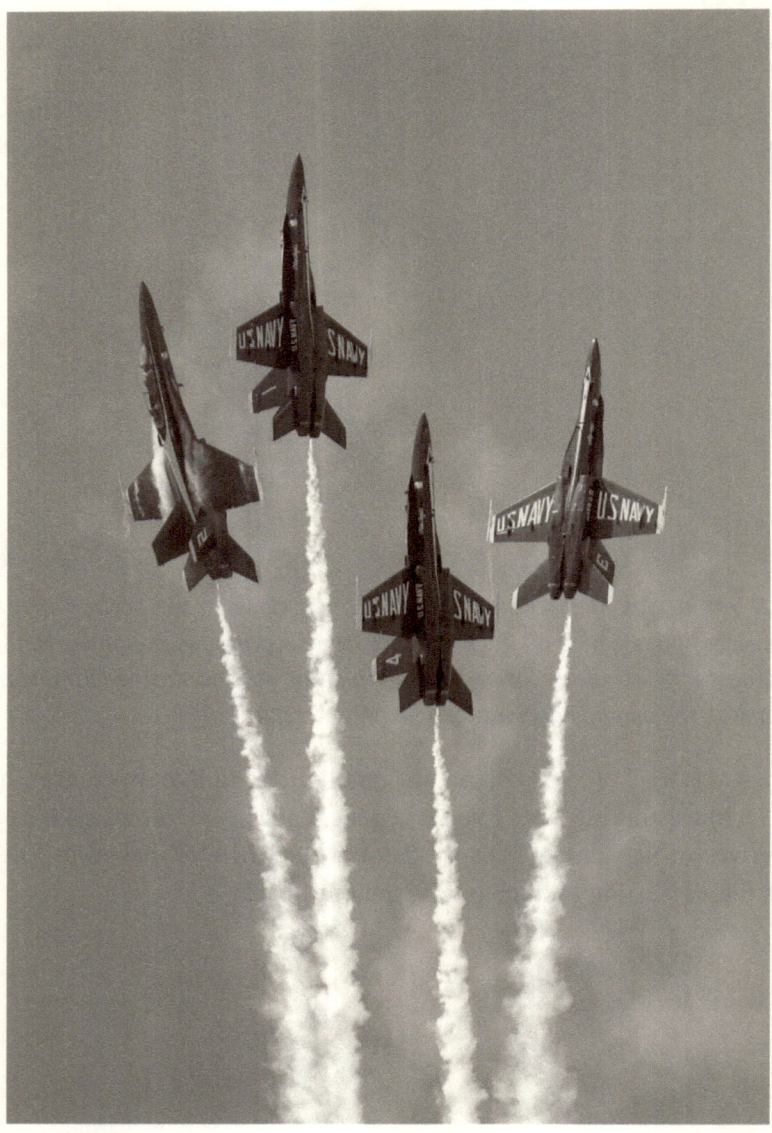

No tiny specs here. Straight-out-of-camera .jpg from the A6500. The planes were literally overhead, making this the only shot where the light was good. 11 fps and AF-C mode was enough to capture the right moment.

Post Processing

Now then, the bad light. There were a few situations where I had warnings that the planes were coming behind me; for those I could turn around and for a precious few seconds I had good light. That's the A6500 image posted above. The rest I had to shoot RAW and post-process to brighten the shadows (since the planes were backlit, they were ALL shadow).

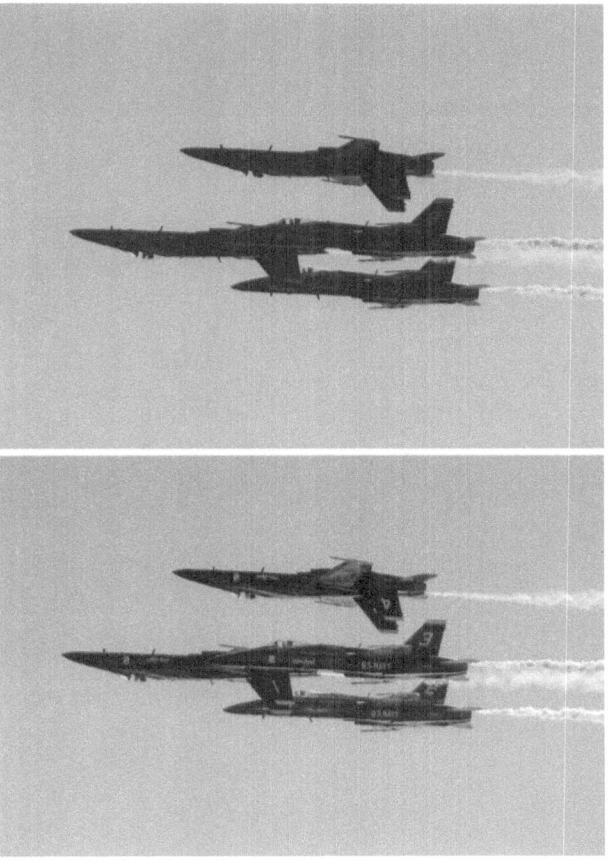

Here's what the controls looked like:

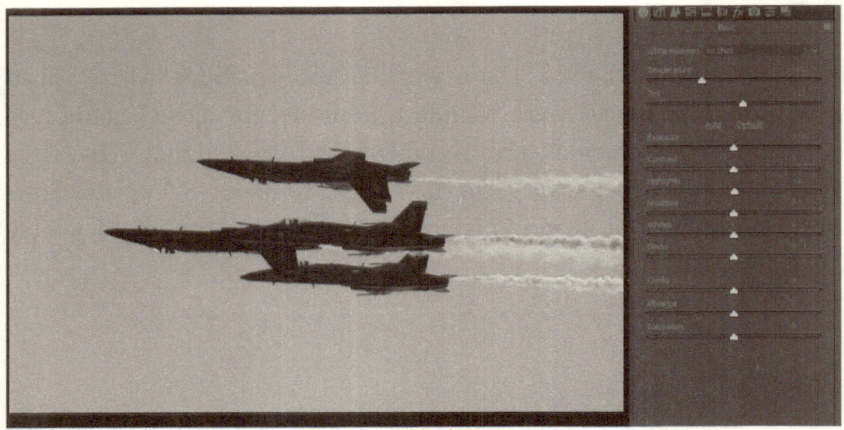

Here's the initial RAW file with no adjustments.

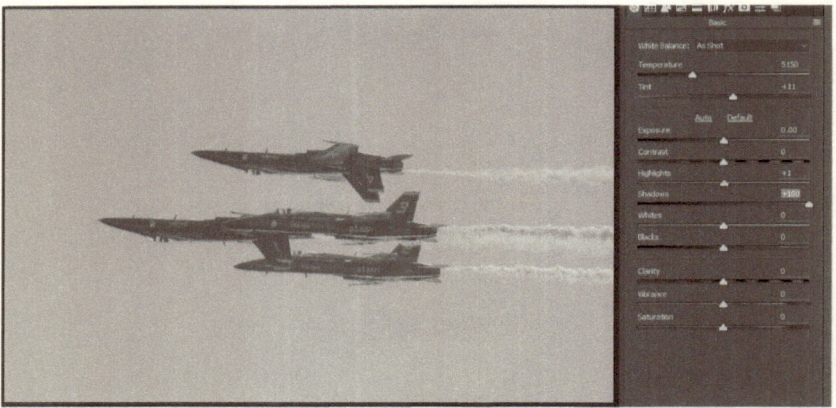

Step 1: Move the "Shadows" slider to the right, lightening the shadows.

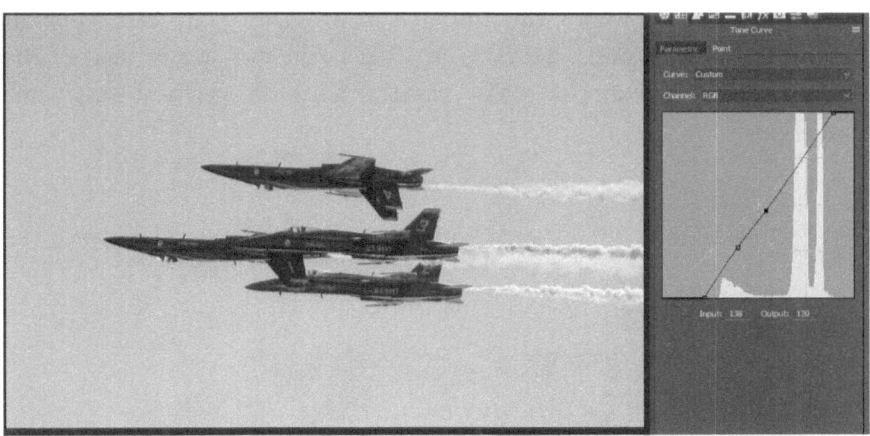

Step 2: Use the curves tool to increase the contrast: Lower-left-hand-corner of the curve moved to the right to raise the shadows to (almost) match the blackest point of the input, upper-right-hand corner moved to the left to do the same for the whites. Sometimes I drag the middle of the line upward to increase the brightness of the midtones as well.

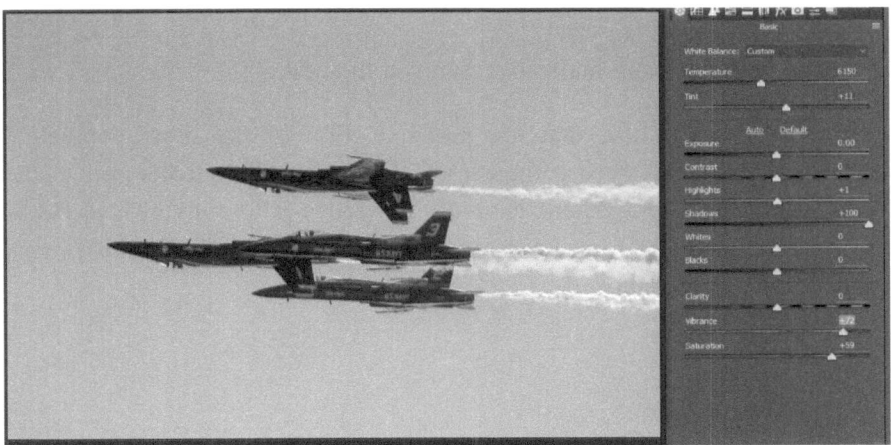

Step 3: Back to the "Basic" panel, increased the saturation and vibrance, and moved the blue-yellow slider away from the blue to let the other colors stand out.

Here's a situation where shooting RAW provides your best hope of having the images pop. Or does it? Let's edit the .jpg instead of the RAW using Photoshop's RAW camera filter to perform the same operations:

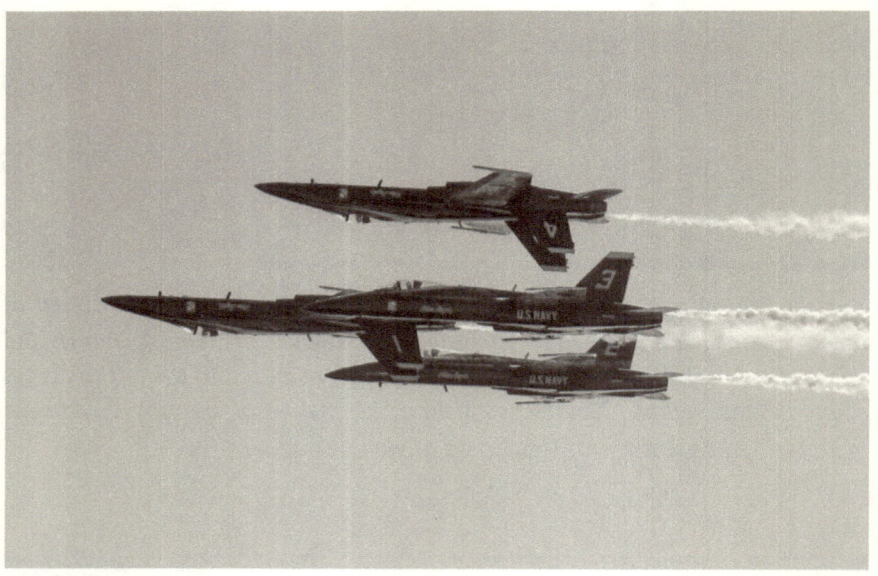

Moral: .jpgs are more malleable than you thought. :-)

So now I have shots that are just like 98% of the other competent photographers that were at the event. What can I do to make mine stand out a little bit? One trick I have up my sleeve is to convert it to B&W ("It's more artistic!") but keep a tinge of color. So I de-saturated most, but not all, of the colors.

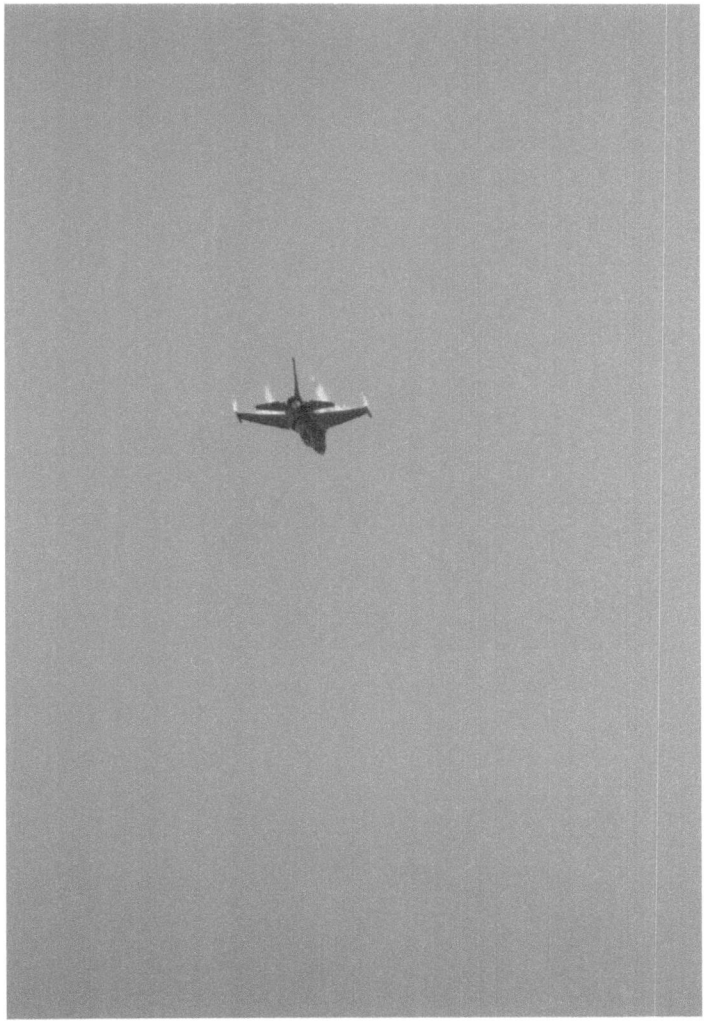

Here's the original image.

After cropping, here's what I did in Lightroom:

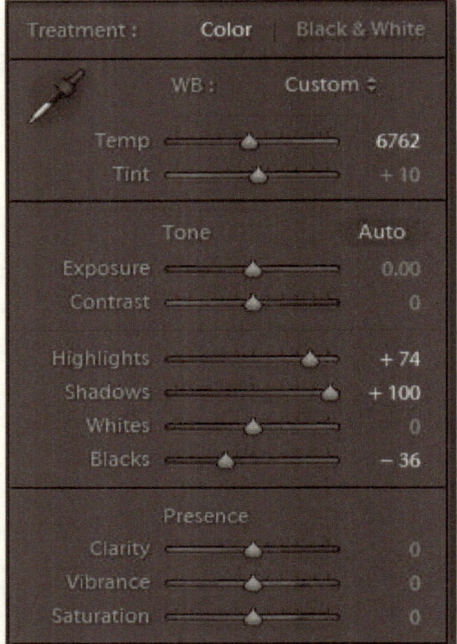

Raise the shadows, and darken the blacks.

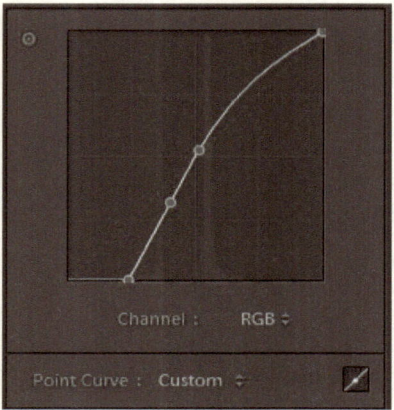

Played with the curves until it looked "right" to me.

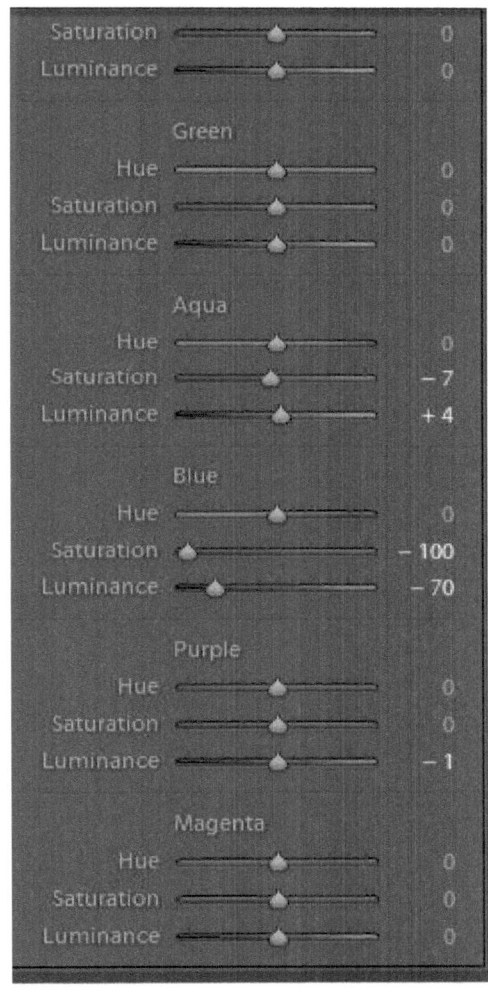

Under HSL / Color / B&W, I clicked on "Color"
and desaturated only the blue channel

And voila!

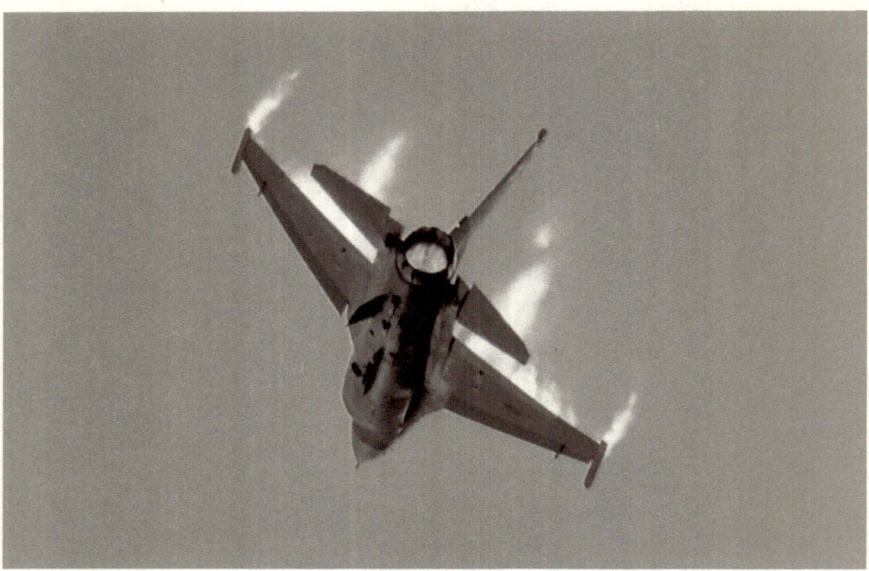

3.5   SHOOTING STAR TRAILS

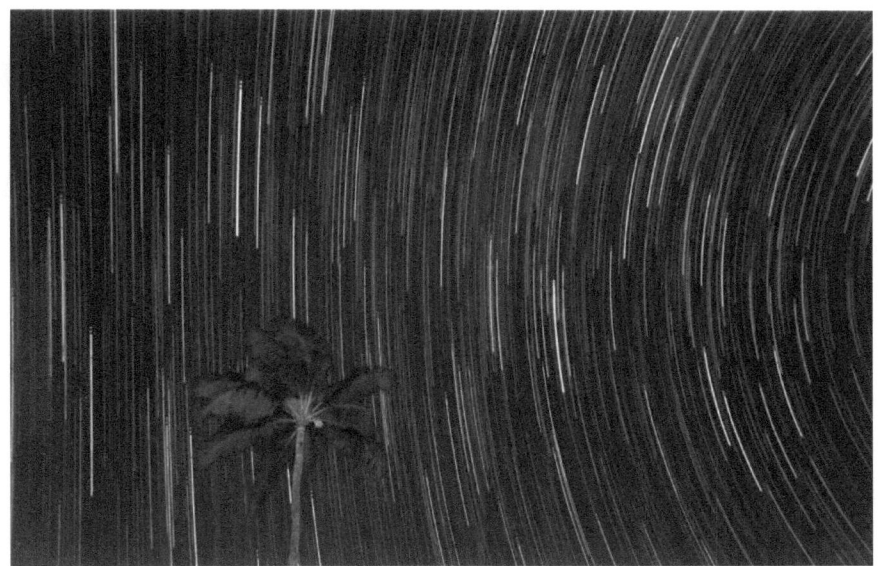

Believe it or not, I've never attempted this kind of a shot before. Maybe because I thought it was too cliché; maybe because I grew up in Southern California where we never really had clear enough skies. But whatever the reason, the first time I tried it was last week, while on a family vacation in Kauai, Hawaii.

Back in the days of film, this kind of a shot was straightforward: Put your camera on a tripod, set the shutter speed to "B", use a locking cable release and keep your shutter open for an hour or two. Not so with digital. Leaving your shutter open for so long will develop so much noise that people looking at it would cringe.

For digital, we have to borrow from the techniques developed by astrophotographers – take a lot of shorter exposures and merge them all on your computer. For this image, I took about 90 pictures at 30 seconds each, ISO 1000, at f/2.8. Then I merged them on my computer using a great, free program called StarStaX (www.StarStax.net).

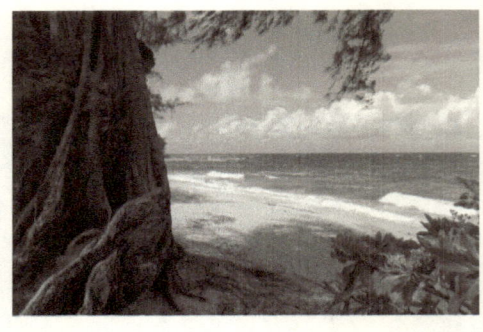

Because this was a family vacation, I brought one of the best cameras ever designed for family vacations: The new RX-10 II. (You probably haven't heard much about it because the whole world is going GaGa right now about the Sony A7r II.) I also took the RX-100 IV, which is essentially the same camera but without the longer-reaching lens. I'll post some other vacation shots I took with these cameras throughout this blog post to keep you from getting bored.

The first challenge to overcome was that of framing and focusing the shot using an EVF. To get shots like these you have to be in a place that is extremely dark – so dark that, even when amplified, your Live View image looks black. How is one supposed to focus and compose under these conditions?

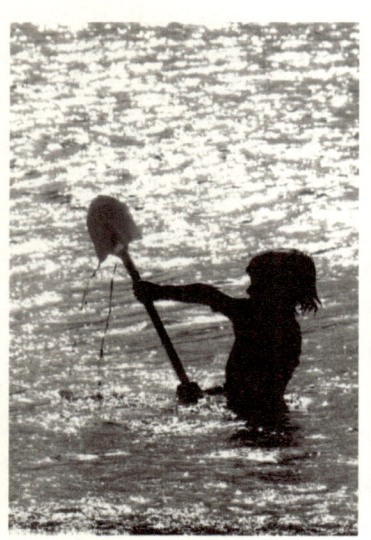

Short answer: For focusing, I set the focus mode to Manual Focus and set the focus distance to infinity. For composition, I had to guess. I pointed the camera in about the right direction and took a test shot. Then I had to manually adjust the focusing a little bit, because apparently "infinity" means "a little further out than infinity". (Lots of lenses behave this way intentionally, to allow them to fully function when thermal expansion happens.)

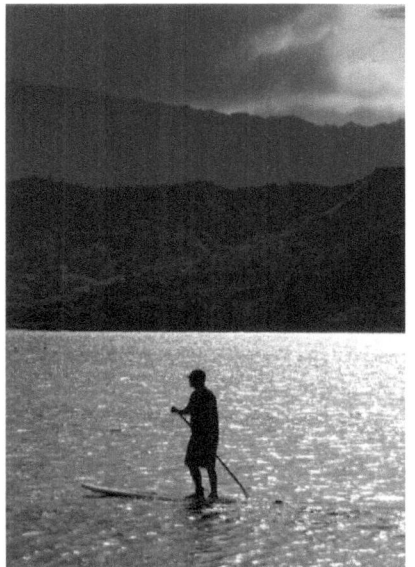

With the shot composed the way I wanted, I used a RM-VPR1 wired cable release, set the camera to continuous shooting, and locked the cable release in the "down" position for about 45 minutes.

Then the fun part commenced. Because I knew noise would be a concern, I shot in RAW, and reduced the noise on all of the images using Lightroom. Then I took the resulting .jpgs and ran them through an easy to use program called StarStax.

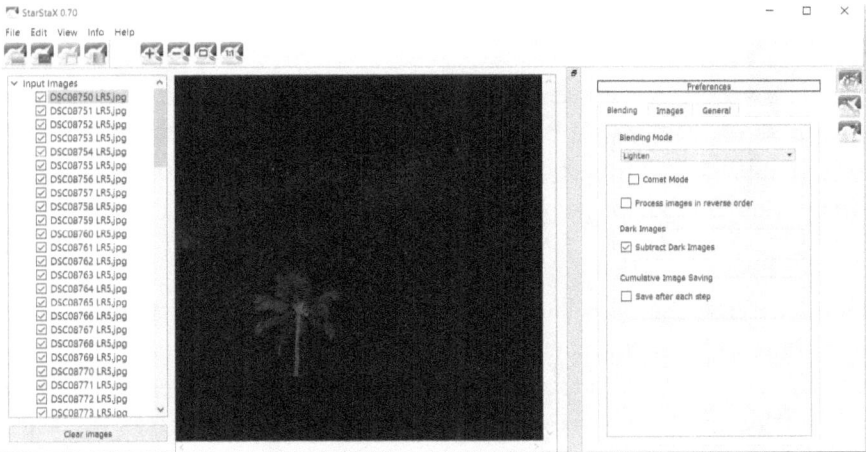

The StartStaX user interface

With StarStax, you just drag all the images you want to merge into the left panel, and hit EDIT --> Start Processing, and wait. (There are more options and controls, but for this image they weren't needed.) I then took the final product, did a slight curves adjustment in Photoshop, lightened the palm tree a little, and that was it!

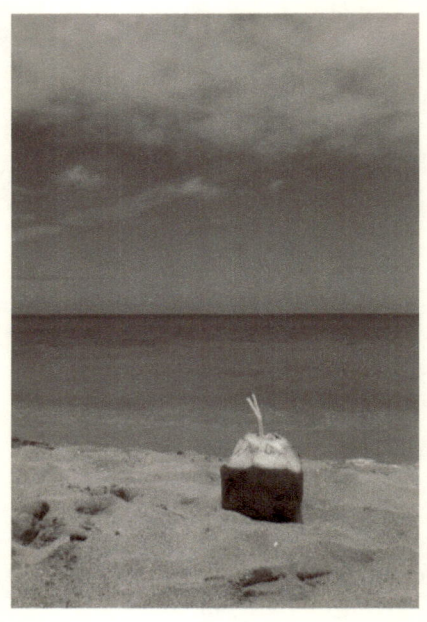

I know what some of you are going to say: "Gary, I've been reading that Sony uses a compressed RAW format whose artifacts can show themselves under precisely these conditions. Weren't you gnashing your teeth in anguish about this issue?"

The answer is no. I consider this an art image, and if there are compression artifacts visible around the bright-to-dark transitions, I sure wasn't able to see them. On the other hand, I'm not an astrophotographer doing this for scientific purposes. If I was, I'd probably be more concerned.

But there is a question that threw me initially: I had expected all of the star trails to form concentric circles around Polaris, the North Star (out-of-frame, to the right in the image). This does indeed happen on the right half of the image, but as you look from right to left you see the stars' paths look straighter. Here's the image again:

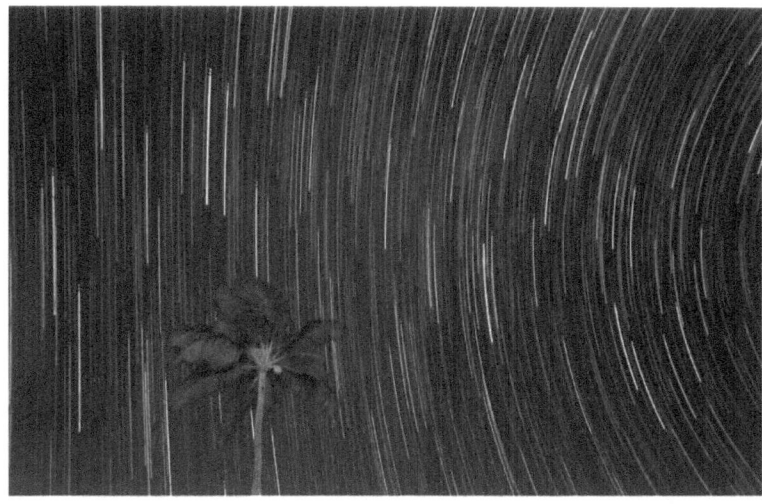

What's going on? I put out the question on Facebook, and sure enough, David Kilpatrick (renown photo magazine publisher, including Cameracraft) provided the necessary insight:

"You're inside a big sphere, in effect, and the stars which make straight lines are directly overhead (moving like the sun does at the equator, if you aim your camera exactly east or west - from horizon to horizon straight over the top). The stars to your left and right will appear to make ever tighter circle until any star perfectly aligned with the earth's axis

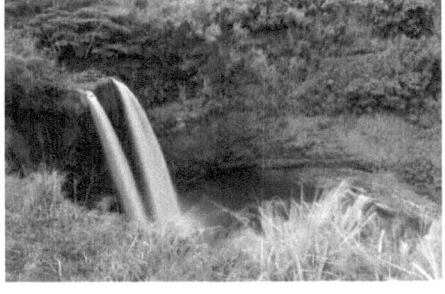

(Pole Star for north? more or less) will not move at all and will record as a point. But you have to be able to see that to record it. Not sure about Hawaii. In Scotland it's easy enough to put the Pole star centre shot and get complete circles. Close to the equator it is probably below the horizon or just above it."

I've said this before, and I'll say it again: That man is a fountain of knowledge.

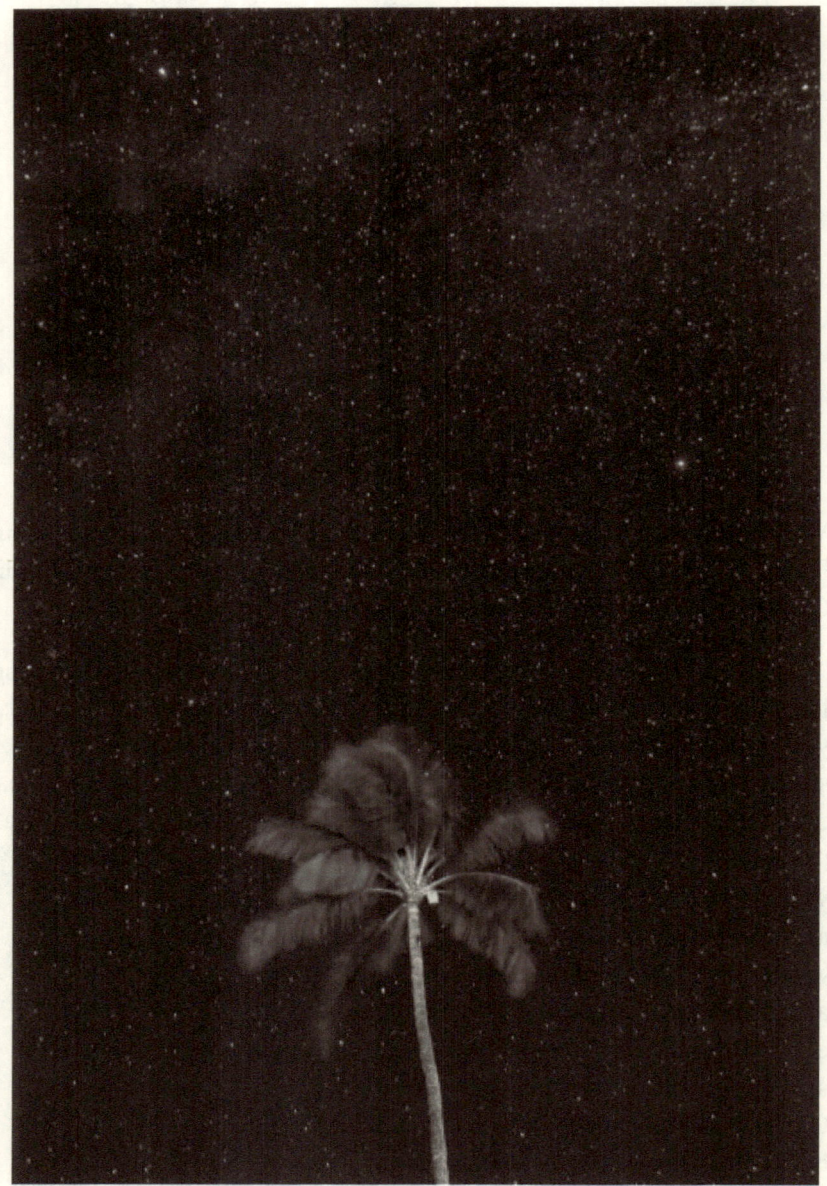

RX-100 IV, 20s, f/1.8, ISO 1250. Slight curves applied to increase contrast but that's it. You can't take a picture like this in Los Angeles.

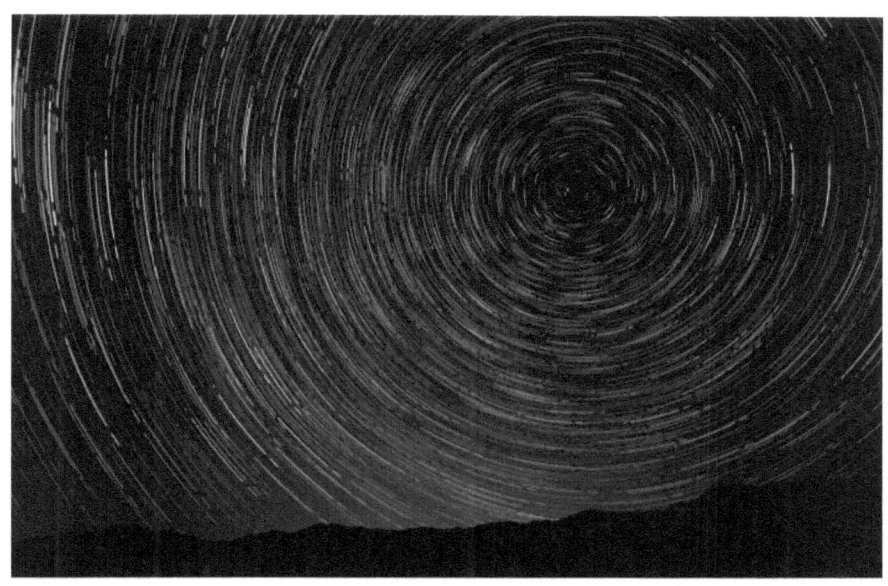

Another result using different settings: A7R II, 28mm lens, 20s f/3.5, ISO 400. 151 images merged using StarStaX.

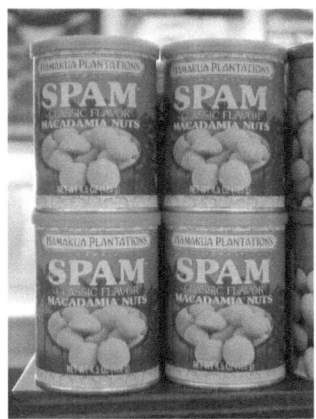

These are SPAM-flavored macadamia nuts... and looking at the ingredients, there's no actual SPAM in them. Some scientist somewhere spent years developing a spam-flavored seasoning. This is what we get from the space program. Welcome to Hawaii!

3.6   THE   PUBLISHED   PHOTOGRAPHER'S PERPETUAL NIGHTMARE

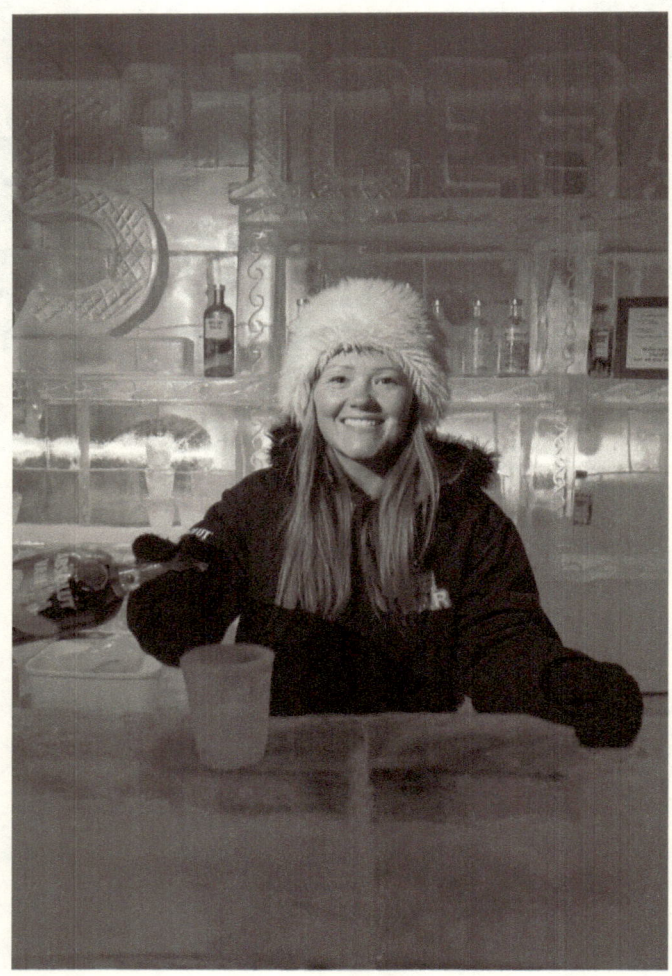

I love environmental portraits. Here's the manager of the Minus 5 degree Ice bar in Queenstown, New Zealand. Everything here is made of ice - even the glasses!

The shot above took a long time to take, for as impressive as the frozen room was, the ever-changing light just wasn't great for the camera.

Here's how I created that image, step by step:

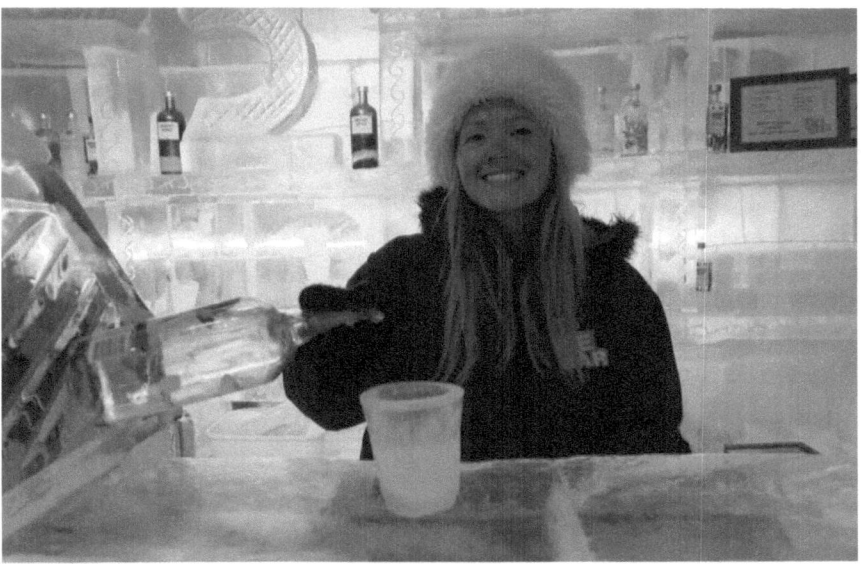

No flash

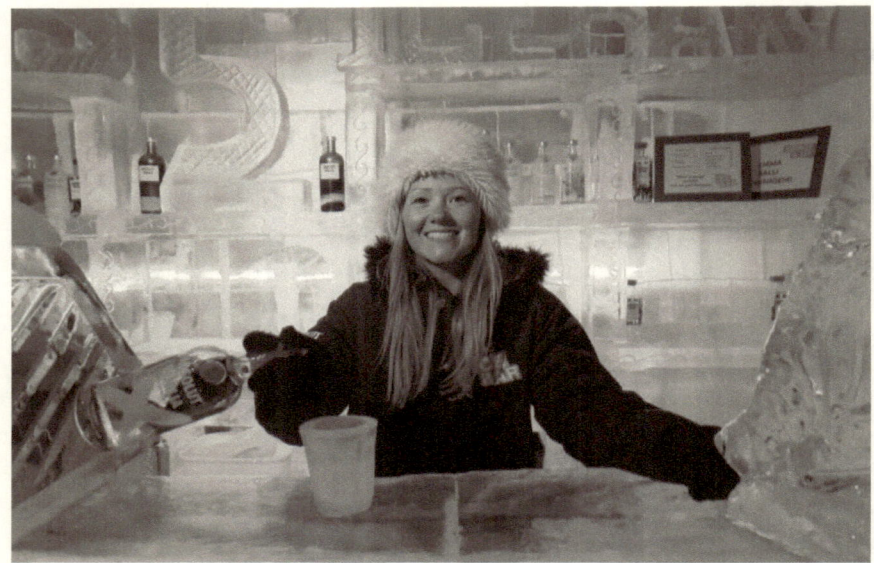

Flash (held by an assistant) but auto white balance

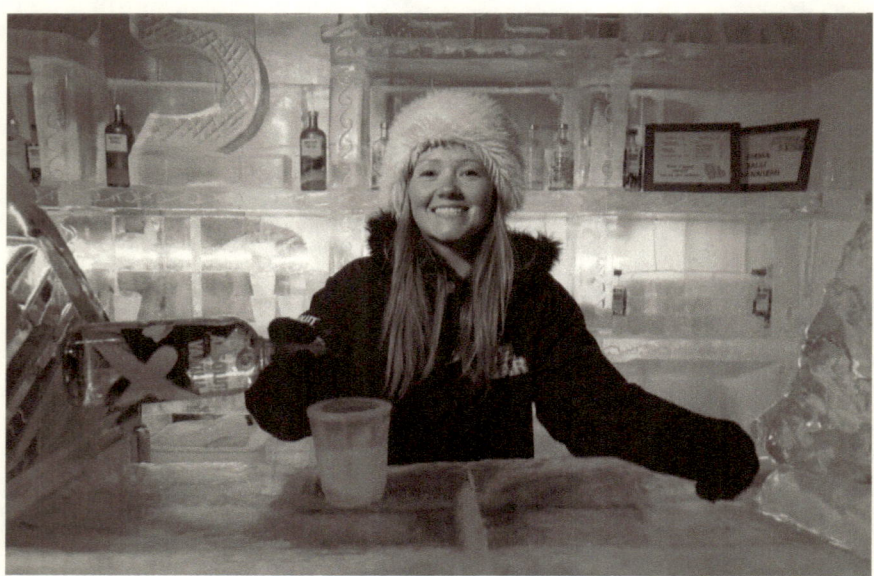

Flash and white balance set to "Daylight"

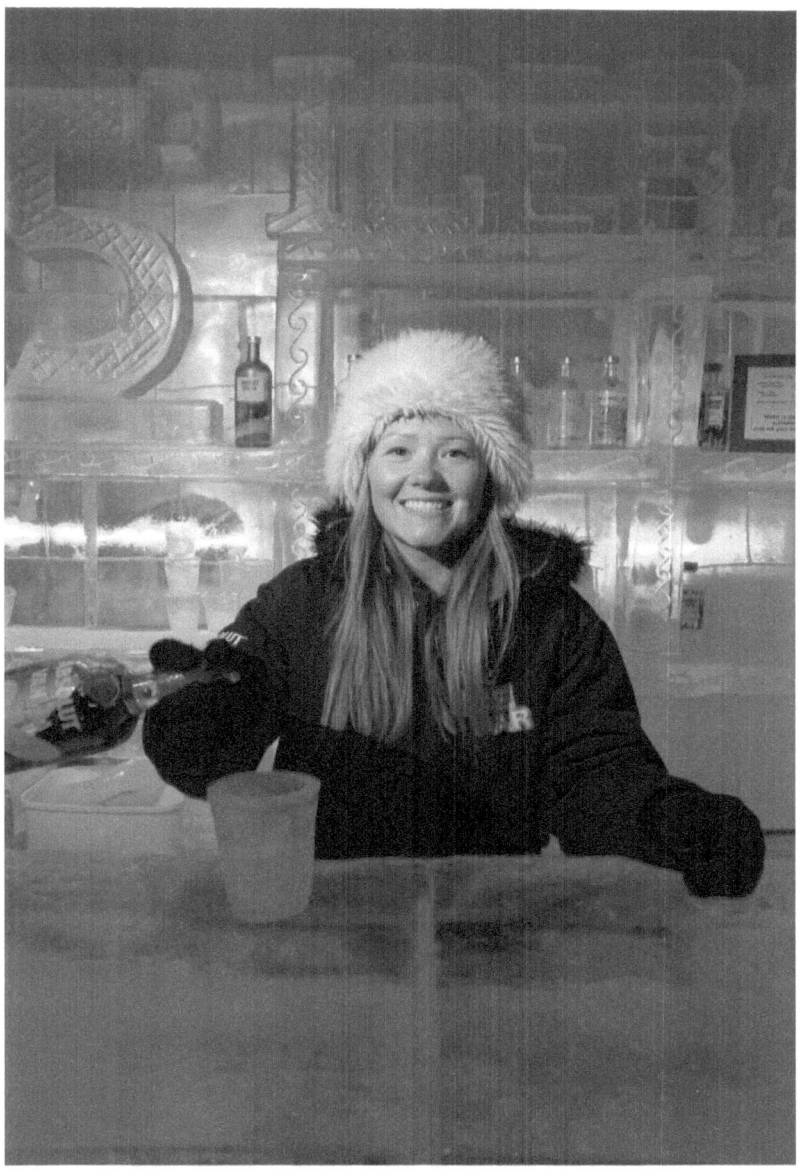

Once I nailed the light, I waited about 2 minutes for the ambient light to change color to this (great color contrast can draw your eye to the shot).

Problem over, right? Nope. If you're going to have the image printed in a magazine (as this will be in the next issue of f2 Cameracraft), you have to take into account that if you convert this image to CMYK mode (the four colors used in offset printing) the image will look NOTHING like it did on the screen! The screen creates its colors using additive light (combining different amounts of red, green, and blue), whereas the printing press by necessity uses the opposite of these colors (cyan, magenta, yellow, and then black for extra contrast). Not all methods can represent all colors, and this picture, as luck would have it, has lots of colors that just fall "out of gamut":

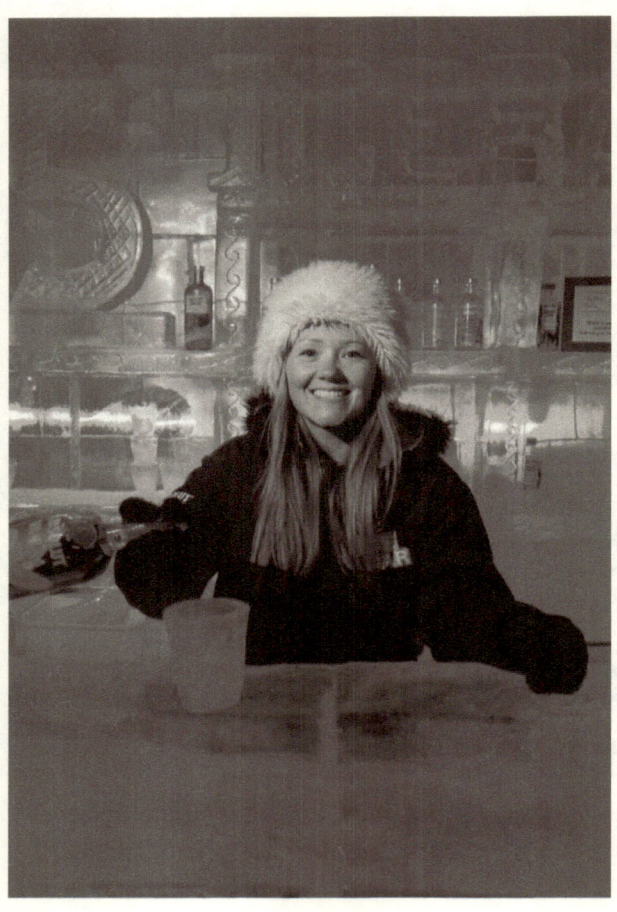

That beautiful blue which makes the shot is all muddy!!! Yuk! Most print houses would just print the version above, and the client would then be furious at the bad repro.   David Kilpatrick, publisher of f2 Cameracraft and king of all things printing, cares about the output so much that he spent 10 minutes tweaking the image in Photoshop in CMYK mode (something most print houses would simply never do) to make it look close to the original. Here's what he did, in his own words:

"To get the big shifts needed in each colour channel, I use the 'Camera Raw' filter option first for processing the opened JPEG and changing the camera calibration - I had to make the blue a lot less purple and the reds more orange less magenta. Highlights and contrast needed adjustment too. I created an adjustment brush (in Camera Raw filter) which lifted the highlights and deepened shadows and also added exposure, and painted this over the ice without going over the bar attendant, until I felt that the ICEBAR logo and the texture of the ice was going to reproduce well. I worked on the image in RGB, but used the 'Proof Colors' options in Photoshop to see how it would print in CMYK, and returned to this between adjustments.

I find the Camera Raw filter very useful for working on JPEGs and prefer it to using layers. It's actually the same as using some very complex layers, but much faster. It's even better if you start with a 16-bit JPEG or TIFF, as these are nearly as good as an original raw file."

Below is the result which prints the same way it appears on screen (although it doesn't look the same when you see it on a screen ☺):

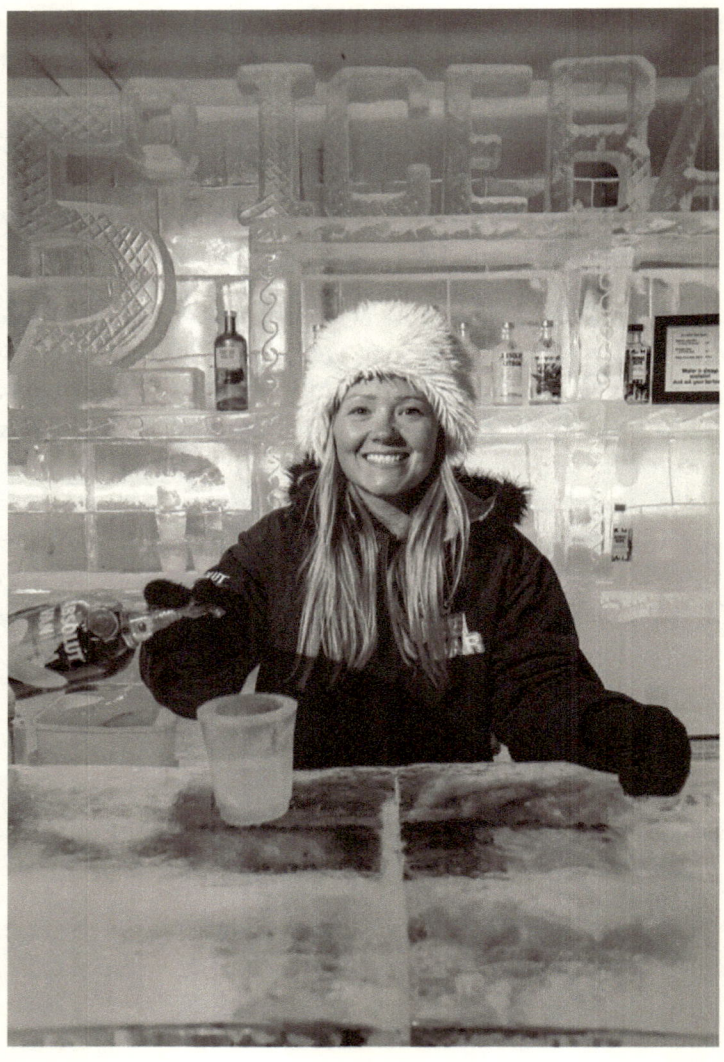

THIS is why professionals care about color matching between screen and print! Had David not corrected this I would have been a bit miffed.

3.7 MYTHBUSTING!

First published August, 2015 in Cameracraft Magazine

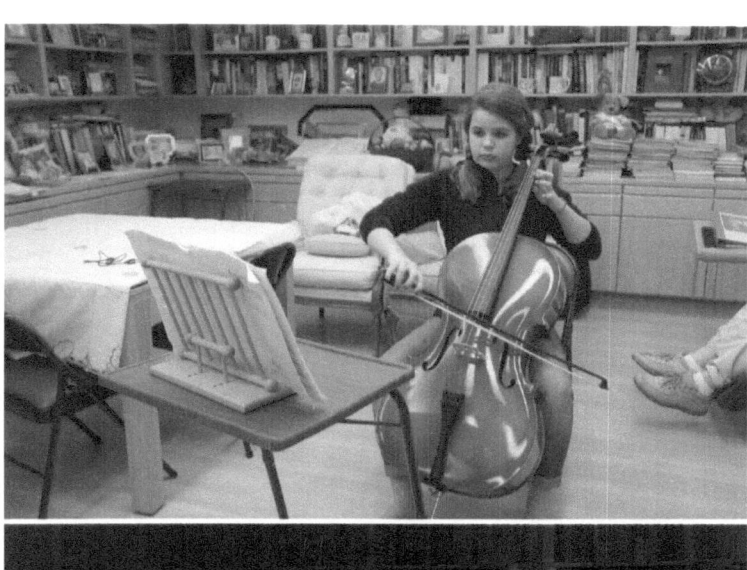

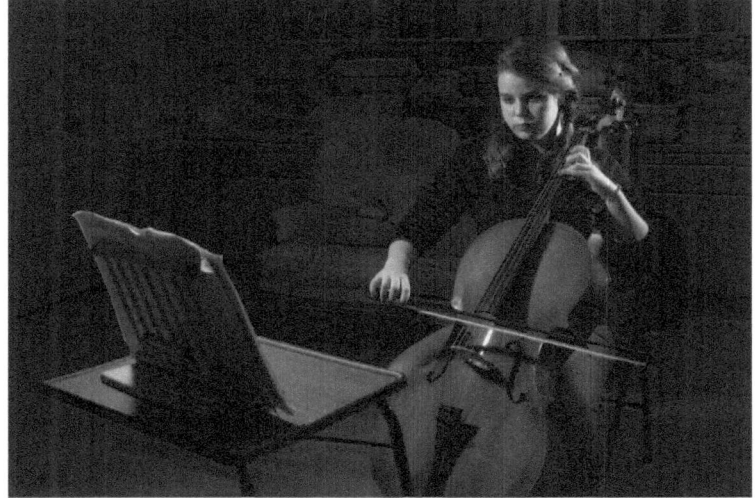

Light and composition are the keys to images which work.

In the last edition our illustrious editor made an eloquent rant about how the world is unjustifiably going nuts over the new breed of overpriced lenses. That article paved the way for this one.

Some background: Most people know me and my work through my camera-specific ebooks. They're a hit with people who buy cameras, as everyone wants to know what all those complex-sounding functions do. And people seem to like my explanations, so that's nice.

BUT there is a deep-rooted myth I've been trying to dispel for a decade now: The implicit assumption that once you learn what all of your camera's features do, your photography will somehow magically improve overnight. The other implicit assumption is "Learning Photoshop will make my pictures better".

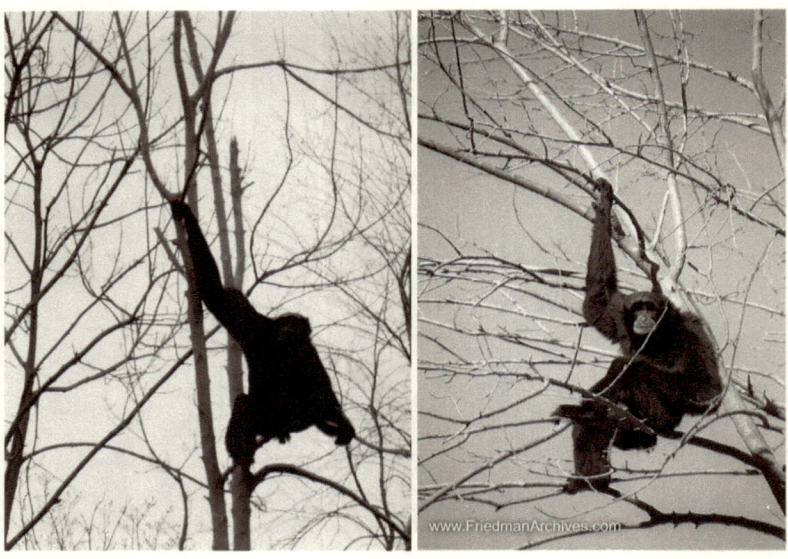

There is no magic button on your camera that can go from the left image to the right. You just have to wait for better light.

Well, you've been brainwashed. Buying an expensive camera by itself does not make you a better photographer. Nor will shooting RAW or learning Photoshop. These things are a few percentage points in what makes up a great picture. In fact, the two greatest components of a "Wow!" photograph are 1) Light and 2) Composition. If you don't have these two components nailed down, none of the other things will matter. Bad light makes high-price lenses impotent.

Neither RAW nor Photoshop can do anything to improve the first picture of the cellist. But lighting – well, you can see exactly what lighting does.

And for the gibbon in the tree ‑ there's hardly any point in taking pictures from the wrong side in the wrong light. Be patient, wait for the light, and find the best way to use it.

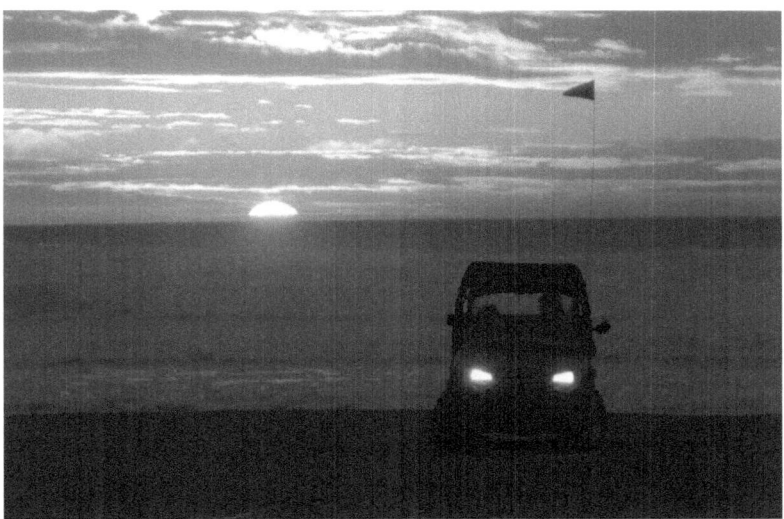

Shooting in P mode, RAW+JPEG, will produce great results most of the time. Exposure is best fine tuned in-camera (±EV control) for sunsets.

So important are these fundamentals that I had devoted an ENTIRE DAY to teaching it in my 2-day traveling seminars. By the time Day 1 is over, attendees leave re-examining long held beliefs about what they thought was important in photography. Good.

In an effort to reach more people I had a seminar professionally videotaped, and last month a streaming version of Day 1 was brought to market. Shortly after that the feedback started rolling in. Many raved about it, but the ones that stuck in my mind were the negative ones. The worst of these can be summarized thusly:

"Your course was OK, but I wanted to know what camera settings to use in order to get better vacation pictures!"

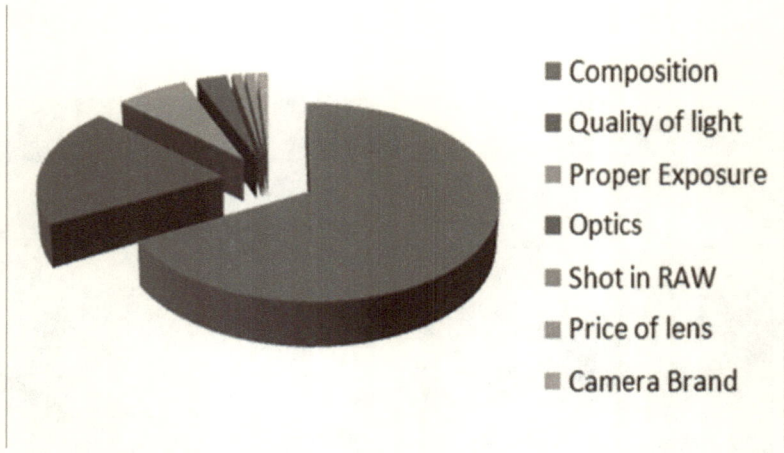

Gary's pie puts composition top...

Grrrrrr…. In the course I talked about that at length, with lots of examples. I also showed lots of examples where having a fancy camera wouldn't have helped, like the gibbon in the tree. If you're not happy with your vacation pictures, knowing your camera's settings won't necessarily help you much. Apparently my message went right through these customers.

On the one hand you could say I failed as a teacher to get my idea across. Or you could, just as correctly, say that some people just don't want to hear it. "Light and Composition seem just too simple, and since I didn't mention any of these oh-so-important camera features, obviously I'm only telling half a story. Will you talk about all that in Day 2?"

Don't be like them. I'm populating this article with lots of examples of great pictures taken with an old point-and-shoot on Auto, as a reminder that in the old days we never had these features or Photoshop, and yet we still managed to get great pictures using the very simple techniques I tried to instill in my seminars. The things we are told as being important (resolution, 14-bit uncompressed RAW, High-Dynamic Range feature, no pincushion distortion in the optics) are meaningless unless your

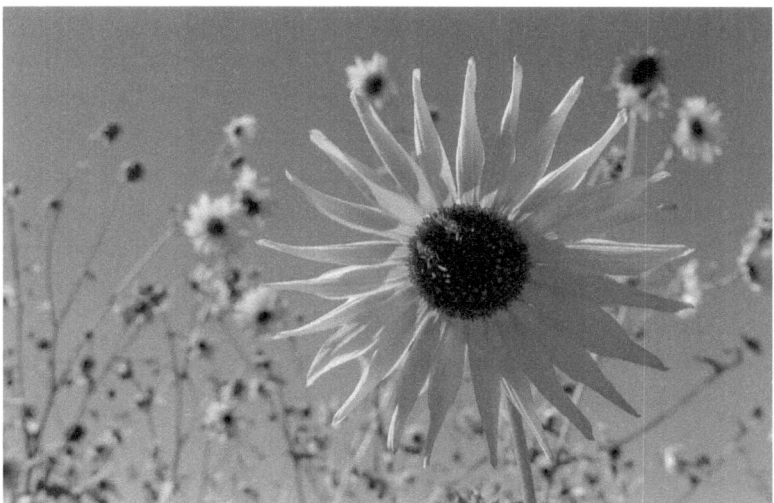

Cameras with tilting rear screens (like this, taken with the RX100 MkIII, 8.8mm) let you find angles and viewpoints from ground level upwards.

light and composition are strong. If you want to improve as a photographer, that's what you concentrate on.

I'm not the first to complain about this. It's been true forever. Many businesses recognize it and leverage it for immense profit (case in point: most popular photography magazines, gear review websites, and the whole ecosystem that sprung up around Photoshop). I think that's one reason I covet my association with Cameracraft so much – it's an oasis of vision in a sea of people obsessed with gear.)

So in the spirit of furthering this message, allow me to additionally bust five myths commonly associated with improving photography:

1. *"A-mode is best for walkaround photography."* - Actually, for walkaround photography I find myself shooting in Program mode and Auto ISO most of the time. This allows me to get the shot very quickly – letting the camera do what it does best while I concentrate on what I do best. Once I get the shot, if I have the luxury of a second chance, I'll ask myself "How can I make that shot better? Is the exposure right? Should the background be more out-of-focus so the subject pops more? Should I use a different shutter speed to cause more of a blur for artistic purposes?" Then I will exit P mode and then go to whatever mode helps me achieve my vision. But I always start in "P" mode because it increases the odds of me capturing a fleeting event quickly.

2. *"You're not a serious photographer unless you shoot RAW."* - There's a great irony in this, as only the photographers who really know what they're doing can get away with shooting JPEG only. I usually shoot RAW+JPEG all the time just to have a safety net in case something goes wrong. When I get back to my office I'll put the RAW files in a separate directory just in case I'm not happy with how the JPEGs turned out. 99.999% of the time the RAW files never get opened. While that's bad for my disk space usage, over the course of my life I've probably saved two years' worth

of work not having to tweak the RAW files so they look as good as the JPEG. Life is short, and I'd rather spend it shooting than tweaking. The quality of today's JPEGs are so good compared to 10 years ago that if your light is good, and your exposure is right for that light, then your images will not benefit greatly from shooting RAW. See my blog posts elaborating on this subject here: http://bit.ly/1dvjQgA and http://bit.ly/1g0MzVd .

3. *"Expensive cameras take better pictures."* – The entire camera industry is built upon perpetuating this premise. It's only true if you have nailed your light and composition. Without those, your 50 megapixel Canon EOS 5DS with L-series glass will only take mediocre pictures. And if your light and composition ARE wonderful, then I would argue that, as long as you're not enlarging to auditorium-sized prints, it doesn't really matter what you shoot with any more – all of today's cameras are amazingly good. National Geographic photographers are now shooting with the low-light capable 12 megapixel Sony A7s and they print just fine.

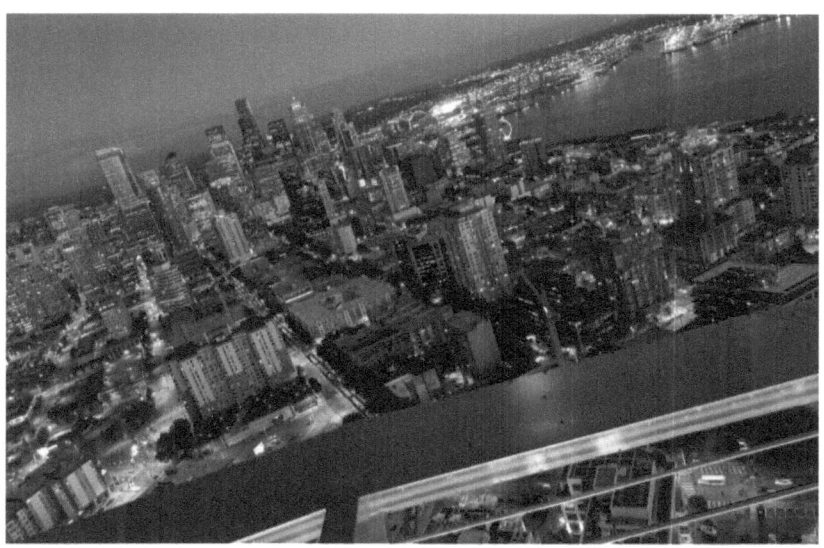

I've had many full-page commercial images printed that I took with my six megapixel Konica Minolta 7D.

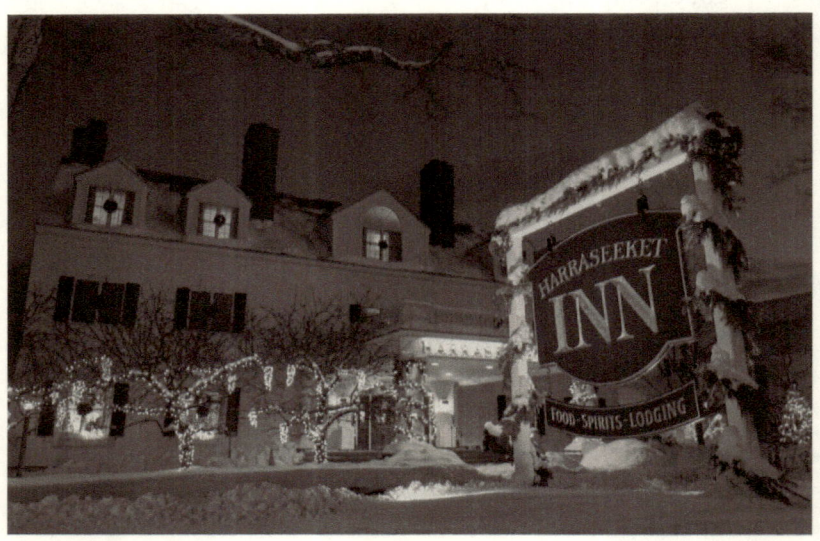

Today's pocketable cameras can tackle almost anything: top, Sony RX100 MkII at ISO 160. Pro cameras go further even with the kit lens, Harraseeket Inn was enlarged to wall size from 36MP from a 28-70mm basic zoom.

4. *"Primes are essential for great photography!"* – See the previous paragraph. What's actually true is that today's cameras (bodies and lenses) are so good that in order to see any difference between them, you have to pixel peep with an electron microscope. No reasonable person does that. Some of my best pictures taken with the original Sony A7 were shot using the kit lens. And some shots are much easier to take with a zoom!

5. *"I think the reason I'm not happy with my pictures is because I don't understand all of my camera's features."* – Seriously, no. The overarching truth is if your light sucks, so

will your pictures. Those features only come into play once your light and composition are good.

Okay, my rant is over. But I still don't know what I should be doing differently to help get this important message out to the world. Maybe life would be easier for me if I gave up and just conducted Photoshop classes.

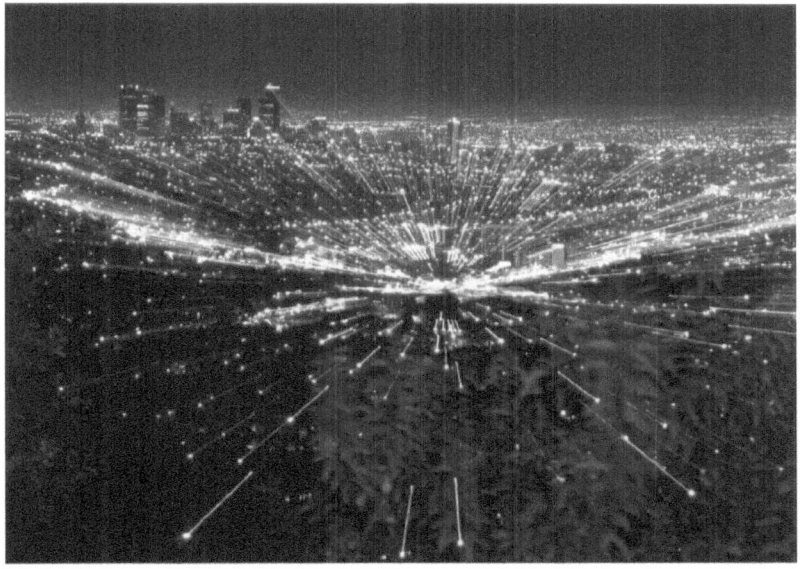

Zooms are actually essential for some shots!

3.8   FUN WITH GREEN SCREENS

First published September, 2015 in Cameracraft Magazine

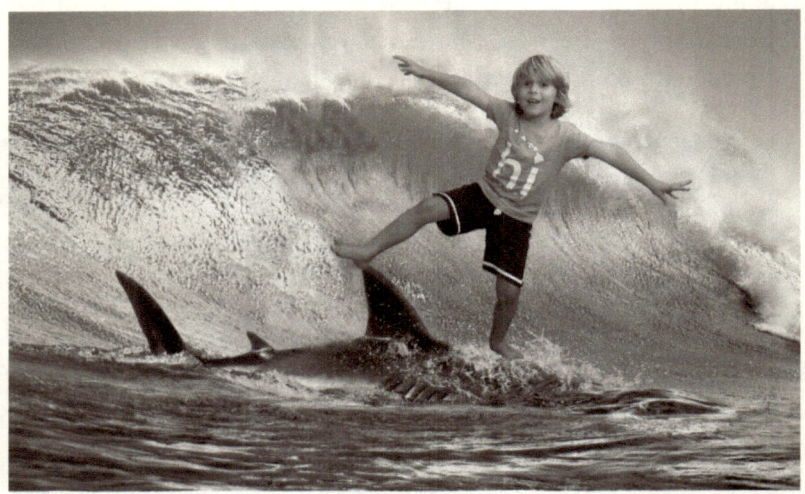

A lot of people think shooting chroma key (now commonly known as "green screen") is difficult and expensive. Not so! At a bare minimum, all you need are two speedlights that can operate in wireless mode, and a green cloth. And thanks to some free software I'll talk about shortly, the creation of these composites are not at all difficult to do!

Formally called "Chroma key", the idea of being able to remove a solid, known color and replacing it with something else was actually invented in the 1930's. It didn't come into its own until the 1960's, where it was adopted en masse by television news. Blue screens gave way to a less-naturally-occurring green color after several embarrassing situations where the anchor's blue clothes or blue eyes caused the audience to see right through them.

So here's what you need:

1)   A bright green cloth

2)   At least two light sources. (You can get away with one if your subject is far enough away from the background).

3)   A free Photoshop plug-in called "Easy Green Screen" (download link below).

4)   Ummm… Photoshop. ☺

You may well ask, "Why is special software needed? Why can't I just select the green color using Photoshop's magic wand tool, then remove it using the eraser leaving a transparent background?" If you've ever tried it you'd know the answer: This technique fails miserably when it comes to fine details like hair. You see patches of leftover green everywhere. (See three examples of Mark Stewart, who tours with Paul Simon and is the world's best Xaphoon player, next page).

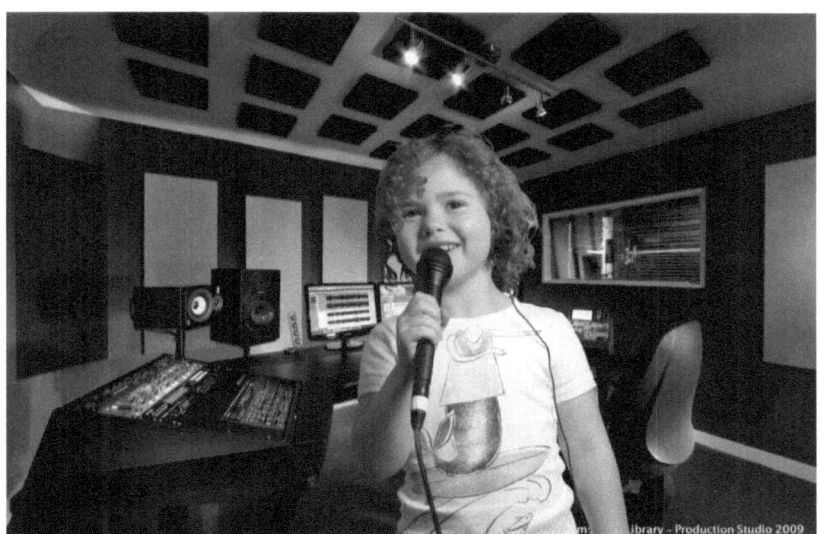

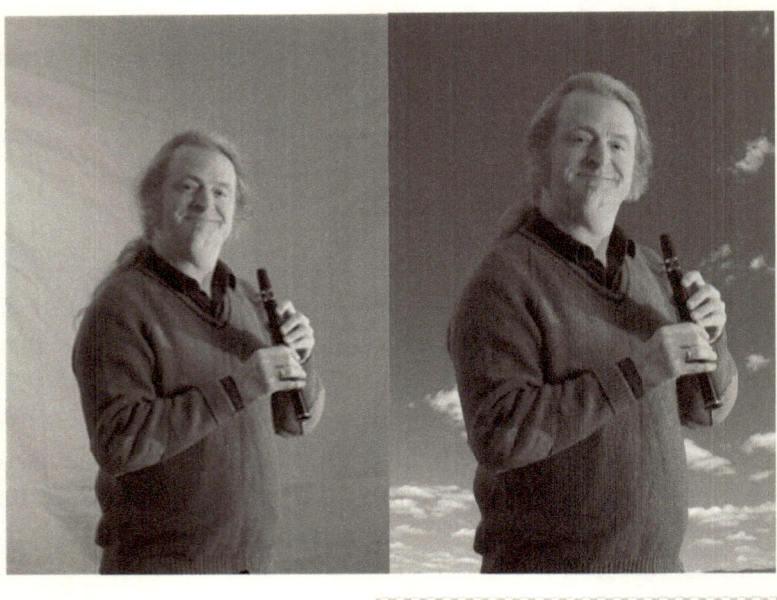

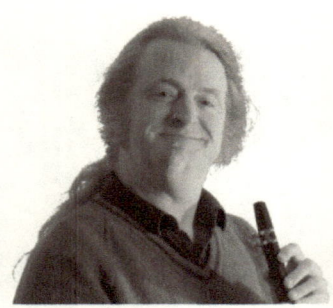 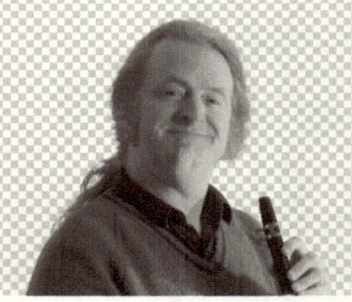

From top left: Original out-of-camera shot, and final product: drop-in a cloud background. Bottom row: removing green via Photoshop's magic wand tool (yuk!); and removing green using EZ Green Screen. See how much cleaner it is around the hair?

This is taken care of brilliantly by a product called "EZ Green Screen" (http://www.ezgreenscreen.com) and what it does is far from trivial. This software employs several steps, including the creation of a superior mask layer. It also adds a special "spill

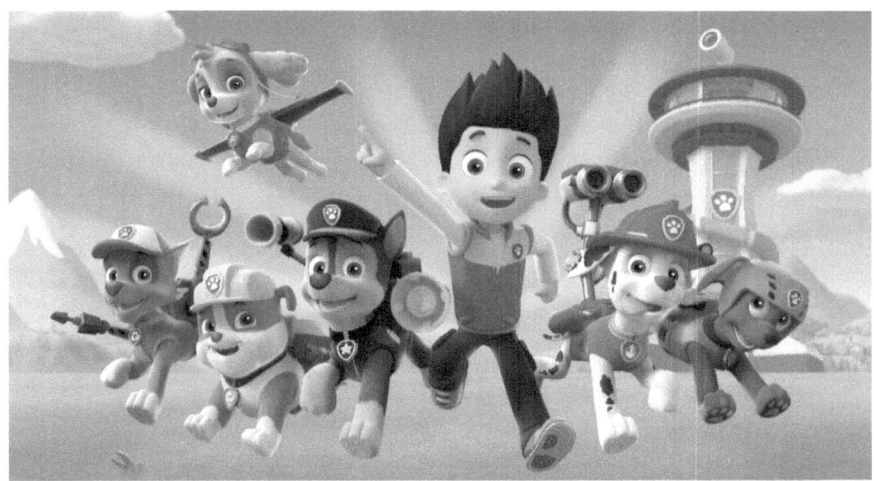

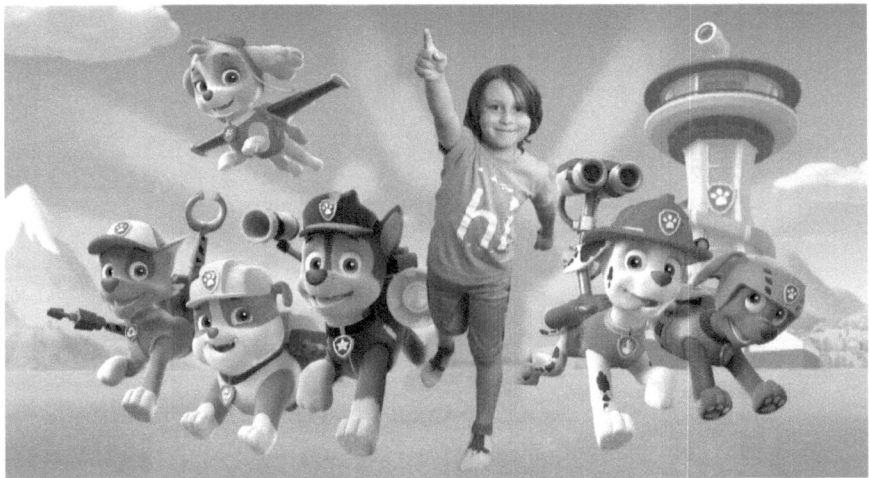

What kid wouldn't want to be included in his favorite TV show?

correction" layer which gets rid of green that may have reflected off the subject into the camera (it happens a lot!) This makes for a very fast masking process that is more accurate than if you were to do it manually.

Normally the software sells for $169, but you can download a free trial version from here: http://bit.ly/1KunDHK (this works on both Windows and Mac).

Now then, the lighting setup… the examples I show here use two wireless speedlights. One pointing directly at the background, so as to make background removal easy and shadow-free. The other is placed behind a softbox that will be lighting the subject. Both flashes are on manual output.

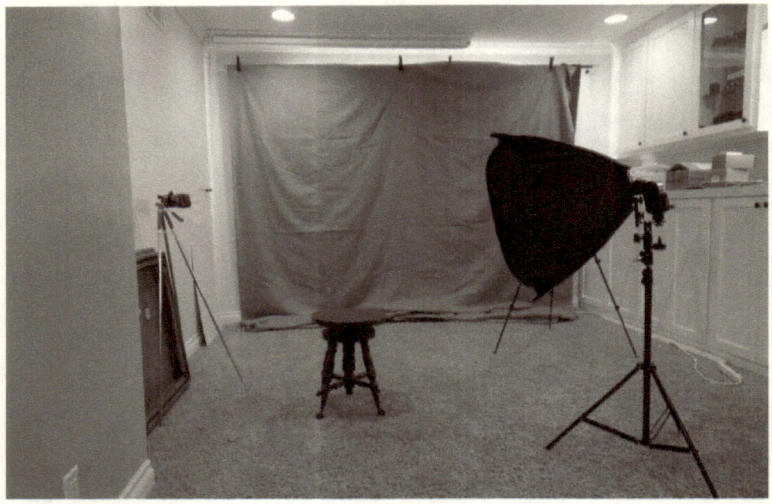

It's usually best to identify your background image first, that way your subject knows what's going on and won't look quite so out of place once the new background is added. If you're like me you're likely to start dipping into all of your beautiful images whose compositions stand on their own, only to discover that this can be a horrible choice since they result in two subjects vying for the viewer's attention! Since my first green screen I've started to shoot differently out in the field – in addition to getting well-composed shots I'll then shoot with backgrounds in mind – landscapes with no subject, pure textures, shots that are just boring.

Another great resource for backgrounds is Google Images; however this source comes with two potential pitfalls: 1) High-res images from Google Images can be rare, but they do exist and can save you a lot of time. 2) Many times you may find that a subject needs to be removed from the image in order to make it work for you. Photoshop has numerous tools (like Content Aware Fill and Move tool, and the patch tool) to help facilitate the removal of subjects. These tools work either magically well or not at all. If not at all there's always your old friend the rubber stamp tool.

Shots like these evoke more "Wow!" (in person) or "Like" (on Facebook) than your average family shots, which is a pretty good metric for your photography. One thing I can say for certain – these shots bring a smile to customer's faces more than any other kind of studio work I've done!

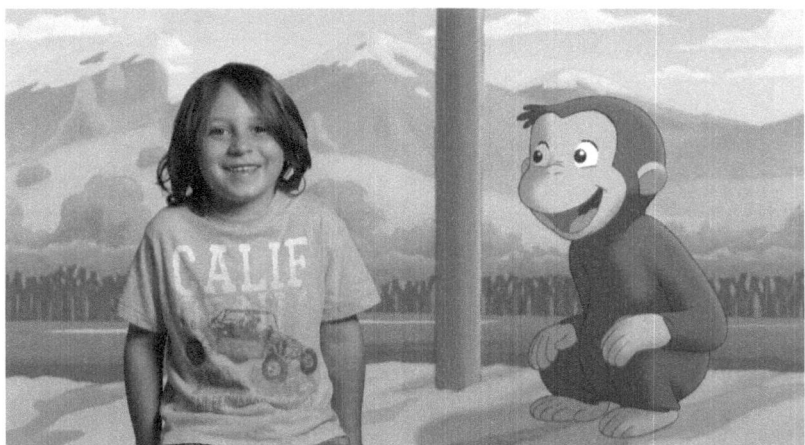

3.9   SHOOTING YOUR FIRST WEDDING

First published April, 2015

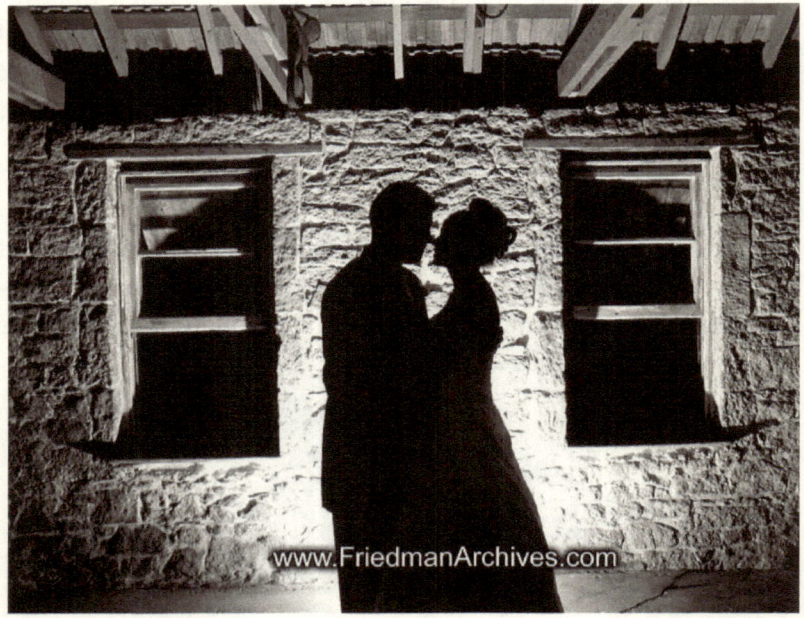

Can't overemphasize the importance of wireless flash for those "Wow!" shots!

So, your friends have noticed that you have a fancy camera, and they've asked you to photograph their kids' wedding.   Or perhaps, confident of your skills, you're brave enough to enter the crowded field on your own.   Either way, congratulations! As a former wedding photographer, let me share with you some tips to help ensure the happy couple is ecstatic with your results.

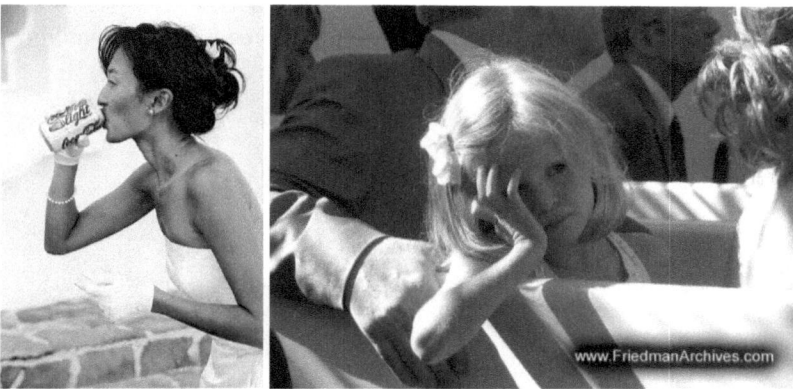

2nd shooters can sometimes be free to catch unscripted events.

The first few things you need to know involve a paradigm shift – for YOU. Know that your customer has NO IDEA what a wedding photographer actually does. 99% of people think your pictures come out better because you have a bigger or more expensive camera. So they will try to negotiate down on price because it's clear that the teenage kid next door will do it for less and he would get the same results if he owned your camera too.

Furthermore, you should know that what's important to the photographer and what's important to your customers are completely different, and neither party is aware of this fact. Photographers covet great light, clean composition, classic poses and technically excellent prints. Most of those things don't register with low-end customers; they care only about having a good memory jog so they can lament about how youthful they used to look later on. A great snapshot taken by a guest with a mobile phone will rank equally in their minds (sometimes more) than the technically perfect, posed picture you're delivering. Your customers are blissfully unaware of the differences between snaptshots and photographs.

What to do? Believe it or not, the most important thing you can do to build your value in your customers' eyes is the pre-wedding

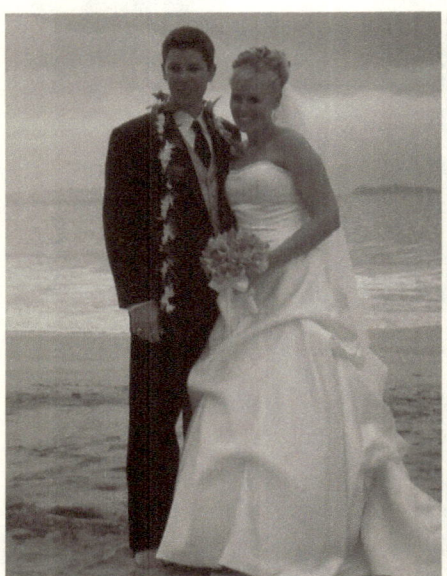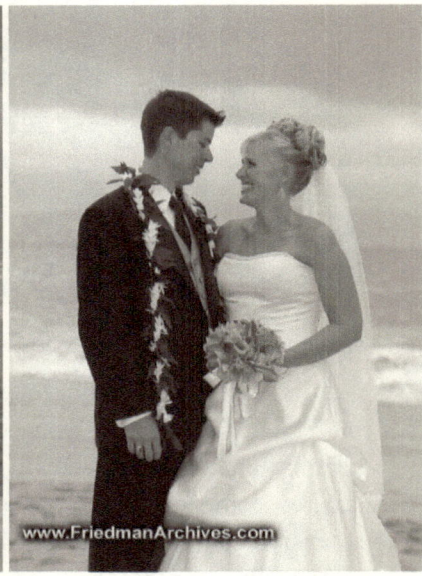

Cameras can often be thrown off by open shade and overcast lighting, wanting to make everything look 18% grey. Using an accessory flash with Flash Exposure Compensation set to -1.5 can fix a lot of problems without it looking like you used a flash.

meeting(s). Ask thoughtful questions, explain to them what you'd like to do (and why), and make a plan. Have them scour the internet for wedding images they'd like to duplicate (you do the same), then strategize in front of them what it would take to get that shot. Have them come up with a list of family group shots before the event (very important!), and have THEM identify the person who will be gathering the right people to execute these shots. Shooting engagement shots too? That will get them even more comfortable with you and they will start to understand your value more readily.

Wedding photography can be very stressful or not, depending upon how much pressure you put on yourself. I took it too seriously, knowing how important this day was, that it would never happen again, and it was my job to "capture the spirit" of the event. That kind of pressure can lead to the equivalent of writer's block, where you're constantly wondering "What should I be shooting next"? So I had a shot checklist to make sure I covered all my bases in making a nice wedding album. Here's the list that I used:

http://friedmanarchives.com/~download/cameracraft/wedding_sh ot_list.pdf

Outside of the list, you are essentially a photojournalist, and your job is to be aware of your surroundings, anticipate what's going to happen next, and be ready for it (right place, right lens, right settings). A 2nd shooter is a wonderful asset to have to ensure you meet this requirement!

Scout out the location ahead of time, at the same time of day the wedding will occur. What's the light like? Will the reception take place in a blah hotel conference room with only the lights from the DJ to create ambience?

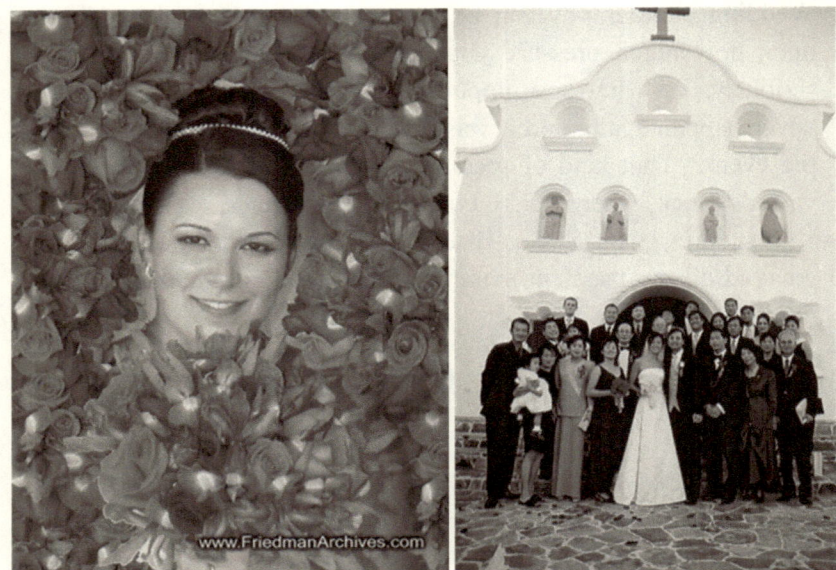

Left: Bridesmaids would hold their bouquets of flowers all around the bride for a nice frame. Right: Shooting in open shade. I overexposed slightly and used fill flash. (This was especially challenging since this was shot on film and I was shooting blind. In those days you really had to know what you were doing!)

Technical Settings

I found that I had three general camera settings – one for indoor candids, one for outdoor candids, and one for outdoor posed. All three settings use flash with a large bounce card to throw the light everywhere and make things look a little more natural. Flash can make poor lighting tolerable and if used properly it can make your pictures look "happier". And shoot RAW so you can better keep detail in the black tuxes AND the bride's white dress – the extended dynamic range can help here.

<u>Dark Indoor candids</u>: Manual exposure mode, f/stop set to around f/3.5 - f/5.6, shutter speed = 1/15th, ISO AUTO, Flash Exposure Compensation = 0. The goal here is to help ensure that the background isn't pure black; that you retained a sense of place. It is dangerous to use your fancy f/1.4 lens and shoot wide open because very, very little of your people shots will be in focus – maybe an eyelash, but not a nose or an ear. And if you're shooting multiple people very little of what's important will be in focus. In these non-artistic situations, it's better to use a boring lens to get more in focus and make sure your subjects don't move (otherwise with such a slow shutter speed movement will look blurry).

<u>Outdoor, candids</u>: Program mode, ISO Auto, flash exposure compensation = -1.5 so it doesn't look like you used a flash.

<u>Outdoor, posed</u>: For selective focus, shoot wide open and concentrate on just a part of the image – just the ring, just the eyelashes, etc. 85mm f/1.4 lenses are great for wedding shots like this.

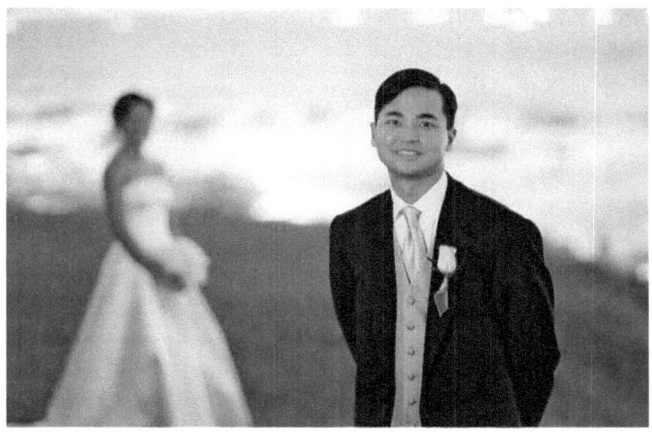

Outdoor, posed: shallow depth-of-field.

How much to charge?

No wrong answer here; whatever the buyer and seller agree upon is the right amount. But do NOT give in to the oft-heard request to "just hand over your camera's memory cards at the end of the day". A big part of your value is delivering great pictures, and that includes cropping / tweaking / recovering highlights. (Brides with white dresses force you to really work to place your whites where you want them without blowing anything out.) There is a near certainty that you know how to make your pictures look better than they do, so do not leave this very important step in the hands of amateurs.

Finally, be prepared for bitchy brides. (The term "Bridezilla" didn't just evolve out of thin air, you know.) With them, nothing you ever do will be right, which is why it's very important to get a non-refundable 50% down-payment up front before the event. Afterwards, be glad you don't do this for a living.

If you're a subscriber to some of Icon Publications' sister magazines like Master Photographer, you may be intimidated by the high-end, award-winning wedding photography images you occasionally see gracing their pages. Although inspiring, these kinds of images should not be your reference point when it comes to judging the quality of your own work. The sample images I included in this article are more than good enough.

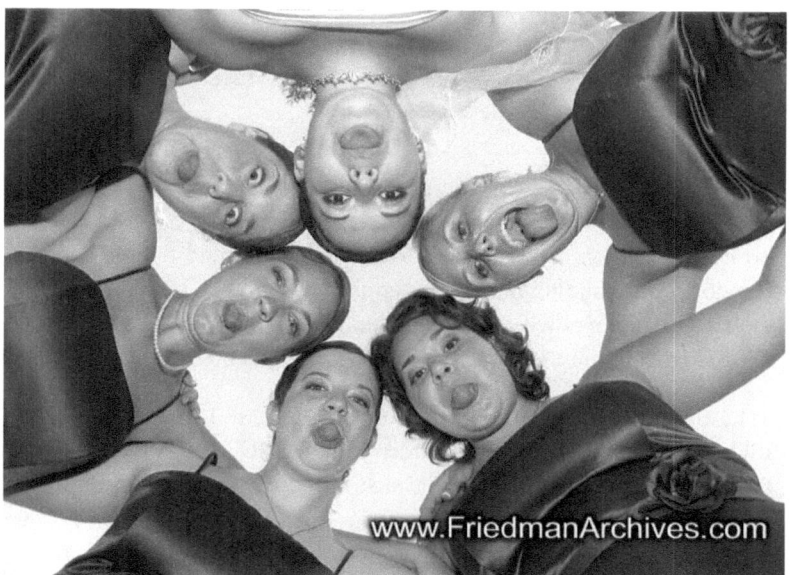

3.10   FULL-FRAME   VS.   SMALL   SENSOR (DON'T LAUGH...)

First published March, 2017

So here I was, on my way back from Las Vegas, and I came across a run-down old building that has a certain "character". I pulled over and took a few pictures with my A99 II and Zeiss 24-70 f/2.8, then started to head back to the car. Then I hesitated.

"These conditions are pretty good. Strong light, so I can shoot at a low ISO with a small f/stop. I wonder how the RX-100 V compares in these ideal conditions?". I went back to the car and tried to duplicate the shots I just took using a small-sensor point-and-shoot. Then I drove home.

The subject matter and the lighting were so good that I suspected enlargements from the two cameras would be indistinguishable. (Click on any image to see a larger version.)

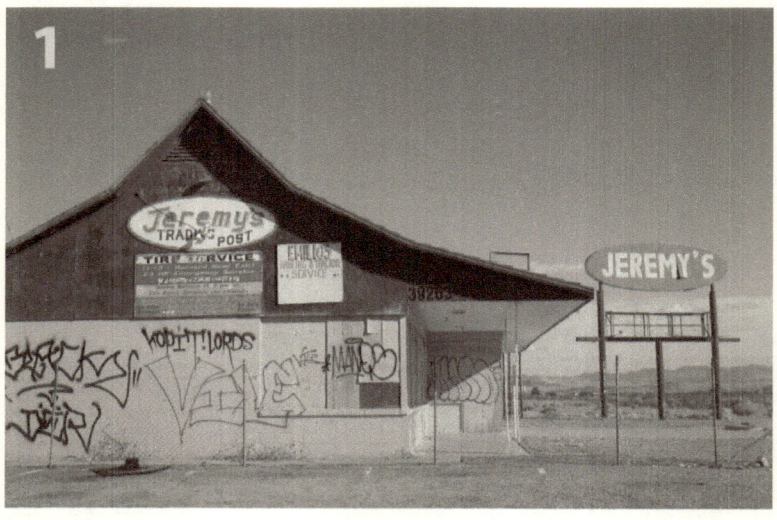

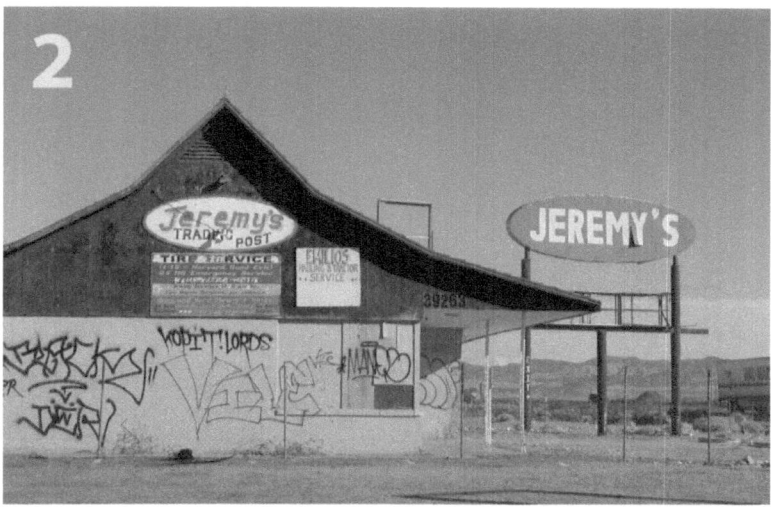

You can download and examine the images for differences yourself. Here are the links:

http://friedmanarchives.com/~download/blog/Vegas_RX-100_V_DSC05978.JPG

http://friedmanarchives.com/~download/blog/Vegas_A99_II_A990968 1.jpg

Before I go on, I should mention that in my seminars I always say that no matter how tempting it is, pixel peeping is not an appropriate way to evaluate image quality. The better, more time-honored way is to make a giant enlargement and then view it from a reasonable distance.

And so I blew them up to poster size and examined them. I was right. Not only me, but nobody at the Seminar I did in Tuscon could tell which camera took which image.

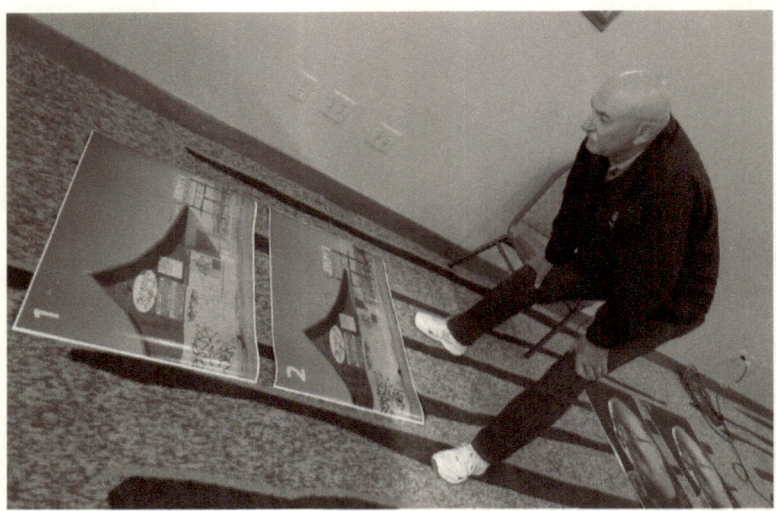

A seminar attendee examining the enlargements closely. We had to put the posters on the floor because nothing would stick to the walls of that venue.

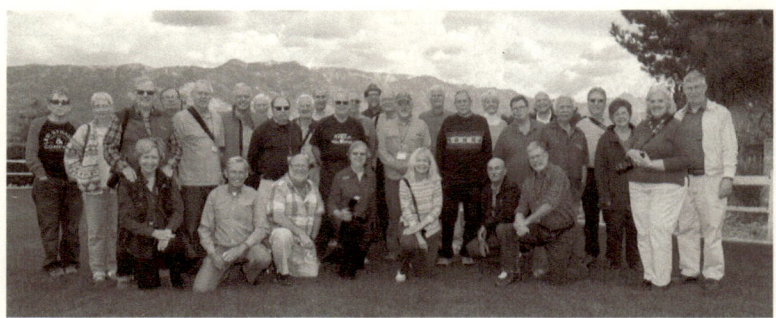

Lots of people attended. :-)

Okay, how far can I push this? I knew that at this size, the high-end cameras would have an edge with close subjects having a lot of detail that were well-lit. So I called a 20-something-year-old friend of mine, "Come to the studio on Saturday and don't shave for a few days!". My goal was to give this even more of an acid test: a highly-detailed, high-frequency (not shaven) subject shot with the A99 II and the Zeiss 135mm f/1.8 lens, vs. the RX-10 II (which is essentially the RX-100's small sensor with a superb 24-200 lens thrown on it) under ideal conditions.

My friend called in sick, so I had to be my own subject. Could attendees tell which camera took which picture?

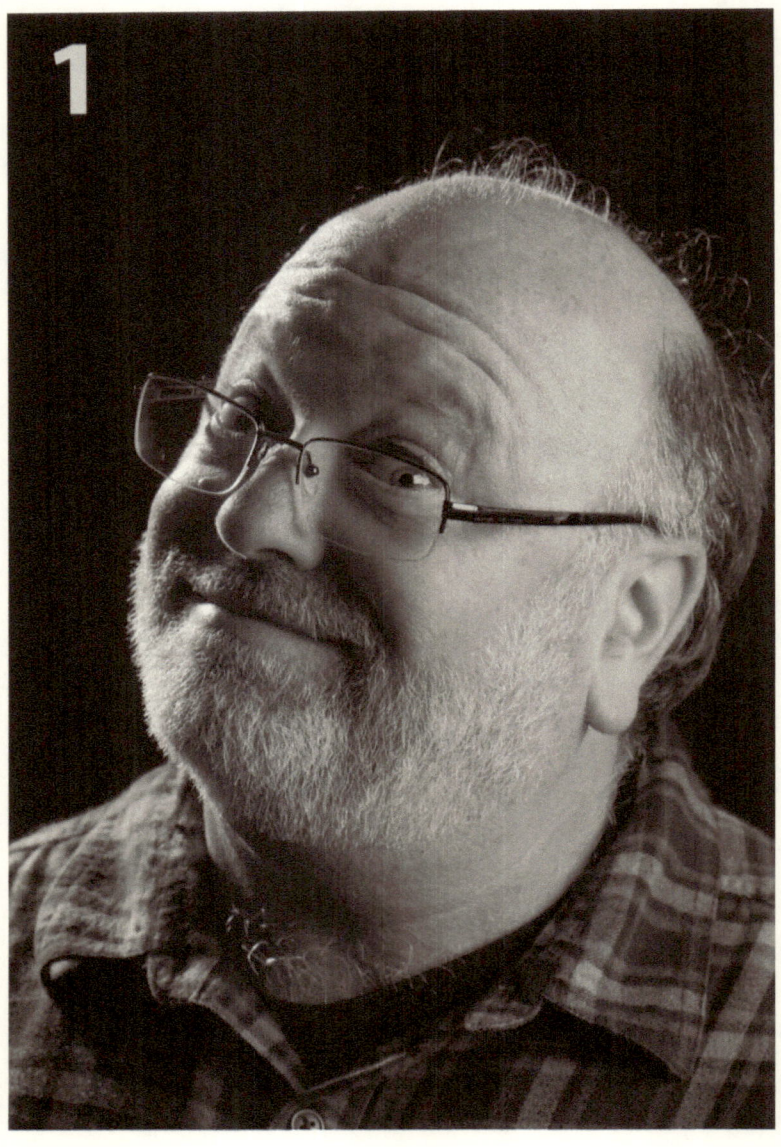

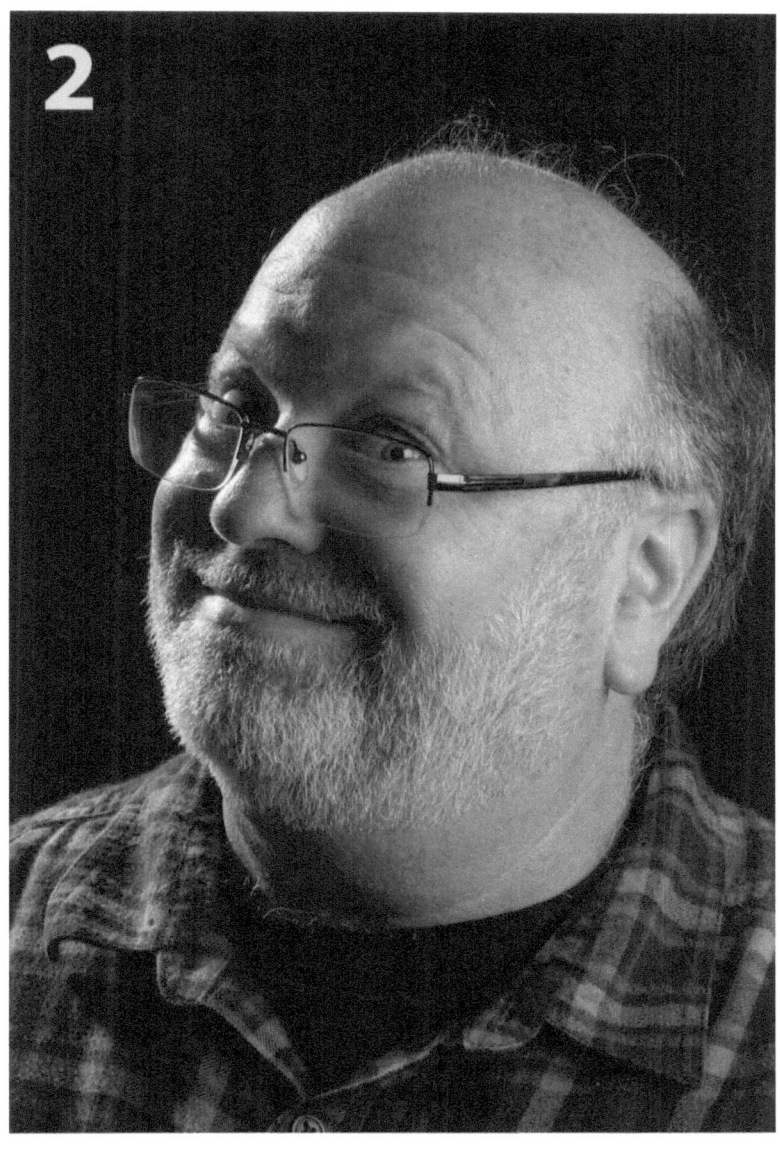

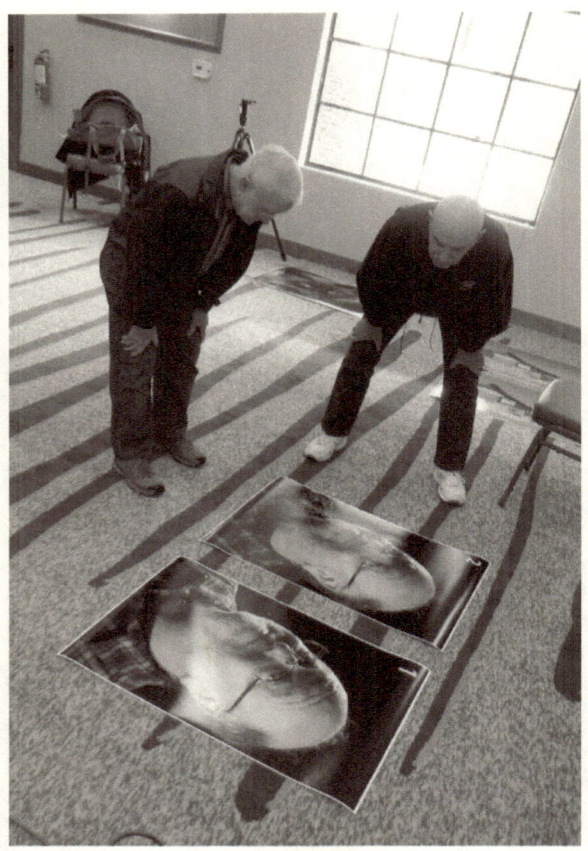

"One of these pictures was taken with $5K worth of equipment", I announced to the room, "and the other was taken with a $1200 camera. Is one image 5x better than the other?"

Here are the two download links:

http://friedmanarchives.com/~download/blog/Studio_A99_II_A990994 7.jpg

http://friedmanarchives.com/~download/blog/Studio_RX-10_II_DSC09453.jpg

While one image was twice the number of megapixels as the other, when enlarged and viewed from a reasonable distance, the two images were very close indeed – in fact, nobody in the room was able tell which camera took which picture. It serves as a reminder that all cameras have been improving over the last decade, even the small-sensor cameras that everyone thumbs their noses at. Under ideal conditions, it's hard to tell the difference.

So who needs a 42 megapixel camera and high-end lenses then? I continued my sermon:

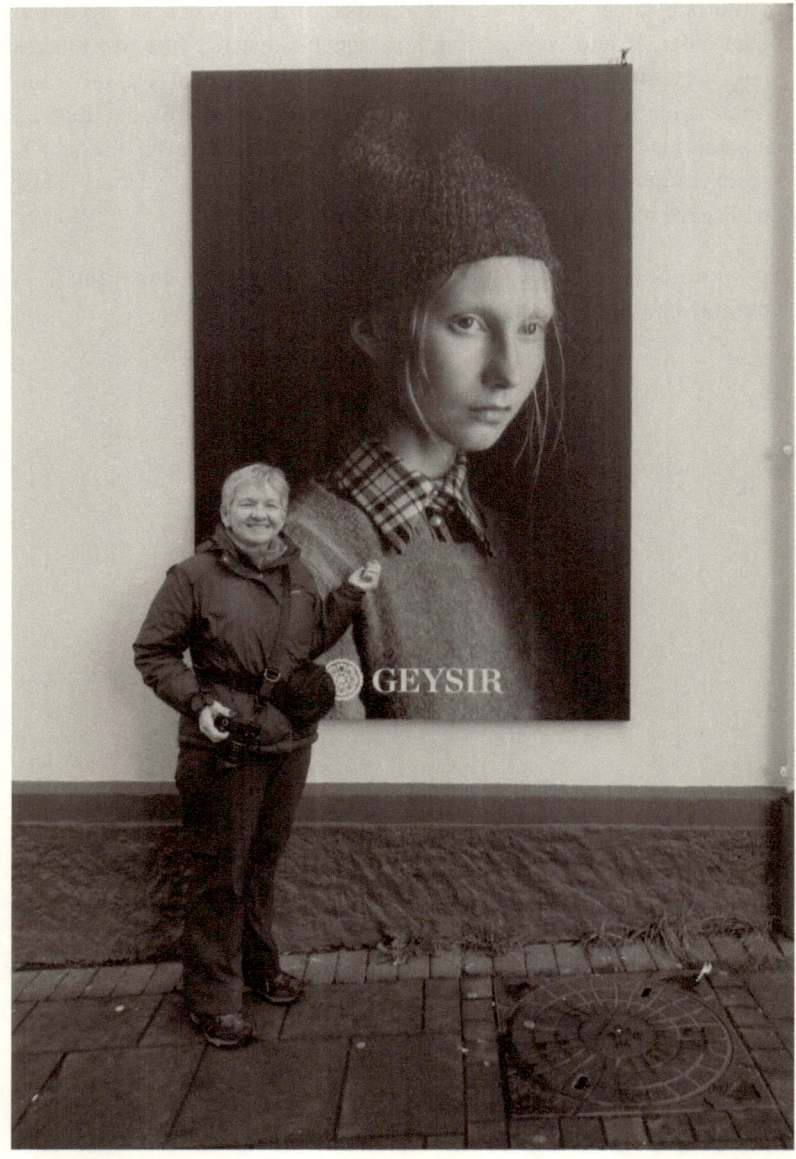

"You need the more expensive camera when you're making much bigger enlargements..."

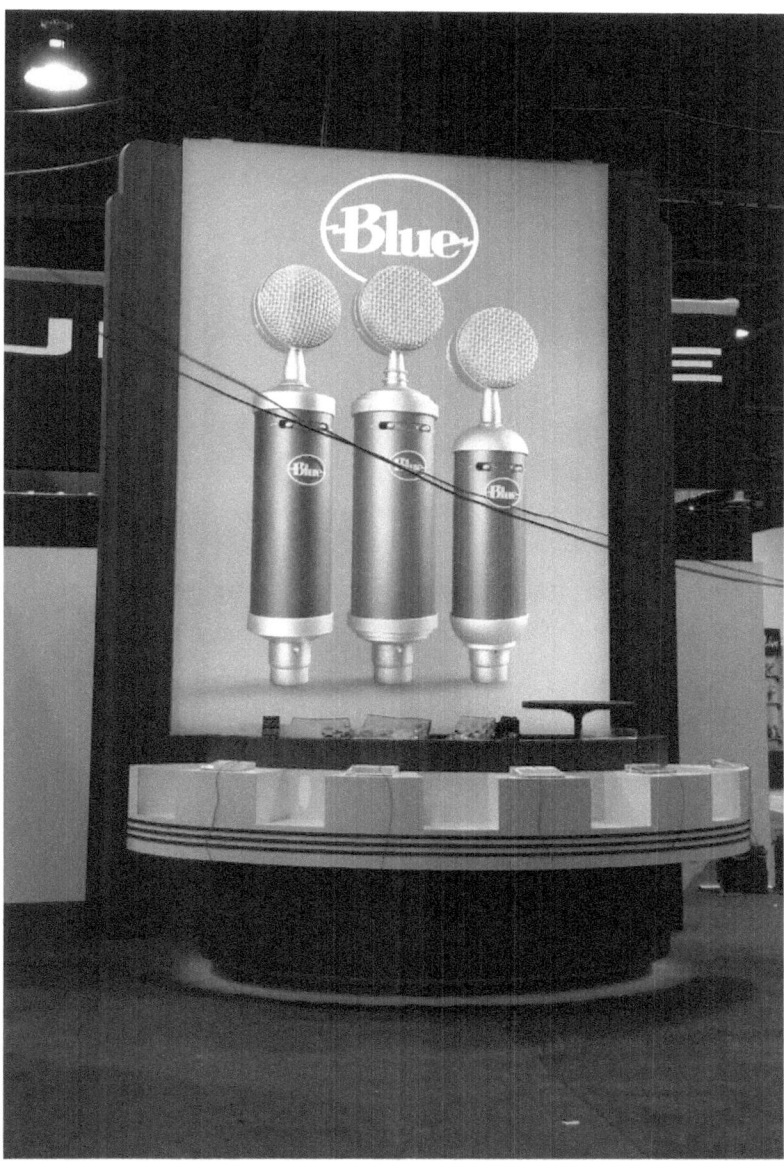

"...I mean REALLY big - places where medium format was once required."

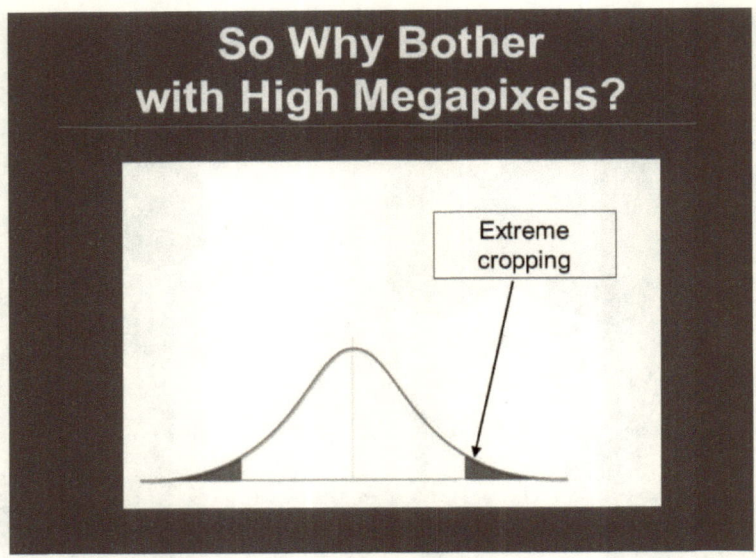

When you want more cropping options, or want to do extreme cropping.

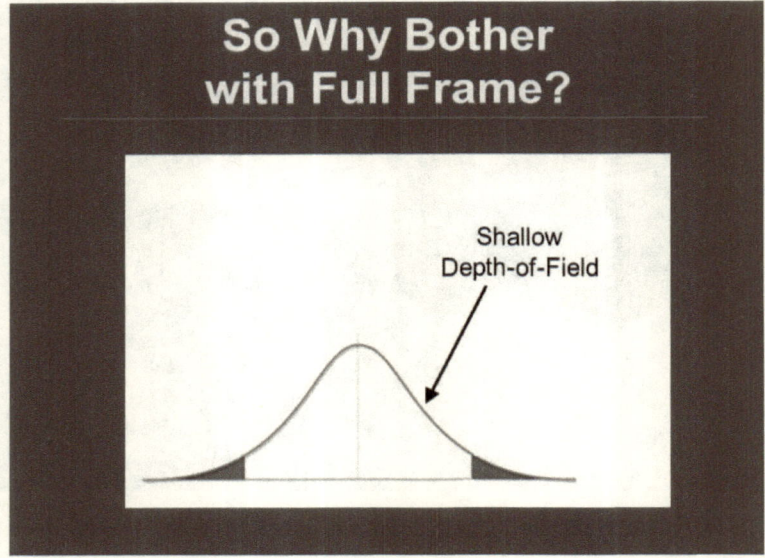

If you covet shallow depth-of-field.

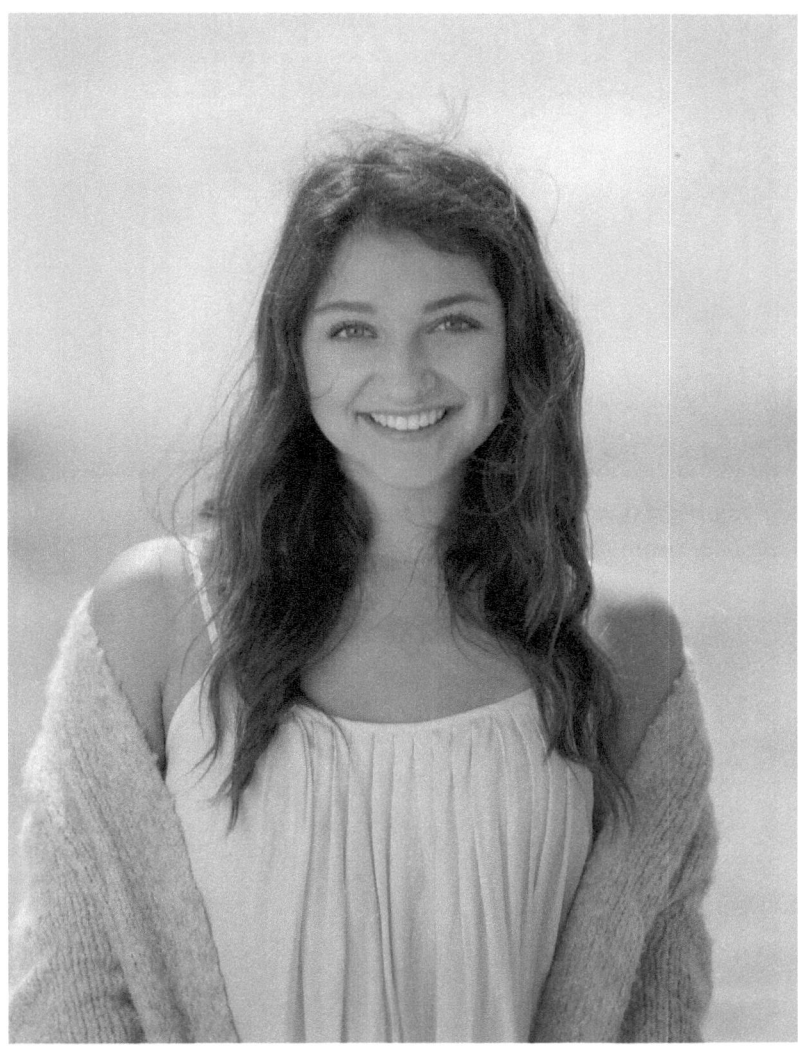

Like this. :-)

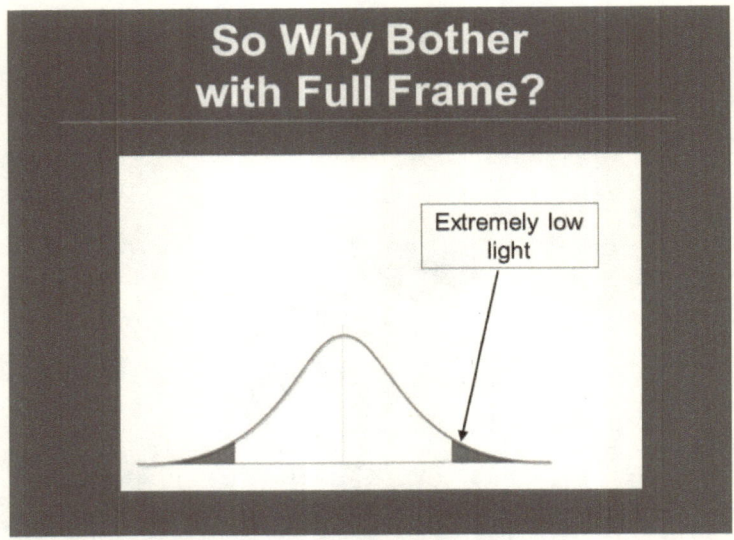

If your light is not as ideal as in these examples (in which case you'll probably want the Sony A7S II).

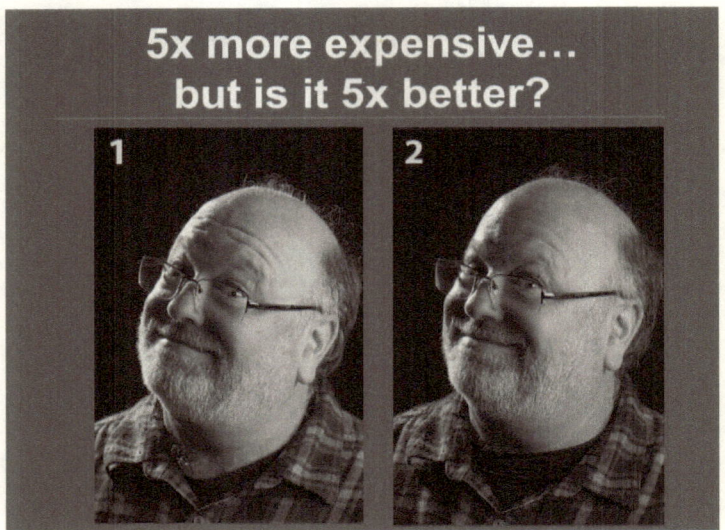

I will say this... with the small-sensor camera the chest hairs are also in focus. :-)

Pretty surprising how close these two cameras performed in this acid test, right? Now you understand why I've been singing the praises of the RX-100 and RX-10 cameras for so long.

3.11   A REAL-WORLD EXAMPLE OF INDUCED MOIRÉ

First published October, 2016

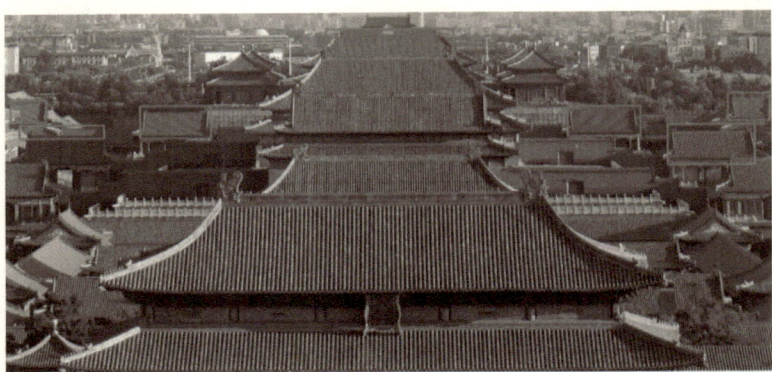

A lot of the world's high-end cameras have been boasting about the lack of optical low-pass filters in front of their sensors. And while most hail this as a wonderful thing to help increase the detail in your images. it comes with a theoretical downside: your images might become more susceptible to a phenomenon called "induced Moiré".

Moiré interference patterns happen when two similar, regular arrays are not quite aligned properly. In early television, Moiré patterns would show up a lot when cameras pointed at presenters wearing pinstripe suits or even finer-lined patterns. The interference came from the interaction between the clothing and the 525 lines in the TV camera. In color TVs the interference patterns had a lot of color burst associated with them as well.

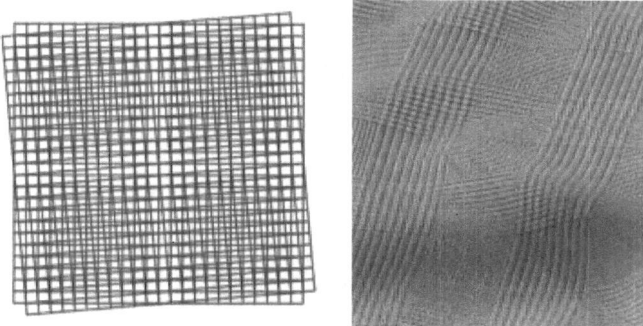

Two screens of a similar square size ("frequency") will develop an interference pattern when one is slightly misaligned with another (left). Since the pixels in a sensor are arranged in an array similar to a screen, it's possible that such a "induced Moire" pattern can develop when photographing another array of a proportional density (right). Sometimes the effect is accompanied by color bursts. (Right image courtesy Foveon.)

Two screens of a similar square size ("frequency") will develop an interference pattern when one is slightly misaligned with another (left). Since the pixels in a sensor are arranged in an array similar to a screen, it's possible that such a "induced Moire" pattern can develop when photographing another array of a proportional density (right). Sometimes the effect is accompanied by color bursts. (Right image courtesy Foveon.)

Early digital cameras would have suffered the same fate had designers not tried to avoid the problem by installing what's called an anti-aliasing or low-pass filter in front of the sensor. Without going into the mathematics behind the design, it can safely be summarized by saying "the filter fuzzifies the image a little bit, eliminating the annoying interference patterns and making both consumer and professional photographers very happy". (Of course I'm oversimplifying this a lot.)

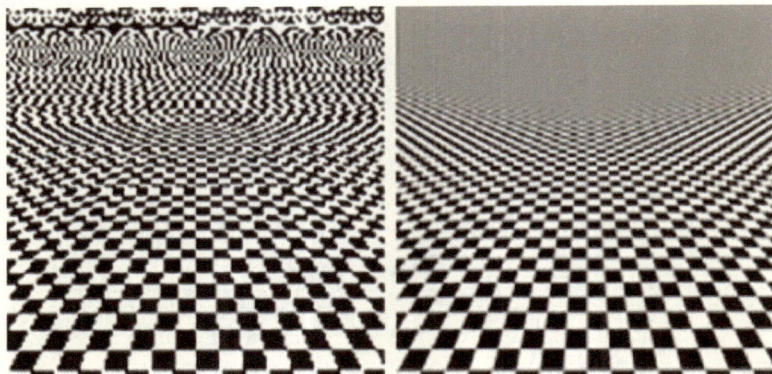

Example image courtesy Wikipedia.

Time passed. Pixel densities increased. A higher pixel density is the equivalent of a finer-pitched screen. Finer-pitched screens don't induce as much Moiré (well, it all depends on the subject being photographed, but in general it won't produce as much) and so manufacturers have been experimenting with taking the anti-aliasing filter away, thus not intentionally fuzzifying the image and allowing all the detail of the subject to be properly captured.

Over the last few years as part of my explanation of this feature in my books, I tried very hard to actually create an image where such induced Moiré occurs, and, try as I might, I have never been able to create such an example. (And so I always ended up using exaggerated examples from companies like Foveon which you would never actually see in the real world.)

Then last month I received an email from a reader:

Dear Gary,

due to your great eBook about the Sony a7R2 I'm confident you know a lot of about the camera and how the camera works. [...] To cut a long story short, I'm living in Beijing and made some pictures of the Forbidden City while I was on the Jingshan Park behind it.

I used a Sony a7R2 and a Zeiss 16-35mm lens. I took some pictures of the Forbidden City and recogized some serious image quality issues in the area of the roof of some of the buildings. I would like to ask you if you could tell me why the roof looks that bad and how I can avoid these kind of effect.

You are the only one I know who understands how this camera works and probably can explain to me what happend. The Sony feedback service proposed me to clean the lens

Thank you very much in advance! D. Winkelmann, from Germany

I had a look at his attachment, and was gobsmacked - the worst case of Moiré I had ever seen in a modern digital camera. The red rectangles show off the problems pretty nicely:

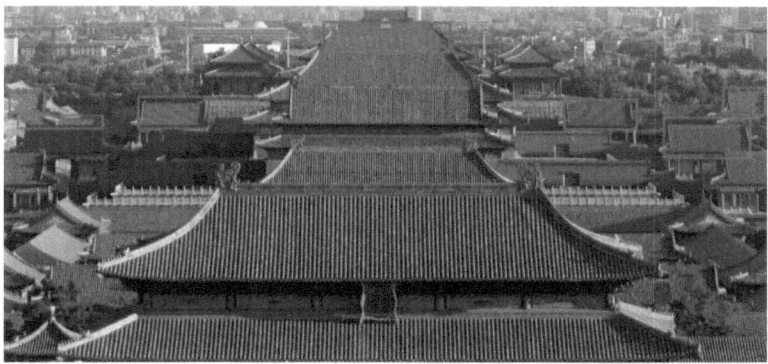

But how was he able to get such a great example when I had tried and failed to get examples like this for years? The answer came later when he sent me the original, uncropped image:

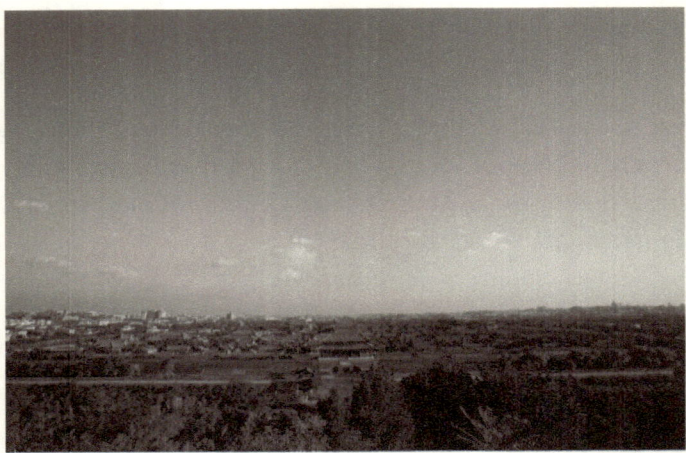

Yup! He had to pixel peep just to see his subject. :-) Of course this is one advantage of high-megapixel cameras and high-resolution optics, but it instantly explained why my previous efforts to create an example had failed: I had misunderestimated (to quote a presidential term) the actual distance between pixel rows and columns on the sensor. Just look at how close the rows and columns need to be in the image in order to produce this undesirable artifact! And look at how closely you had to examine the image in order to see it!

So there's a very good chance you'll never see this problem in your images. But what can you do if you're unlucky enough to have it? Well, the Sony guy's recommendation of "clean the lens" certainly won't help (although in theory making the lens dirty might fuzzify the image a little bit, emulating the effects of the anti-aliasing filter). In the real world, Adobe Lightroom has a tool for reducing the rainbow artifact and you can see examples of how to use it here: https://photographylife.com/how-to-reduce-moire-in-lightroom-4 . Getting rid of the actual interference pattern is more complex and you need a stronger tool such as Photoshop: https://photographylife.com/how-to-remove-moire-in-photoshop .

3.12   TURN YOUR IPAD INTO A HIGH-RESOLUTION FILM SCANNER

First published Feb. 2017

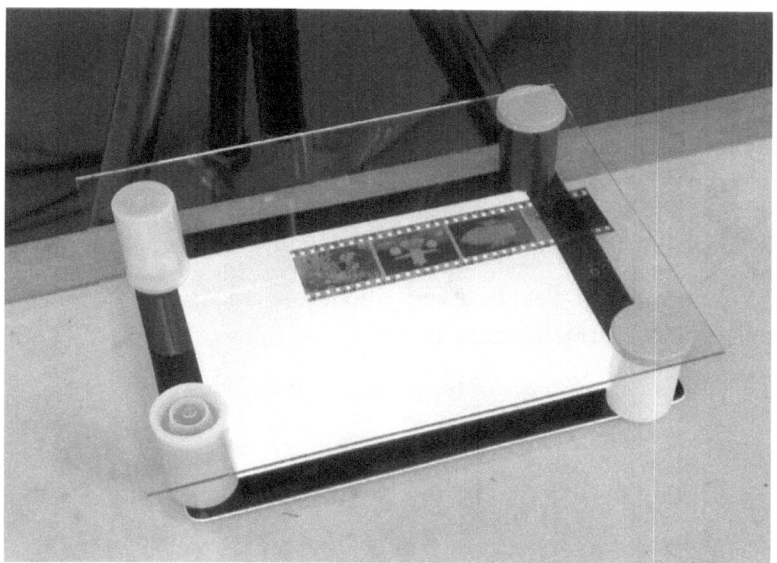

(Okay, that's a misleading headline, since you also need a camera and a macro lens as well. But it works and the results are great!)

This method works much better than the dedicated film scanners that were once available: Using a 24 megapixel camera, you get a larger file size: 6000 x 4000 pixels versus 3779 x 2522 of the Nikon Coolscan LS-2000 (which continues to gather dust under my desk). If you use an even higher megapixel camera, you can easily see just how unsharp your old film lenses were.

Here's what you need:

- A camera with the ability to shoot things that are close. Ideally this would mean a dedicated macro lens that can fill the frame with a single negative (like a 90 or 100mm macro); worst case it can be an RX-100 zoomed out all the way if you just want something quick and dirty.

- An iPad (or other tablet) with a "flashlight" app that can turn the screen white. This is a good example (although by no means the only one).
- An 8x10 piece of glass with some spacers

Here's what to do:

0.   Use the spacers to mount the glass a few inches above the iPad, and put a negative strip on top. (I'll explain why the glass is needed below.)

1.   Turn on the flashlight app. Point the camera at the iPad so the screen fills the camera's frame.

2.   Put the camera into Manual Exposure Mode.

    a.   Set the ISO to 100.

    b.   Set the f/stop to f/8 (the sweet spot of most lenses)

    c.   Set the shutter speed so the camera tells you you're overexposing by 1.7 stops.

    d.   Shoot in RAW or RAW + JPG, as you'll probably need to do some extreme manipulation later on.

3.   Perform a Custom White Balance, so the white will really look white. (This will really be essential if you're shooting color negatives.)

4.   Now compose your shot with one frame of the film strip and make sure some of the sprockets are in the frame.

5.   Using the camera's self-timer, take a picture.

6.   If you shot a negative, you have to turn it into a positive again and make adjustments. I'll explain how to do that later on.

Now then, you're probably wondering why the sheet of glass and the spacers are needed. Why not just put the negative right on top of the iPad? Well, I'll show you:

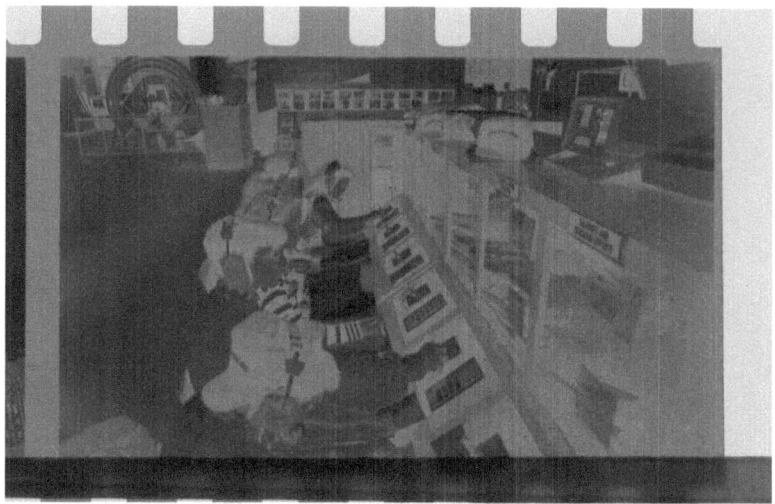

Don't see the problem yet? Here, have a closer look:

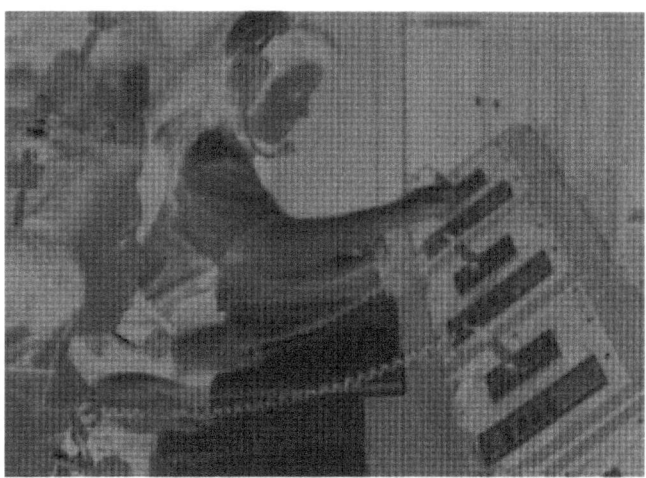

That's right! You can see the pixel resolution of the retina display. Not good!

What about using an intermediate layer, like tracing paper?

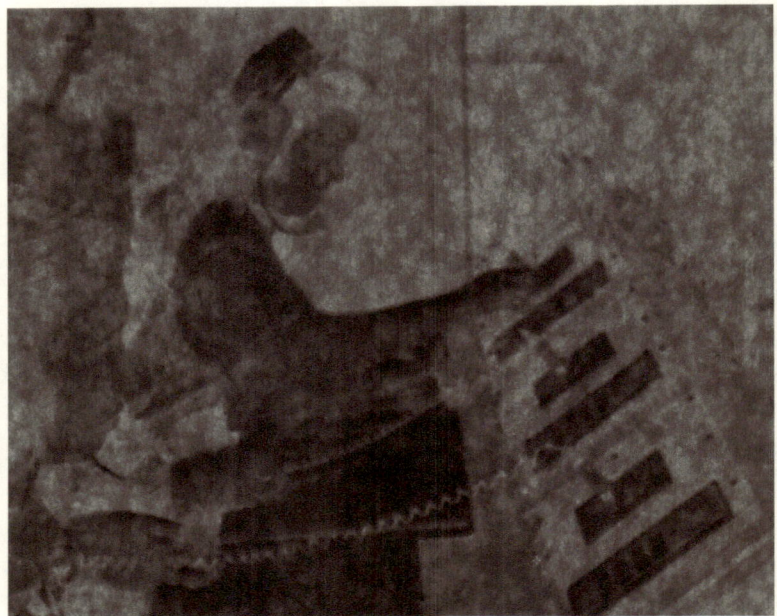

Worse. I suppose I could have used some white plexiglass, but who has that lying around? I ended up using a piece of glass I borrowed from a picture frame, and using old film canisters as spacers. (I knew I saved those for a reason!) The idea being if you're focused on the negative, the retina display behind it will be out of focus and therefore rendered as a blurred, smooth continuous background.

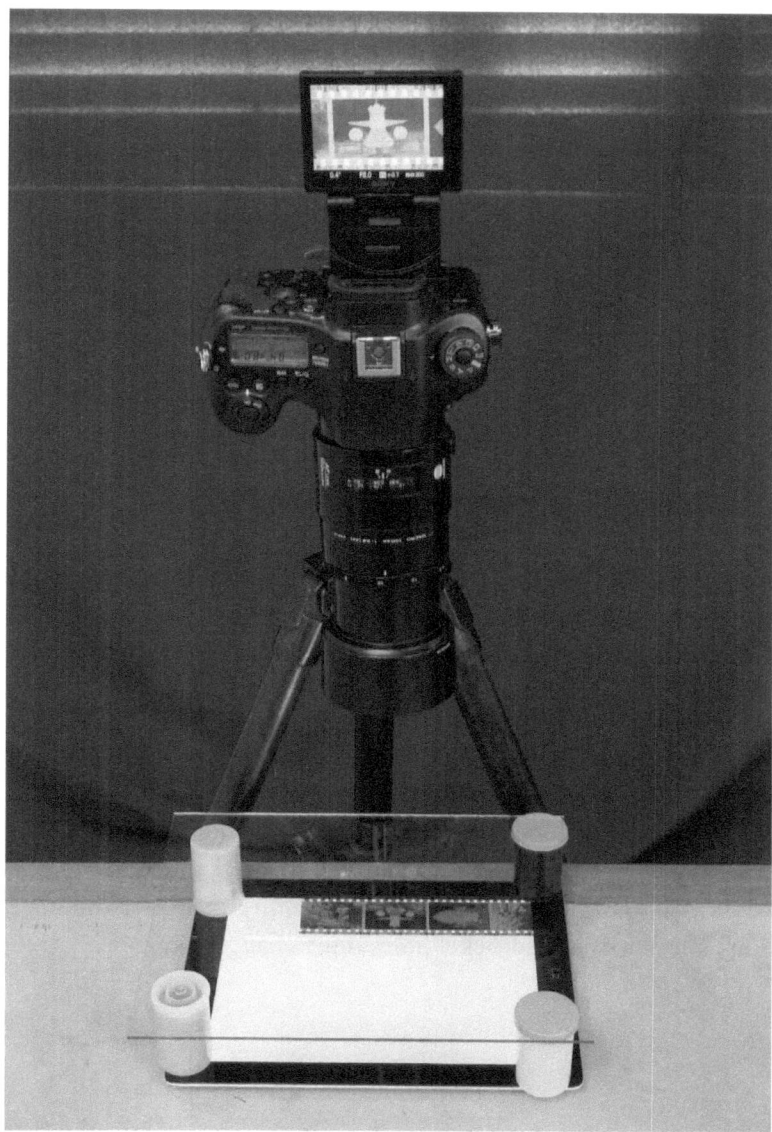

Okay, so you've shot a close-up of a negative with a really good backlight. How to make it useful? Here's what I did. These negatives were from a visit to the NASA Space Camp in

Huntsville, Alabama from 1992. Let's process a gratuitous snapshot of me in front of a Saturn V rocket, shall we?

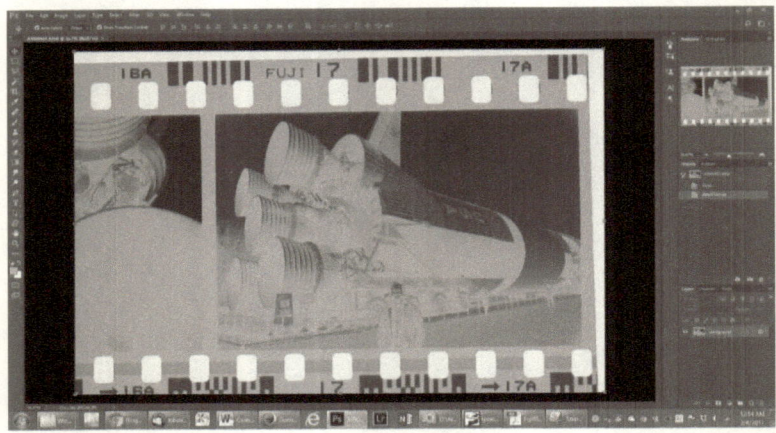

As you can see I didn't quite fill the frame with the negative - I included some sprockets on purpose. Our first step is to try to nullify the orange cast as much as possible.

Using IMAGE --> ADJUST --> LEVELS, I clicked on the the rightmost eyedropper in the pop-up box, and then clicked on an orange area between sprockets, essentially telling photoshop "add whatever colors you need to add, and take away whatever colors you need to remove, in order to make this part look white". It applies the correction to the entire image. (And no, I don't know why the sprocket holes don't change color.)

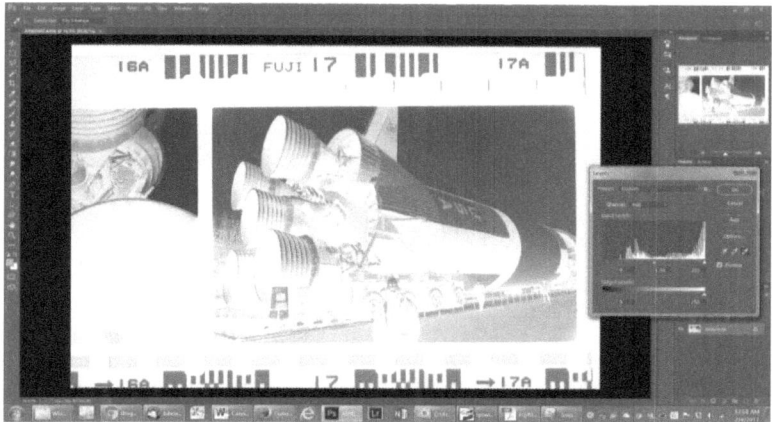

Next, do IMAGE --> ADJUSTMENTS --> INVERT and it goes from a negative to a positive:

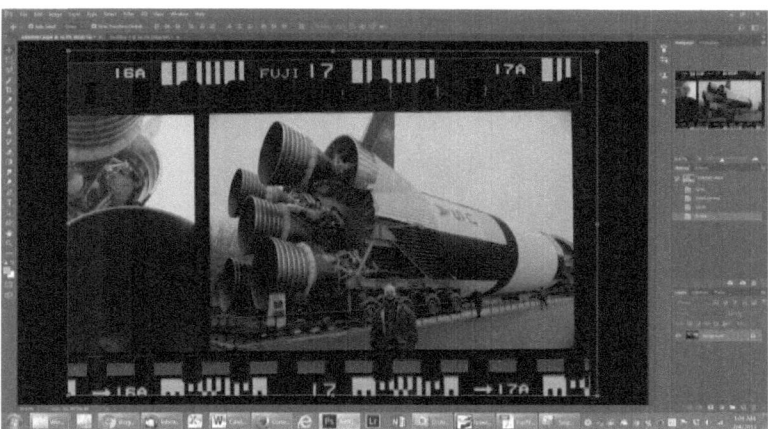

Still needs work. I'll crop and straighten, adjust the color balance, and some curve action to bring out the blacks:

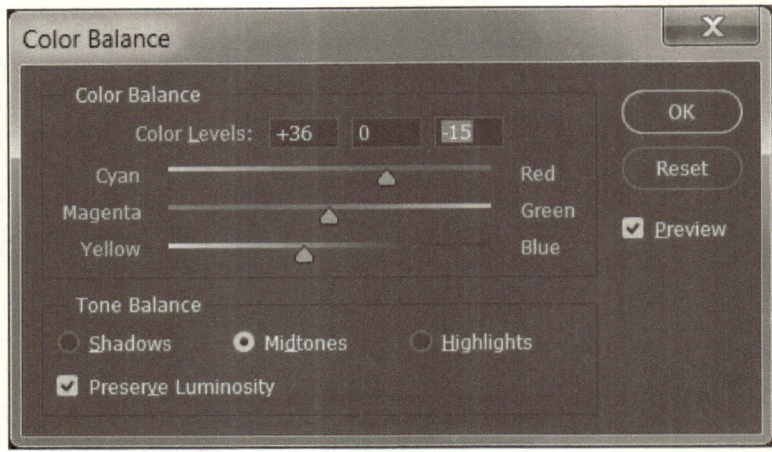

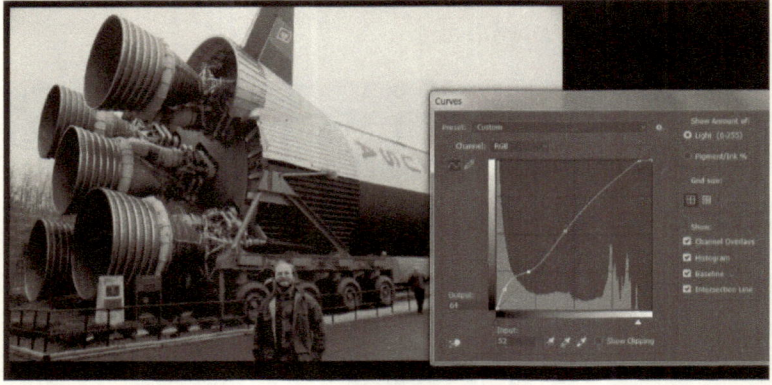

A few more tweaks of color balance and curves and we have a
final product!

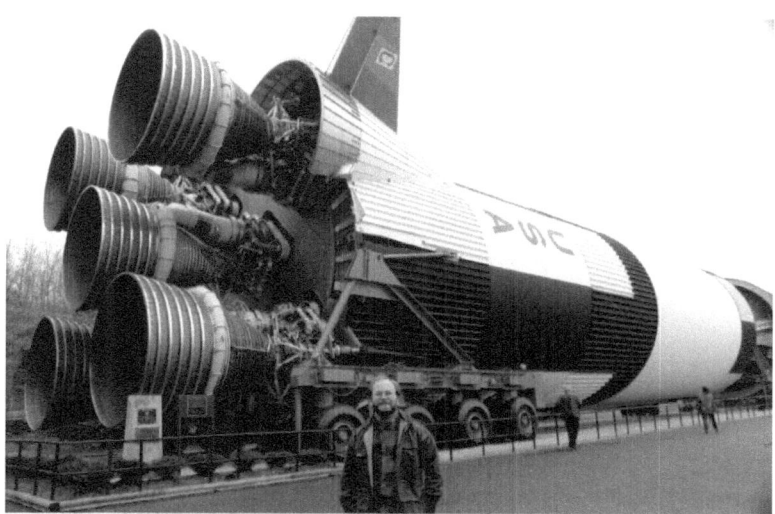

Voila! So that's a quick-and-dirty slide scanner for those who don't want to invest in expensive dedicated hardware. If that's too much work, there are actually a lot of photoshop plug-ins which can help automate much of the conversion process for you. I haven't tried any of them, so feel free to list your favorite tool in the comments section.

3.13   My Personal Workflow

First published August, 2017

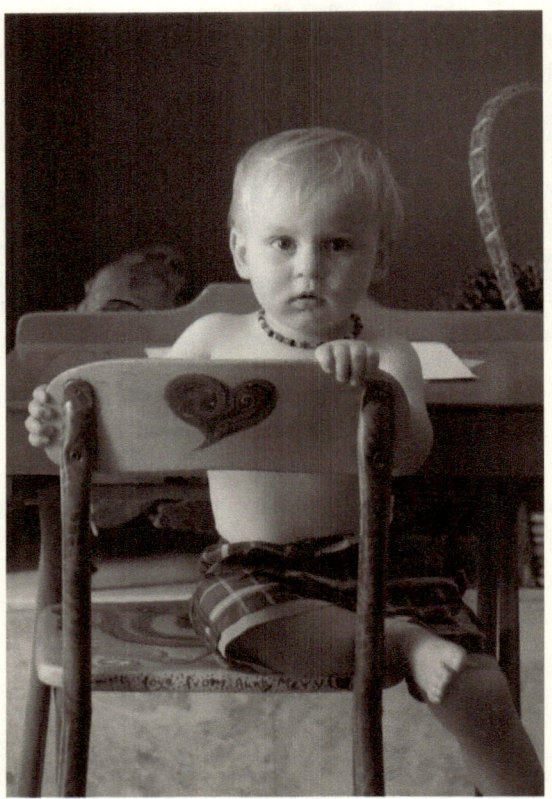

I get a lot of emails asking what my personal workflow is when it comes to processing hundreds of images from an event. So here it is.

Standard Disclaimer: Just because I do it this way doesn't mean it's the best way or that it's the right way for you. Just as there's no "best" way to configure your camera, there's no "best" way to process a ton of images.

Despite Adobe doing everything in their power to annoy me off their platform (slow software, can't do anything else while it starts, constantly changing UI behavior, subscription model, still not knowing how to handle rendering the workspace in Windows 10's high-resolution screen), I still use Lightroom for processing large batches of images, and Photoshop for tweaking images and doing special things that Lightroom can't do.

Because Lightroom is so very slow (not just for pre-rendering, but also for switching between adjacent pre-rendered images on my laptop), I also use a 3rd program called ACDSee which is one of the fastest .jpg viewers I've ever seen. (I understand Photo Mechanic is in that league as well.)

So here's what I do, from the minute I get back to my desk to the minute I hit "upload to Google Photos" to share them with my clients:

1.   Offload the memory card using Sony's PlayMemories Home. (Hey, don't judge me!) This program automatically knows where to pull in movie files from the different obscure directories they're stored in (different formats are stored in different places.)

2.   Make a backup of the imported files, and turn the backup drives off when finished. Experience has taught me to always have two copies of anything before I start work on it in case disaster strikes.

3.   Sort the photos by type, and move the RAW files to a separate directory, and the video files into yet another directory.

a.   If your light is good and your exposure is right for that light, there's no great benefit to shooting RAW. (http://friedmanarchives.blogspot.com/2012/08/where-anti-jpg-bias-came-from-part-2.html) (Read below for what happens when your light isn't so good)

b.   I rarely ever touch more than 1% of the RAW files I shoot, so I keep them in a separate directory just in case. That's true even if I'm shooting with high ISO – starting with the A6300, Sony's high-ISO noise reduction is very close to what I can do manually with PS or LR. So this saves considerable processing time and import time in Lightroom. I'll access the RAW files if I need to pull up some shadows or need to recover some highlights or do some other form of extreme manipulation.

c.   I don't pull video files into Lightroom because LR will insist on re-rendering everything, even if nothing was done. With 4K video clips that can cost me $10/month just in extra electricity (and I have solar!), and makes my computer work harder than it needs to.

4.   Fire up ACDSee and start to mark my favorite images. 500 times faster than culling them using Lightroom, and don't have to worry about bloating up the catalog as fast either.

5.   Move the culled images to a new directory. This way if I ever stop using ACDSee I can still identify the favorite images I selected.

6.   Start up Lightroom and import the new culled directory. (That process can take some time, so while they're importing I'll often log in to Facebook and marvel at all the confirmation bias.)

7.   Start Developing in Lightoom, further narrowing the selections as I go.

8.   If I have images that need special attention, I'll dig up the RAW files and process them separately in Photoshop.

9.   Export and Share everything via Google Photos. Exceptionally good ones (usually less than 0.1% of what I shoot) get added to the FriedmanArchives.com stock image website.

===

Better High ISO Jpgs

Earlier in this blog post I mentioned that I hardly ever touch my RAW files anymore. Here's a good example as to why. First, let me show you a high-ISO, out-of-camera .jpg example from a camera circa 2010:

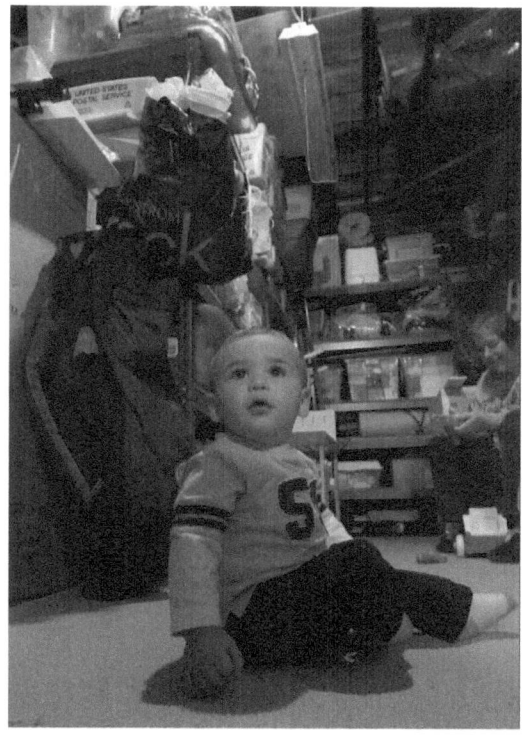

The original file. Camera circa 2010, ISO 10,000

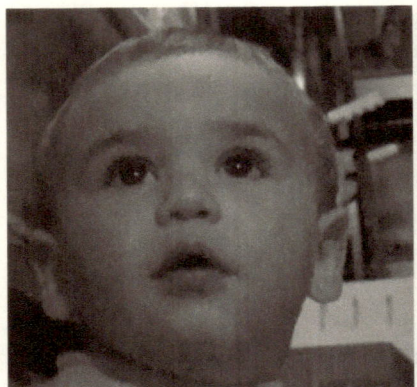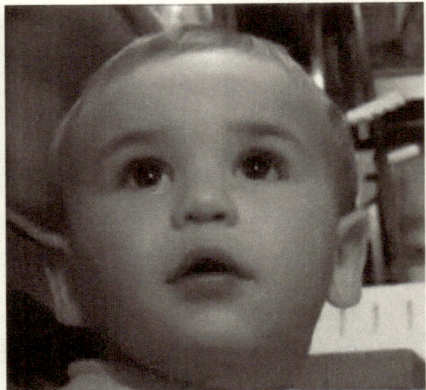

Out-of-camera .jpg on the left. Cleaned-up RAW on the right.

In the old days, the noise reduction algorithms for high-ISO .jpgs were so overzealous and watercolor-y (that's a word!) that these situations practically demanded that you shoot RAW and post-process later to control the noise.

Now let's look at a new camera. Yesterday I took this low-light portrait at ISO 25,600 using the new Sony Alpha 9. Of course I shot RAW + JPG.

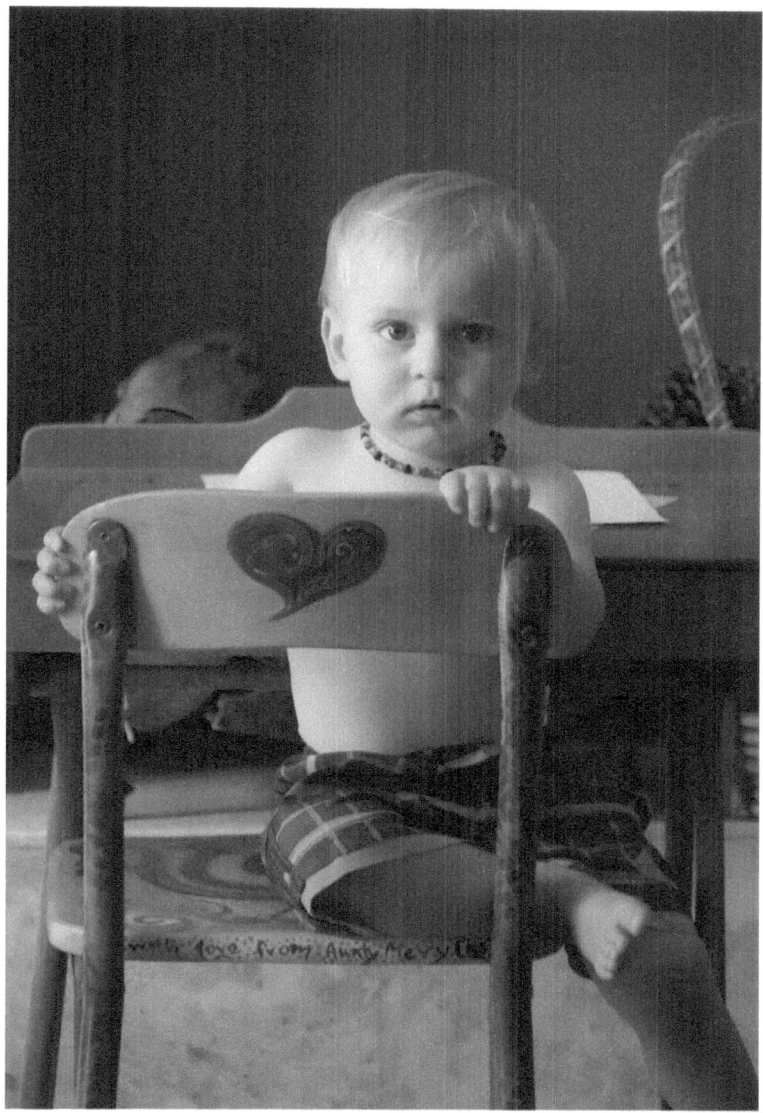

Today the high-ISO .jpgs are so good that in order to see any difference at all you have to pixel peep:

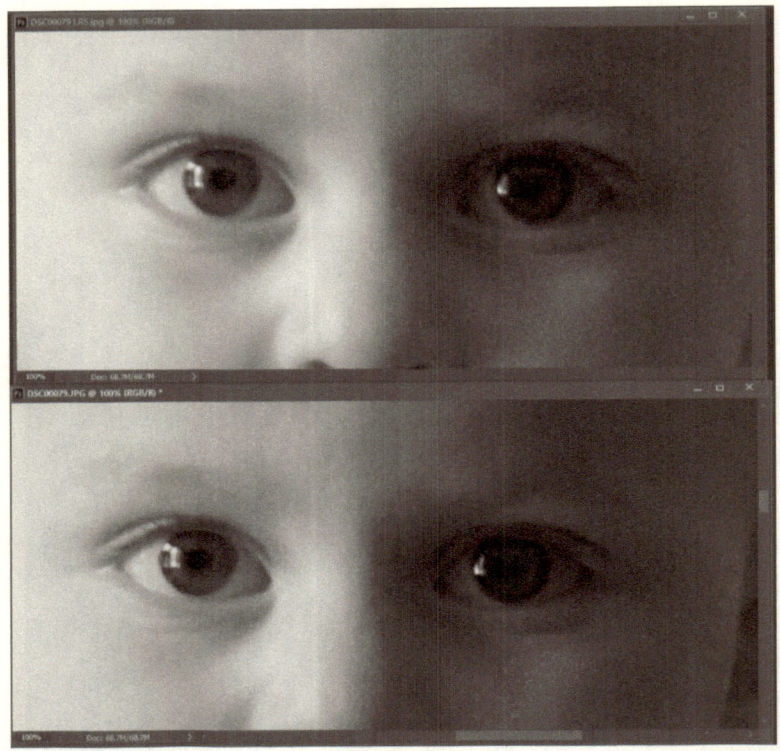

The RAW is still better, but by a much narrower margin than just 5 years ago. And when printed, these small differences pretty much go away. The time spent cleaning things up in RAW is rapidly getting to the point where it becomes wasteful. We live in amazing times.

3.14 ETTR REVISITED

First published August, 2016

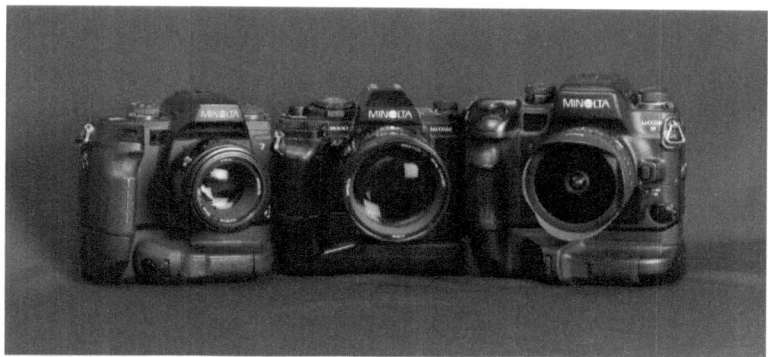

Once upon a time there was an esoteric technique for reducing noise at high ISO called "Expose to the Right". It worked like this: You overexpose the image by about a stop or so (but not so much that you'll blow out the highlights!), and then bring the exposure back down in Photoshop. This technique reduced the noise by about 1-2 stops' worth, which was pretty good. Since those days, modern camera manufacturers have changed the way brightness values are represented in RAW files for efficiency, and some have claimed that this makes the ETTR technique less effective.

Is this true? I decided to find out.

I dusted off my old Alpha 700 (12 MP, APS-C) and compared it to a modern-day A6300 (24 MP, APS-C) using the same setup and the same lens. Since noise is always most pronounced in the dark areas of an image, I figured I'd shoot a relatively dark subject. Three classic Minoltas should do the trick.

The first two shots were taken with the A700 using ambient light (vs. the image at the top of this post which was done with studio strobes). ISO was set to 3200, which is the camera's highest native ISO. The two images below were shot "straight" and with exposure compensation set to +1.3:

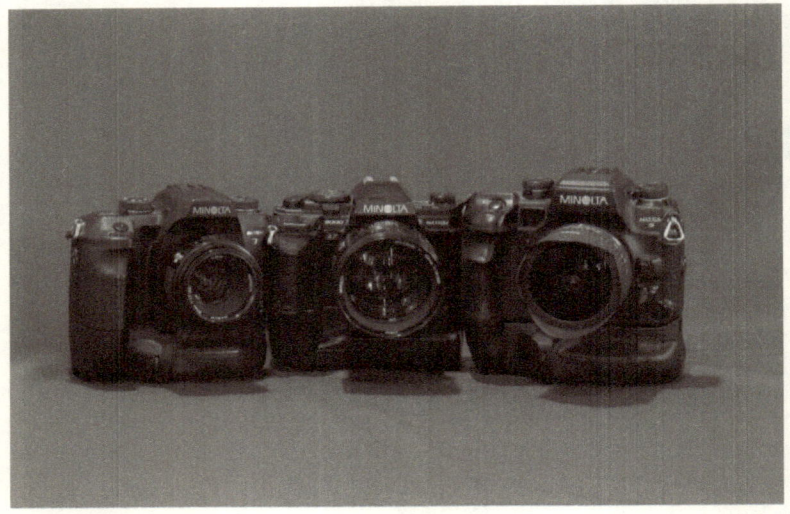

A700 EV0

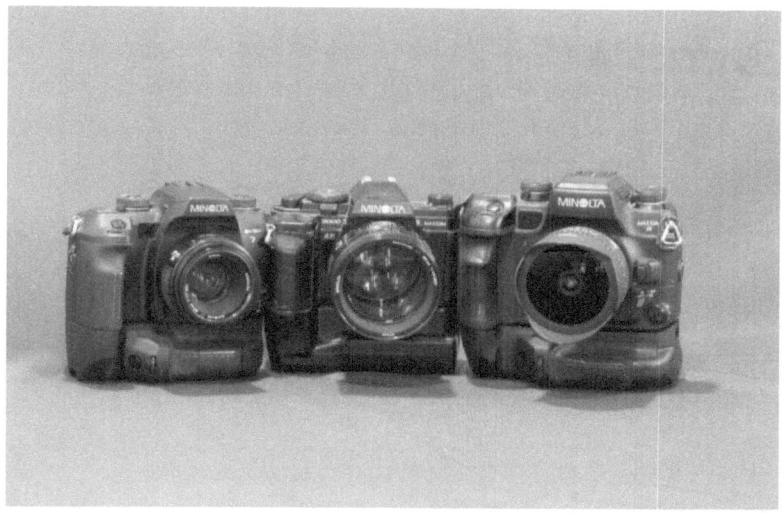

A700 EV+1.3

I opened up the RAW files, and adjusted the overexposed image. No other adjustments (i.e., noise reduction) were performed. Now let's look at the noise via 100% close-ups :

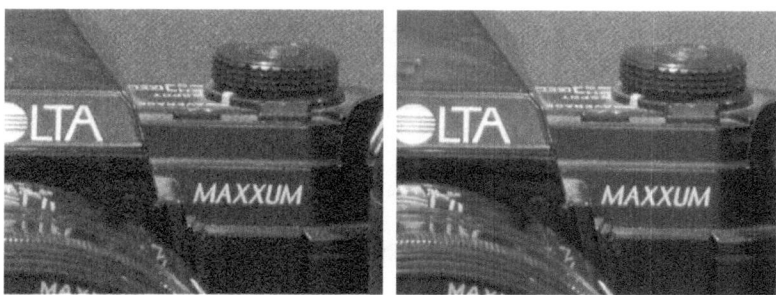

Left: Straight exposure. Right: +1.3 and corrected in photoshop.

This technique was invented by the late Michael Reichmann of LuminousLandscape.com to help bring more detail in the shadows for early Canon users, for if you were to lift the curve in Photoshop to lighten the shadows, it often resulted in ugly noise and banding (yuk!). At low ISO the technique would also result in finer gradations to allow your RAW file to be manipulated a bit more.   The reason it works has to do with the way the brightness values of the image are stored in the RAW file. For a good tutorial of how this works, there's a good summary here: http://digital-photography-school.com/exposing-to-the-right/

Okay, let's do the same test again using the A6300 at ISO 3200:

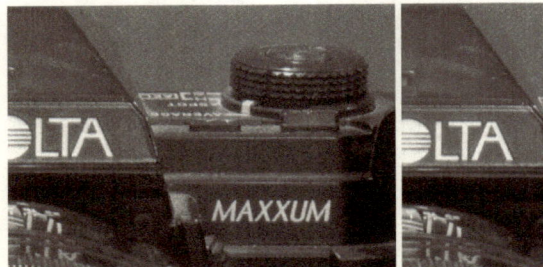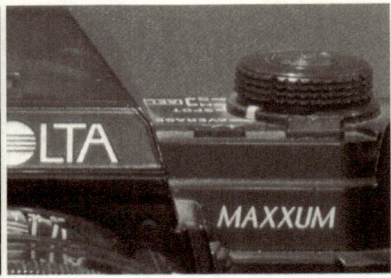

Left: Straight exposure. Right: +1.3 and corrected in photoshop.

The first thing to notice is how much lower the noise is with the newer sensor. (Shouldn't be a surprise, really, but sometimes it's good to look back and see just how far we've come in 9 years.) The 2nd thing to notice is that the improvement wasn't as dramatic. Is that because the theory is right - that the technique isn't as effective as it once was with modern RAW file formats? Or is the difference less pronounced because the noise was amazingly non-terrible to begin with?

Let's try it again at a higher ISO - say, 25,600, which is the A6300's highest native speed.

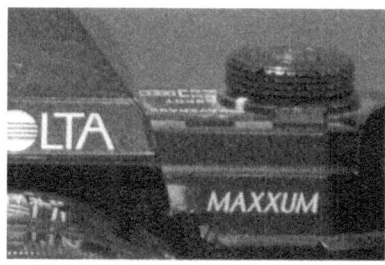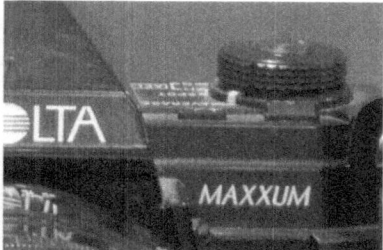

Left: Straight exposure. Right: +1.3 and corrected in photoshop.

My subjective verdict: The technique still works, and is about as effective as before.

"Isn't it better to just shoot at low ISO to begin with", you may ask? I tried this experiment many years ago to find out. Below is a 100% crop of a test image taken with an A100 (remember that?)

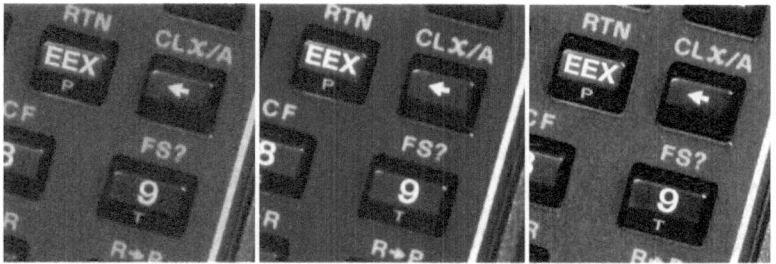

Left: ISO 1600. Center: ISO 1600 using ETTR. Right: ISO 800

Basically, over-exposing by one stop then correcting it in post-processing results in LOWER noise than if you had just shot with one-stop less ISO in the first place. Quite counter-intuitive.

So do I ever use this proven noise-reduction trick in real life? No. If my light is so bad that I have to crank up my ISO to such levels, it means also that I don't have the luxury of overexposing by a stop or more. It's a good technique to know, but tripods coupled with low ISOs is a cleaner solution.

SECTION 4 NOTHING TO DO WITH PHOTOGRAPHY

4.1 POSSIBLE SOLUTIONS TO THE HOT SHOE DESIGN PROBLEM

First published January, 2016

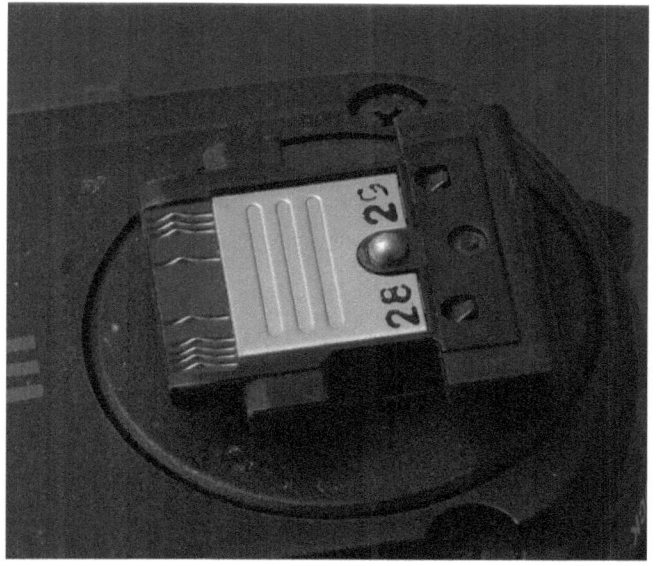

It's no secret that, <u>while I understand why Sony redesigned the camera's flash hot shoe</u>, I am not a fan of the new flash foot. The pins are too vulnerable and too easily bent with casual use. Instead of throwing my flash carelessly into my camera bag during run-and-gun assignments, I now have to stop, search for, and affix that tiny little plastic cover to the bottom. A cover that is small and black and therefore very easy to lose. (I should know; I've lost five of them. The fifth is on a bus on Phillip Island somewhere.) Nuts to that! I wanted to see if I could invent a way to solve this problem, given that Sony is unlikely to change this new specification.

My first thought was a simple tether, like the kind that attach to lens caps to prevent them from getting lost. That's still a bother - I want to eliminate the time spent protecting those pins each time.

Next, I started thinking about protective covers that would be automatically moved out of the way once the flash was mounted to the camera:

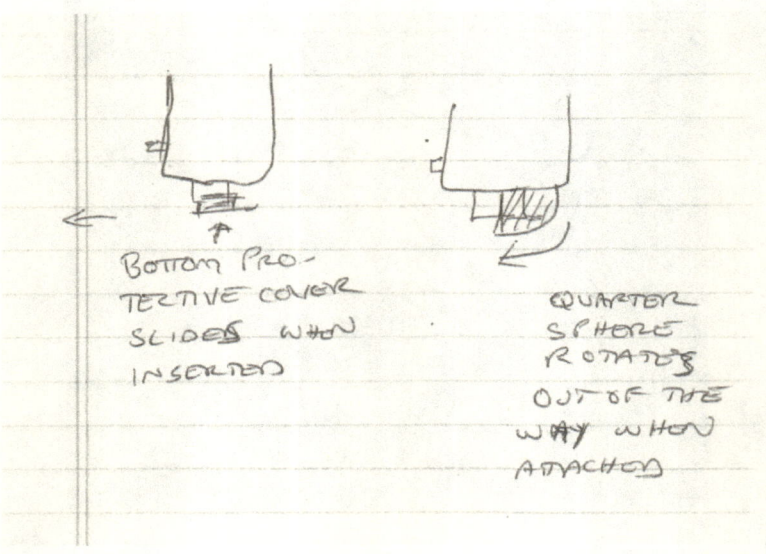

All of my sketches look like this. That's one reason why I became a photographer.

Not too easy to affix it as a 3rd party product, and the whole concept seemed like a flimsy solution.

Then I thought about creating an intermediate connection layer - a piece that was affixed permanently to the bottom of the flash foot, and another piece which affixed permanently to the camera's hot shoe. This would solve two problems - the vulnerable flash pins, and <u>the pins in the hot shoe which can be prone to shorting out when moisture is present</u>. Great! Now all I have to do is devise a reliable 4-conductor mating mechanism.

Oh, wait. Such a 4-conductor mating mechanism had already been devised, and it's just the right size! I'm referring of course to the Minolta hot shoe design which Sony abandoned due to market research feedback. But my solution would have to be strong as well as low-profile in order to be usable.

A prototype appears below. (Photoshop makes prototyping oh-so-much easier than the old days!)

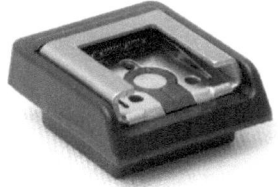 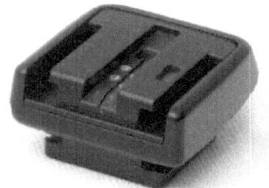

The left one gets permanently attached to the bottom of the flash. The right one gets permanently attached to the hot shoe of the camera..

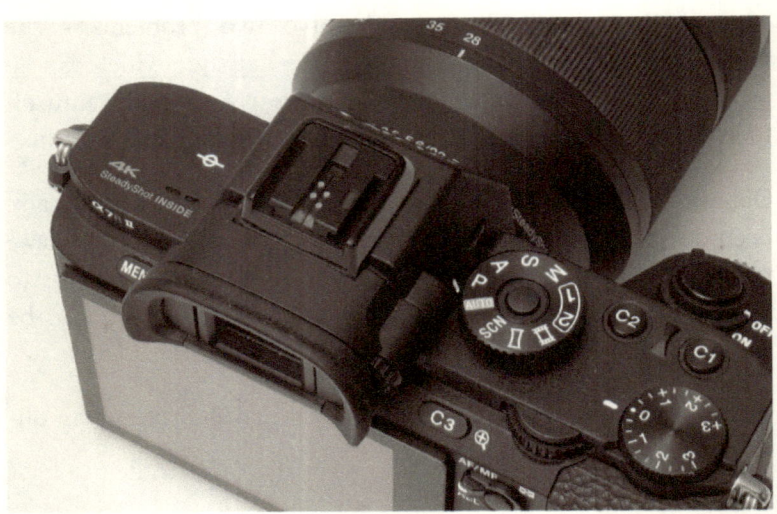

This is what the right one would look like on top of the camera. Sleek, low-profile, and most important: strong enough to support a heavy flash when camera and flash are carried using a BlackRapid strap.

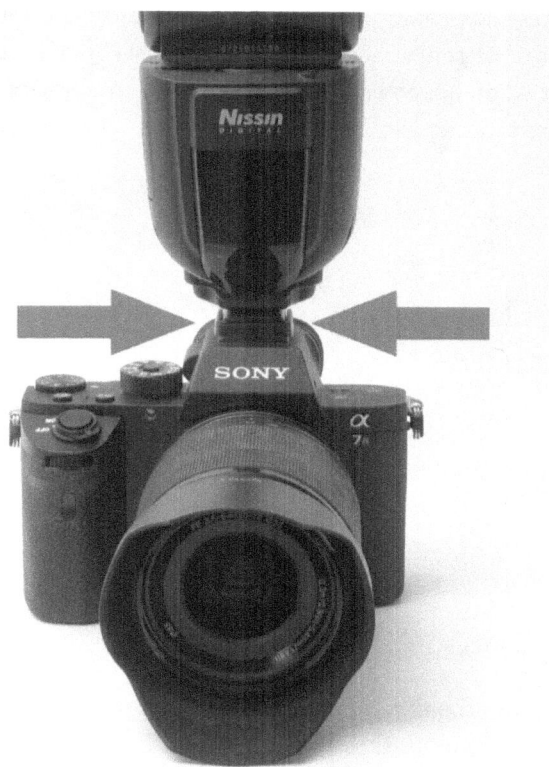

When the flash is attached to the camera, the two low-profile adapters are sandwiched together. Nearly invisible to the user and not the weakest link.

Scholarly note: Yes, mechanical locking and unlocking would be a requirement. That is best figured out by the mechanical engineer who also figures out how to make these. This is just an idea.

While the solution was straightforward, I still felt it was too kludgy. Plus, a quick trial balloon on SonyAlphaRumors.com showed that a lot of people didn't understand it (even though it was explained two different ways). Probably not a good commercial venture. Is there a better solution?

A better idea came to me at 3:00 AM (why does all inspiration have to happen at ungodly hours?). "Why not have the pins retract when not in use?" An animated .gif appears below which gets the idea across:

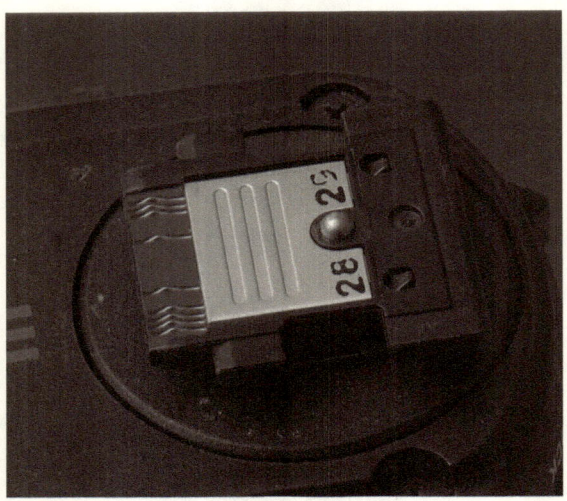

This would require some mechanical engineering work on Sony's side for future flashes - the pins would move using the same mechanism that actuates the locking pins. And with such a mechanism in place, the nature of the pins could change as well - they could be stiffer and could have a solid backing resulting in more pressure. Lots of possibilities here.

I submitted this idea to my contacts at Sony, who tell me that the boys in Japan are open to suggestions for future products. I'm not expecting anything to happen, but I'll let you know if I at least get a response.

4.2   4 KICKSTARTER IDEAS

First published February, 2016

My entrepreneurial days are over (truth be told, it ended here
http://friedmanarchives.com/guitar); but my ability to see
legitimate needs and business opportunities will never go away.
And so I'm giving away four ideas that the world really needs. If
someone wants to go ahead and run with any of them, be my
guest. I will have done my part in helping to make the world a
better place. (And if you want to kick back 0.5%, I wouldn't
mind that either. :-))

Idea #1) 'Uber' for Seniors

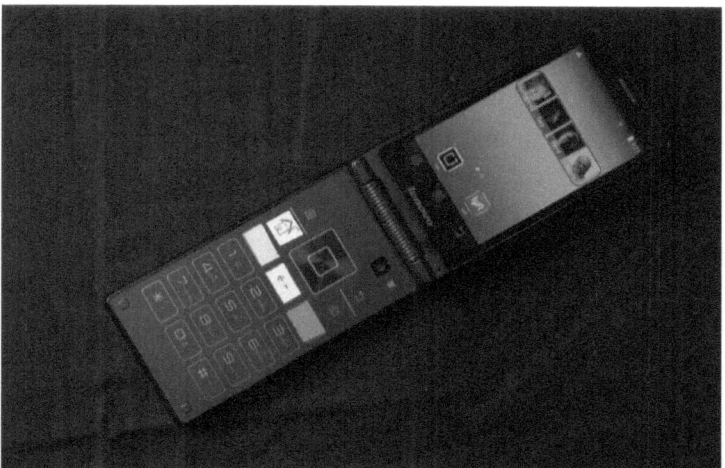

*The smart clamshell phone; configured just for Uber and Lyft, plus one-
button dialing for family members. Simple enough, right? I even put
green and red tape where the Send and End buttons are (which,
frankly, the designers should have done).*

My dad is 88 years old and, god bless him, still teaches Systems Engineering and Constraint Theory as a graduate professor at the University of Southern California. But his driving skills aren't what they were, and the family would feel more comfortable if he were no longer making the commute. Uber seemed like an ideal option for him, and so I got him a hybrid clamshell phone / smartphone (to retain the user interface of the clamshell phone he's used to), and configured it to just have the icons he'll need.

I'll spare you the detail of all the things that went wrong in getting him to operate a smartphone; suffice to say the experiment didn't go very well. As one ages, even an iPhone is too complex to use.

Adding to the problem is that the Uber user interface is pathetic. It requires several button presses, and if your finger wanders a little bit the car will pick you up across town instead of where you are. (How do intoxicated people manage to hail a cab with this app?) Plus there's that "surge pricing" which I prefer not to patronize.   Lyft, which in theory requires only two button presses, presented other problems as the GPS feature thought we were across town. Later, when the car arrived but couldn't find us, we were unable to respond back to the automatic "I'm here!" text. (How useless is that?)

Watching this whole thing unfold was frustrating. I knew how simple the process SHOULD be, and this is far from it. This must have been how Steve Jobs felt when he had in his mind the iPhone but he had to pitch the Rokkr instead.

WHAT THE WORLD NEEDS is an "Uber for Seniors" - a one-button phone with a Come-get-me icon. You press the physical button and a car appears. That's it. (Oh, there might be a status screen saying "your white ford escape will be there in 2 minutes" but no fine motor skills or concepts of modes should be required.) I can see this being a secondary button to the Life Alert pendant - one button for transportation, one button for "I've fallen and I can't get up".

I believe the market for this is huge. All it takes is someone to implement it properly.

Idea #2) .epub and .mobi authoring tools

I've written about this before. (http://friedmanarchives.blogspot.com/2013/01/are-classic-metering-modes-obsolete.html#ERH) The problem still isn't solved. E-readers such as the Kindle were primarily designed for text-only books, and if you want to offer a complex-layout title with figures and tables you have to be a programmer. Yes, there are tools such as Sigil and Calibre but they only takes you 90% of the way there. The last 10% on a 600-page book is an exercise in tedium and an utter waste of consciousness. Currently, publishing houses outsource this to India to have it polished by hand at considerable expense and time.

So if some giant, resource-rich organization were to tackle this difficult-to-solve problem, the world would be a better place for content creators. Microsoft is actually well-positioned to do this, as starting with Word 2007 the entire internal document structure is represented via XML, which is like a higher-order HTML. In other words, they're almost there.

(Want proof about the internal structure? Rename a .docx file to .zip and then open it - you'll be able to see and browse the interior document structure.)

Idea #3) Encryption That Makes Everyone Happy

As often happens with politicized topics, there is much ignorance and lies being spewed by all parties when it comes to the encryption vs. privacy vs. government access vs. security debate. I'm not advocating mass eavesdropping; rather I'm talking about legitimate law enforcement needs to solve murders and kidnappings in cases where a warrant has been issued. (Traditionally, warrants have been the mechanism to keep a power-hungry government in check.)

If you've been following this subject at all in the media, you'll be hearing two major arguments:

1) "Strong encryption prevents the government from preventing terrorism, therefore manufacturers must install 'back doors' to the encryption that the government can use to eavesdrop". (This has been proven to be propaganda, as there are no demonstrated cases where not having access to an encrypted channel would have prevented anything.)

2) "We want to help law enforcement, however if such back doors were to be installed, hackers would be able to access it too, allowing no shortage of evil to take place. Plus, the NSA and other officials have demonstrated that they're not as concerned about due process when it comes to overstepping eavesdropping authority. It would be a public policy disaster and U.S. tech companies would lose international business as confidence in their security drops."

The above set of arguments is what's called a false dichotomy; it implies that these are the only two options available. Throughout this argument, nobody - not even encryption experts - has talked about existing encryption algorithms which can meet everyone's legitimate needs without necessitating a back door. It's called (m,n)-threshold encryption, and it works like this:

Instead of having one key (that can both encrypt and decrypt), or two keys (one to encrypt and another to decrypt), you can encrypt anything using m of n keys, meaning you can have multiple keys floating around, and any 2 or 3 (or whatever combination you choose) of those keys can decrypt the contents. You can also configure it to have just one of the keys lock but two of any of the other keys will be required to unlock. It can be custom-tailored to meet specific use cases.

How would this work in the case of a smartphone?

In this instance I would propose issuing three keys, one of which works as it does now, and two others being distributed to the mobile phone manufacturer (let's say Apple for the sake of example), and the FBI. By themselves, neither Apple nor the FBI would be able to decrypt the phone. However, when a warrant is issued the FBI approaches the mobile phone manufacturer with the warrant and their key, and upon verification of the warrant the manufacturer can combine the FBI's key with their own key to decrypt the information. And since each person / phone / communication channel would get their own unique set of 3 keys, if one decrypting key combination were to be stolen or leaked, all the other phones would still be secure.

Of course I'm not familiar enough with the ways key management is used in modern mobile phones. So I emailed a foremost expert on the subject, Bruce Schneier, whose book "Applied Cryptography" has been referenced by me for longer than I care to admit.

Bruce wrote back the next day: "Many people have proposed secret sharing schemes for government access. What you're missing is that the problems are legal, and not mathematical." (Gotta love a busy guy who answers his own email!) Unfortunately he didn't go into more detail, but at least my premise has been validated: This problem has a technical solution which can be a win for all parties involved.

So, this is an opportunity to save the world from an epic political logjam, protect people's information from overzealous snoops and hackers alike, yet still give law enforcement a valuable tool to help track down that kidnap victim when there is a warrant.

Postscript: March 2017

Remember the big brouhaha a year ago, when the FBI wanted to read the contents of a terrorist shooter's phone, and Apple said no? That re-ignited the eternal "Should governments have easy access to encrypted communications?" debate.

Right about that time I proposed a technical solution this very problem, which would break the impasse between the "Strong encryption prevents the government from preventing terrorism" camp and the "If you install a back door, hackers will be able to access it also!" camp.

Shortly after that was published, someone else proposed my very same idea to a reputable engineering discussion forum called risks.org (where engineers discuss potential risks of technology to society in an effort to prevent ill-thought-out systems). You can read that proposal here: http://catless.ncl.ac.uk/Risks/29/28#subj9

So my idea has been vindicated! Although I'm not impressed with the moderator's response: he essentially dismissed it because it wasn't a million percent perfect, while completely ignoring the fact that it was five hundred thousand times better than what we have now.

Idea #4) Class Action Lawsuit Against Credit Card Companies

You know how your credit card companies make you feel warm and fuzzy, saying "Don't worry if you see some unauthorized activity on your bill - just let us know and we'll remove it"? Do you ever wonder who absorbs that loss? I'll give you a hint, it's not the credit card companies. It's the merchants. Merchants like me.

This can be a huge burden if you have an online shop that mails out physical goods, like I do with my other business: Maui Xaphoon Musical Instruments (www.Xaphoon.com). A typical order goes for between $90 and $250 and we ship out physical goods right away. I can't tell you how many times the credit card got approved at the time of sale, only to be reversed weeks later because the purchase was made by stolen c/c info.

Why am I the one who must pay for the weak security of the credit card infrastructure? Why isn't the issuing bank absorbing this loss? Why go to the trouble of getting an authorization for each transaction when the "Approved" response means nothing? Perhaps if the parties involved were to be held liable for all the fraud their weak systems allow, they might be further incentivized to replace it with something that requires more than a 3-digit security code and a matching zip code. (So far the only innovations they've implemented make data theft easier, not harder.)

So I propose all merchants get together and conduct a class action lawsuit against Visa, Mastercard, and American Express to make them absorb the fraudulent transactions that they are approving. I have no idea if you can fund a class-action lawsuit with kickstarter, but it seems to me this would be an ideal way to find out.

(Oh, if only I could just accept bitcoin for payments instead of credit cards, this whole problem could go away. Right now the weakest aspect of bitcoin is their digital wallets, but that won't affect me if I convert them to dollars daily.) (Too bad most customers don't know how to pay with bitcoin...)

4.3   WHY AMERICANS BEHAVE THE WAY THEY DO

First published May, 2016

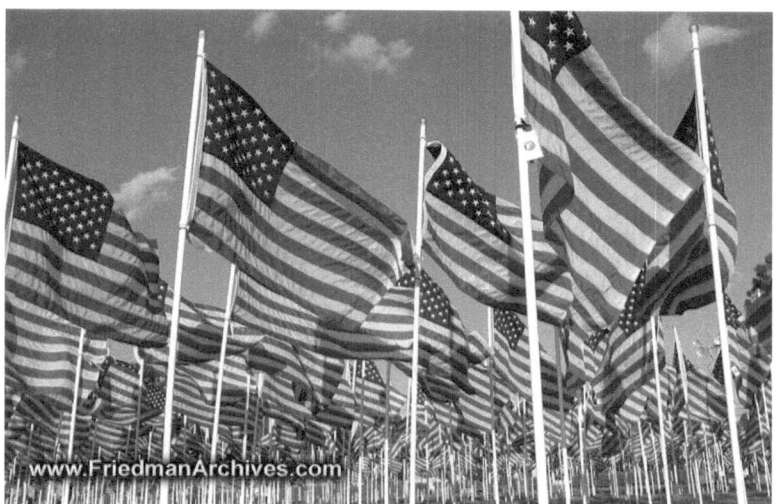

Sometimes in life you come across things that completely change the way you see the world. In the world of business, it was the book "Crossing the Chasm" by Geoffrey Moore, where I learned that we were lied to in kindergarten about building better mousetraps. (Every inventor needs to read that book!) In the world of cinema, it was the art movie Koyaanisqatsi (and its sequels) which changed my view of civilization and how we live our lives. Deepak Chopra's "The Seven Spiritual Laws of Success" taught me the stress-relieving power of working toward your goals while at the same time letting go of the outcome.

Long before those, I happened upon a paper which had an even larger impact on me back in 1988, when I was preparing to visit what was then the Soviet Union. While doing my homework (studying history, and learning as much of the Russian language as I could, in order to become a proper ambassador), I came across a paper written by an agent of the State Department, explaining to foreign visitors why Americans act so strangely. This was not the kind of American-bashing treatise like we see so often on the internet; it was a serious paper which set out to explain *The Values Americans Live By*. If a behavior seems strange to someone, understanding the underlying values which were responsible for that behavior can lead to greater understanding of a foreign culture. A quick excerpt:

For example, when you ask Americans for directions to get to a particular address in their own city, they may explain, in great detail, how you can get there on your own, but may never even consider walking two city blocks with you to lead you to the place. Some foreign visitors have interpreted this sort of action as showing Americans' "unfriendliness." We would suggest, instead, that the self-help concept (value number 6 on our list), is so strong in Americans that they firmly believe that no adult would ever want, even temporarily, to be dependent on another. Also, their future orientation (value 8) makes Americans think it is better to prepare you to find other addresses on your own in the future.

If you are an American, this may allow you to see yourself differently. If you're not an American, this may explain a lot of behaviors for which Americans are traditionally criticized, rightly or wrongly. Here's the paper - it's a short read. http://www1.cmc.edu/pages/faculty/alee/extra/American_values.html

For me it changed how I saw myself in the world and helped me become a cultural ambassador, both with my camera and with my attitudes.

4.4   I KNOW WHAT I DID LAST SUMMER

First published September 2017

Last year I alluded to a major project I was working on that was occupying quite a bit of time. The project was the 2nd edition of my father's book on Constraint Theory, the groundbreaking Systems Engineering theory on which his Ph.D. dissertation was based and which he's been teaching at USC at the graduate level for the last 20 years.

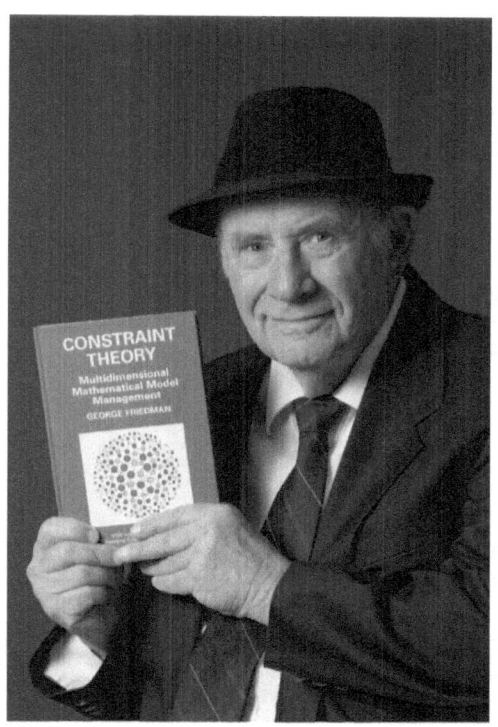

My Dad in 2005, holding the 1ˢᵗ edition. One wireless flash and one umbrella. ☺

What made it a melancholy event is that my Dad has Alzheimer's disease, and the book was finally published a few months after he had to stop teaching because of his memory loss.

Constraint Theory is most useful for extremely large engineering projects, like a military aircraft, where you have millions of requirements and millions of unknowns for which you have to solve. Very often these requirements conflict with each other yet nobody realizes it, resulting in inevitable cost overruns and schedule slips. My dad's theory can quickly identify the conflicts within a computer model of the project, and even offer suggestions on how to resolve them, all without needing to do an exhaustive, brute-force search of all the variables which can take lifetimes via computer, even for systems of low complexity.

Back in 2004 my father and I created the first edition of the book; and last summer I worked closely with one of his graduate students who had taken my Dad's theory to the next level, making it about a trillion times more efficient.

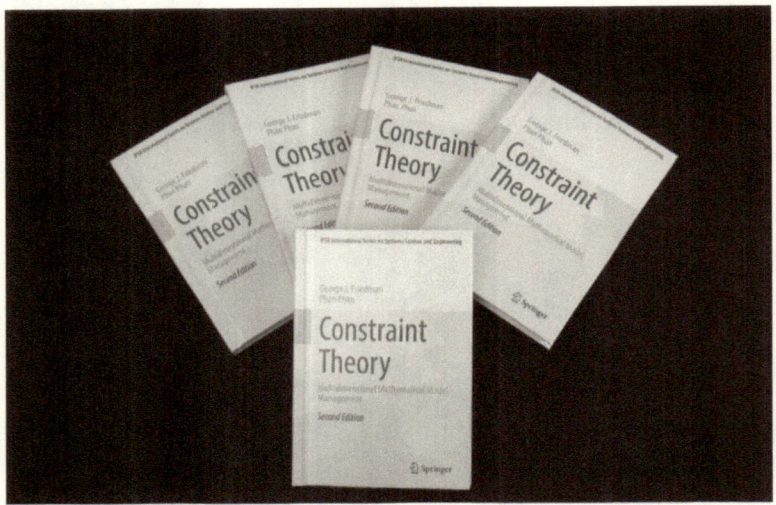

I inherited a lot from my dad, including the tendency to see problems and come up to solutions to those problems long before the rest of the world realized there was even a problem. (A bad thing if you're an inventor! See http://friedmanarchives.blogspot.com/2013/06/my-life-as-geek.html) And so I truly believe that 100 years from now, history will judge my efforts on these books to be one of the most important things I've ever done - even if the world doesn't fully realize that there's a problem right now.

The new edition is now available from Springer Academic Publishers (http://www.springer.com/us/book/9783319547916), and my Dad's groundbreaking theory will continue to be taught at the USC School of Engineering for the foreseeable future.

More detail about Constraint Theory can be found here: http://friedmanarchives.com/CT/

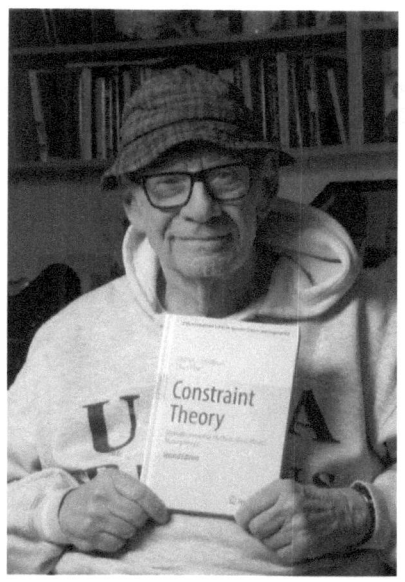

My dad, with the 2ⁿᵈ edition. Same lighting. "Whoever wrote this sure seemed sure of himself!"

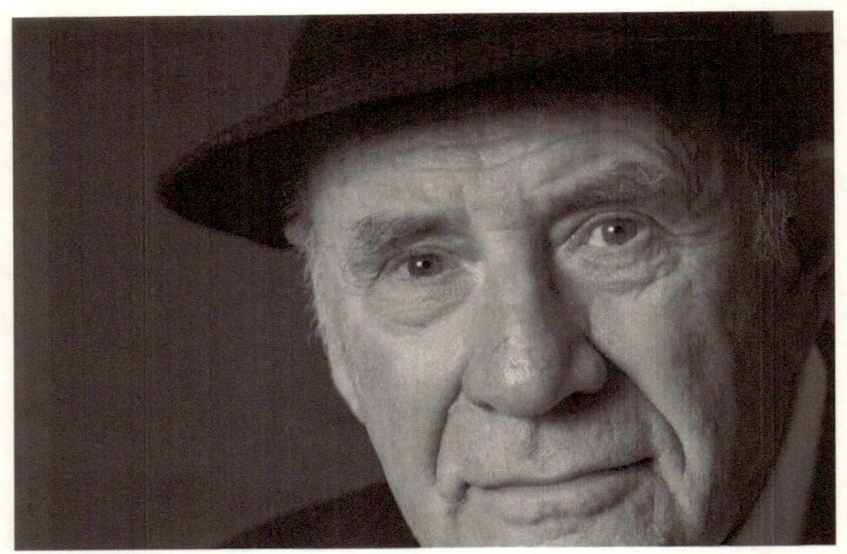

www.ingramcontent.com/pod-product-compliance
Lightning Source LLC
Chambersburg PA
CBHW031835170526
45157CB00001B/311